CHRIST AND HIS CHURCH

through the ages

VOLUME 1 **THE ANCIENT CHURCH** (AD 30–590)

CHRIST AND HIS CHURCH

through the ages

Second Edition

HERMAN HANKO

Edited and Revised by Dan Van Uffelen

REFORMED
FREE PUBLISHING
ASSOCIATION
Jenison, Michigan

Printed in the United States of America

Scripture cited is taken from the King James (Authorized) Version

Unless otherwise noted, pictures and maps are in the public domain from Wikimedia Commons.

Reformed Free Publishing Association
1894 Georgetown Center Drive
Jenison, Michigan 49428
616-457-5970
www.rfpa.org
mail@rfpa.org

Cover design by Erika Kiel
Interior design by Katherine Lloyd, The DESK

ISBN: 978-1-944555-75-7
LCCN: 201893571

CONTENTS

Part Three: The Nicene and Post-Nicene Period (AD 313–590)

FOREWORD

I still remember the first time I heard him preach. It was Sunday, July 21, 1985, and I was seven. Towering over our pulpit at First Protestant Reformed Church in Holland, Michigan, a slender man with a commanding presence, piercing eyes, and a ringing voice introduced his sermon. "I'm going to talk to you children tonight, because this word of God is for children," he began. "We're going to let the parents listen in, and all who are here tonight… but nevertheless I am going to talk to you children." I felt like he was staring right at me. Maybe he was. I hung on every word. As young as I was, I knew I was listening to a great preacher.

His name was Herman Hanko. He was fifty-five years old and in his prime as a pulpiteer and a seminary professor. Based on Colossians 3:20, his sermon that night was titled "God's Word to Children." Opening the scriptures and preaching in terms I could understand as a child, he pointed us to God's providential placement of each unique son and daughter in the right family; he explained the high calling that children have to honor their parents; and he encouraged us to live as God's children in a wicked world. I remember his vivid illustrations, including one with angry children banging dishes around in the kitchen; and I recall the effective acronym he used to make a child's calling to obey his parents stick: "HOLY—Honor. Obey. Love. Yield." That sermon still lives in my soul. It is a case study in effective preaching and story-telling, patterned after the Lord's method of teaching with parables.

Thirty years later, on June 21, 2015, at Hope Protestant Reformed Church in Walker, Michigan, I heard him preach for the last time. That Sunday morning he preached on the theme "A Doxology of Election," based on Ephesians 1:3–4. Before he finished his introduction, he shared a story about his teaching days in the seminary, brought us back to the 1940s radio ministry of the PRC, and used multiple metaphors to appeal to listeners of every age. His sermon declared the comforting doctrine of God's election, extolled the covenantal unity of Christ and his church, and cataloged the champions of sovereign grace through the ages: Guido de Bres, Zacharias Ursinus, Caspar Olevianus, Franciscus Gomarus, and Herman Hoeksema. In his stirring conclusion, he delivered his own doxology of election and declared, "Isn't that wonderful, beloved?" The sermon was his swan song and a microcosm of his ministry.

In the thirty years between these bookend sermons, I came to appreciate Professor Hanko not only as a preacher and a storyteller, but also as a teacher and a writer. When he came to lead an interim course on prayer at Heritage Christian High School during my first year as a teacher, I sat at his feet along with my students as he engaged our hearts and minds. As I struggled to find my way as a church history teacher, I discovered his book *Portraits of Faithful Saints* and found it inspirational and indispensable. In subsequent years, I learned the history of my denomination by reading *For Thy Truth's Sake* and came to appreciate the doctrinal riches of the church by reading *Contending for the Faith*. I found in each of these books a beautiful blend of history and storytelling, doctrine and application, firmness and comfort.

Now, at long last, Professor Hanko has crowned his life's work with a panoramic survey of two thousand years of church history. Entitled *Christ and His Church Through the Ages*, this fresh series unlocks his thirty-six-year goldmine of church history instruction in the Theological School of the Protestant Reformed Churches (1965–2001). Written for the student in the classroom, the theologian in the study, and the layman in the living room, this series imparts a solidly Reformed understanding of the historical development of Christ's church. Brimming with instruction and encouragement, these books were written to help all readers understand and appreciate the biblical foundation of the church, the wonderful works of God throughout history, the trials and triumphs of the saints, and the marvelous theme of sovereign grace. In an age of historical amnesia, this series erects memorial stones to the mighty acts of God (Gen. 28:10–22; Josh. 4:1–9, 21–22; 1 Sam. 7:7–12) and preserves the ancient landmarks of our fathers (Deut. 19:14; Job 24:2; Prov. 22:28).

For those readers who have never heard Professor Hanko preach, and never will, you will catch in these pages something of the passion, conviction, and sincerity of the man. You will enjoy his prowess as a storyteller and his natural ability to engage readers of every age. You will profit from his knowledge of God's word, his application of scripture to church history, and his ability to show the relevance of church history for the church today. You will also appreciate his glowing love of Christ and his church, his call to an antithetical life of holy living, and his comfort for God's pilgrim people as they look toward heaven. These are the qualities I recall from the first time I heard him preach to the last, qualities the Lord has used to make his teaching, preaching, and writing effective these many years.

May God bless those who travel these pages with Christ and his church through the ages, and may God bless the tour guide who captured my imagination when I was just seven years old.

Dan Van Uffelen
Church History Teacher
Covenant Christian High School

EDITOR'S NOTES

PROJECT HISTORY

This church history series is ten years in the making.

Many years ago, I joined a chorus of voices urging Professor Herman Hanko to produce a layman's guide to church history, a textbook for both old and young that would celebrate the great doctrine of sovereign grace and trace the history of the church from the days of the apostles through the history of the Protestant Reformed Churches. When I asked him again in early 2010, he wrote to me, "It is getting rather late in life to start on such a mammoth project." He was, after all, nearly eighty years old. The dream seemed to be vanishing.

But desperate times call for desperate measures. At the time, I was teaching at Heritage Christian High School in Dyer, Indiana; and Gwen Van Baren (now Birkett), a granddaughter of Professor Hanko, was one of my students there. When Gwen mentioned offhand that she often wrote letters to her grandfather, I had a rare epiphany. "Gwen!" I exclaimed. "Ask your grandpa to write a church history book! Maybe he'll listen to *you*." She smiled and enthusiastically agreed.

Just days later, Gwen's mother—and Professor Hanko's daughter—Mrs. Karen Van Baren asked me what I knew about a church history book. Karen shared with me her father's recent message to her: "I have been under some pressure, as you know, to write some sort of book on church history. I would love to do this, but again face an insurmountable task even in the preparation for writing." Gwen's request had put the wheels in motion. Professor Hanko was ready to write! What I failed to accomplish through years of dogged determination, granddaughter Gwen achieved by a simple request. It is abundantly clear to me that Professor Hanko wrote this one for the children and the young people—for the generations to come.

And the rest is history. In early 2011, things began to move quickly. Already in January, at Professor Hanko's request, Karen and I collaborated on an outline for the manuscript. By March, Professor Hanko submitted the first three chapters to us for feedback. In April, I wrote a prospectus to pitch the project to the Reformed Free Publishing Association (RFPA). When Professor Hanko and I met with the RFPA's book committee in June, they loved the concept, expressed a strong desire to publish the book, and encouraged us to proceed. Energized by the meeting, Professor Hanko buried himself in his writing, an activity he once described as "blood, sweat, and tears," and yet a work he thoroughly enjoys. In an interview published in the winter 2011 issue of the RFPA *Update*, he said, "History, especially of the church, attracts me like a magnet attracts a nail, and so writing history is a fascinating occupation." Already in the early stages of writing the manuscript, he wrote to me, "I think we have a good thing going here that, under God's blessing, will be for the welfare of the church of Christ."

By 2013, Professor Hanko had already finished the entire first draft of *Christ and His Church Through the Ages*. I read the draft and offered an initial round of editorial remarks and suggestions. At the RFPA's request and with Professor Hanko's approval, I used the manuscript in my church history classes at Covenant Christian High School. My students offered a wide range of helpful suggestions, many of which were utilized. Over the next two years, I worked my way through the entire manuscript a second time, producing a document of suggestions for revision. Professor Hanko incorporated the ones that he deemed useful and necessary. He also selected fitting Bible verses to introduce each chapter.

In 2015, the RFPA made a formal review of the early manuscript and then asked me to serve as the project's developmental editor. At their request and in conjunction with a master's course I was taking at Calvin College, I began another critique of the entire manuscript, focusing especially on unity, clarity, and historical accuracy, and incorporating previous editorial suggestions into the manuscript.

In 2018, the RFPA decided to print several hundred copies of the unedited first edition to satisfy the immediate needs of several Christian schools and to give teachers time to provide quality feedback on adjustments they would find helpful in the finished product. Based on their experience with the first edition in the classroom, teachers gave corrections and suggestions. In the meantime, the RFPA asked me to revise the manuscript one last time to prepare it for publication, dividing it into multiple volumes and providing further editing, quality introductions, various sidebars, and an array of pictures, maps, timelines, and tables in order "to publish a high-quality work that will be great for any reader and for Christian schools."

In 2020, I finished my work on the ancient period and submitted it for peer review and copyediting. In 2021, *Volume 1: The Ancient Church (AD 30–590)* was ready for the printer. It is my hope that *Volume 2: The Medieval Church (AD 590–1517)*, *Volume 3: The Reformation Church (AD 1517–1648)*, and *Volume 4: The Modern Church (AD 1648–present)* will be available in subsequent years.

EDITION CHANGES

Because my work on Professor Hanko's manuscript has been extensive, it is appropriate that I explain the editorial changes and revisions I have made. I am convinced that these changes to the first edition will significantly improve the book's readability, usefulness, and appeal in our homes, schools, and churches. However, those who would like to read the unedited edition of Professor Hanko's work are welcome to do so. It was published by the RFPA in 2018 to be used on a trial basis in our schools. My revisions of that first edition fall into ten basic categories:

Introductions: Ancient church history is divided into three distinct periods. To introduce these historical periods, I wrote introductory essays, compiled timelines of events (based on Susan Lynn Peterson's *Timeline Charts of the Western Church* [Grand Rapids, MI: Zondervan Publishing House, 1999]), and selected appropriate maps (from Tim Dowley's *The Baker Atlas of Christian History* [Grand Rapids, MI: Baker Books, 1997] and *Atlas of Christian History* [Minneapolis, MN: Fortress Press, 2016]).

Organization: In order to strengthen the organization of the material I occasionally renamed and rearranged chapters; added, renamed, and repositioned subheadings; and even moved paragraphs and blocks of text to different locations in the manuscript.

Development: Although hesitant to alter Professor Hanko's syntax, I found it necessary to add transitions, simplify sentences, remove repeated material, define terms, provide further context, and incorporate various selections from his "Ancient Church History" seminary syllabus (1977).

Fact-checking: Reviewing the manuscript for historical accuracy and consistency, I fact-checked, corrected dating issues, and modernized spellings of names and places.

Copyediting: Although I am not the copyeditor, I did make capitalization, punctuation, spelling, grammar, and usage corrections along the way.

Biographies: I wrote biographical sketches highlighting the ancient heroes and villains of church history and added reading recommendations from Professor Hanko's books *Portraits of Faithful Saints* (Grandville, MI: RFPA, 1999) and *Contending for the Faith* (Jenison, MI: RFPA, 2010). I placed these biographies throughout the book where I thought they fit best.

Sidebars: When something important was missing from the text or was insufficiently treated, I wrote fresh sidebar material (e.g., "The Destruction of Jerusalem," "The Apostles' Creed," "The Decian Persecution," and "Jerome's Latin Vulgate"). Unless otherwise noted, these sidebar materials are my own.

Supplements: At other times, I was convinced that complementary material written by Professor Hanko in other articles and books should be incorporated into this book as well. These supplemental quotations appear as sidebars and include the author's name and original work citations.

Charts: I selected and created charts and tables and recommended placement throughout the book. The selections came from John D. Hannah's *Charts of Ancient and Medieval Church History* (Grand Rapids, MI: Zondervan, 2001) and Robert C. Walton's *Chronological and Background Charts of Church History: Revised and Expanded Edition* (Grand Rapids, MI: Zondervan, 2005).

Pictures: Finally, I chose nearly one hundred suitable pictures, photographs, and maps in order to bring life to the book and widen its general appeal. Most of these resources came from Wikimedia Commons.

SPECIAL THANKS

Many deserve to be acknowledged for their contributions to the first volume of this second edition of *Christ and His Church Through the Ages*.

I express special thanks to my dear wife, Kate, for the sacrifice of my time and attention for this project. Maybe someday she will forgive me for editing the manuscript in the hospital delivery room while we waited for one of our children to arrive.

This book truly was a labor of love. Thanks to my children too, who were at times frustrated when I was slow to pull myself from this work. Their reward will be to read these books in years to come.

Thank you to my former and current high school church history students. Their enthusiasm for church history has fueled my own love for the subject, and their encouragement has motivated me to press on. Their suggestions regarding the rough draft were a great help to me on this project as well.

I thank the church history teachers of our Protestant Reformed Christian schools who were willing to utilize the first edition in their classrooms and who provided helpful suggestions. Thanks as well to the church history teachers who graciously agreed to peer review the revised second edition before it went to the copyeditors: Prof. Russell Dykstra, professor of church history at the Protestant Reformed seminary (1996–present); Prof. Douglas Kuiper, professor of church history at the Protestant Reformed seminary (2017–present); and Mr. Scott Van Uffelen, teacher of church history at Covenant Christian High School (1998–present). They kindly read the revised manuscript and offered detailed suggestions for improvement.

Thank you to the board and staff of the Reformed Free Publishing Association. Their commitment, patience, and deadlines were all necessary to make this book happen. Mrs. Evelyn Langerak provided indispensable direction in the early days of the project; Mr. Alex Kalsbeek's idea to publish an incomplete first edition to garner feedback from the schools was brilliant; and Mr. Jeff Kalsbeek's unflagging commitment to the project saw it through.

Finally, many thanks to Prof. Herman Hanko—my hero, my teacher, and my friend—who through many years has cultivated within me—and countless others—a profound love and appreciation for the history of Christ's church and a sincere desire to declare it to the generations to come. No one has taught me more about church history. I thank him for asking me to contribute to this grand project. Working with him has been a tremendous honor, a remarkable learning experience, and a rich blessing indeed.

Dan Van Uffelen
Summer 2020

AUTHOR'S PREFACE

I am not embarrassed to add another book to the long list of books written on the history of Christ's church. In 1965 the Lord called me from the pastoral ministry, which I loved, to spend the rest of my active years in the Theological School of the Protestant Reformed Churches. One of the subjects that I was called to teach was church history. The seminary curriculum called for four semesters of church history: one semester each for the ancient, medieval, modern, and recent periods.

Preparing and keeping fresh lectures on these four periods required extensive reading and research of the subject. Many works were available, from Eusebius of Caesarea's *Ecclesiastical History*[1] to Bruce L. Shelley's recent book *Church History in Plain Language*. While the books that I read were all helpful in giving the facts of church history, some in considerable detail, I could not find one book that dealt with the history of Christ's church from a biblical and, more specifically, a *Reformed* viewpoint.

The term "scholarly" has taken on a unique meaning in academia. A scholarly work has copious footnotes, extensive quotations from many writers, a thorough analysis of their views, and many conclusions from different writings on a given subject. But a scholarly author does not often test ideas, weigh conclusions, and include his own views in his work. That, it appears, is unscholarly. It is left to the reader to make his own judgments—if, indeed, judgments are even expected.

If the idea just described is truly scholarly, this book on church history is *not* a scholarly work, nor is it intended to be. I started this project too late in life to do such an enormous work. Nor is this necessary in a world flooded with books on church history.

---

1 Eusebius of Caesarea (c. 260–340) was a contemporary of Constantine the Great and the father of church history from Pentecost up to his time.

This work reviews events that belong to the church, errors that were taught, innovations adopted, and views of many men who were part of the history of the church. As I wrote, I have felt free, even compelled, to weigh all things in the light of God's word, the only infallible canon of faith and life. Running through my mind was the apostle John's injunction, "Beloved, believe not every spirit, but try the spirits whether they are of God" (1 John 4:1).

Even then, my primary goal in writing this book was not to give the reader a huge file of facts and dates. Rather, my goal was to write for enjoyment and learning on the part of all God's people. I have consciously tried to make the book enjoyable and worth reading. I firmly believe that God's people ought to know the history of Christ's church, for they are a part of that church and members of the family of God who constitute the church. God's people ought to know the members of their family. It is good to know them now, for we shall live with them in heaven, world without end. Further, throughout the writing, I was conscious that the book will be used in high school church history classes. It is imperative that our children, children of the covenant, know the history of the church of which they are a part.

If God is pleased to use the book for the spiritual welfare of his people, that is to be preferred to scholarship.

This goal required teaching church history from the viewpoint of scripture's teaching concerning the church. Any book on church history has to take its starting point in scripture, and scripture has much to say about the church that was elect from all eternity, redeemed by Christ's sacrifice on the cross, saved by the irresistible power of the Spirit of Christ, and destined for eternal life with God in heaven.

A scriptural approach to church history must include some important points in order to serve its proper purpose. First, it must include the truth that the entire history of the church is God's history of saving his church. The viewpoint must be that of God's work through Jesus Christ. The history must make clear that the Son of God from his exalted position in heaven gathers, defends, and preserves the church.

Second, a scriptural approach to church history traces the church's defense of the faith over against heresy. It is biblical to describe the church by the name often given it: the *church militant*, in distinction from the *church triumphant* in glory. It is the church militant because the devil is determined to destroy it, and one of his most successful methods has been the introduction of false doctrine into the church. The church must fight to defend the truth.

Third, a church history that is faithful to the scriptures defines the crucial doctrine at stake in all the church's history: the doctrine of the particularity and sovereignty in God's work of grace in gathering his elect church through Christ. The doctrine of God's sovereignty was the issue on the floor at the Council of Nicaea. It was the burden of Augustine's ministry. The Roman Catholic Church corrupted the doctrine throughout the Middle Ages. It was restored triumphantly and emphatically by the works of all the reformers. It is written large on the pages of the Canons of Dordrecht and the Westminster Confession of Faith. It has been the chief point of dispute in one form or another in the history of Protestantism from the Reformation until today.

Finally, a scriptural approach to church history must point out that the church built the imposing body of the truth on the basis of the teaching of the apostles and prophets recorded in holy scripture. The church in any age and in every age builds on the foundation of the doctrine confessed by the church that lived before it. Christ promised his Spirit, the Spirit of truth, to the church, so that he from his throne on high might preserve his church through the one work of the one Spirit given to and possessed by the church of all ages. He has and does now lead the church into all truth. That truth is her life and her blessedness. A faithful church history has to be written on the foundation of these biblical givens.

The high schools established by Protestant Reformed parents throughout the denomination are staffed with Reformed teachers. Many times over the years these teachers of church history have asked me to write a textbook from a biblical perspective—not because there were no other books available, but there was nothing that they or I could find that was written from a Reformed viewpoint; that is, one that applies the truths of scripture to every aspect of the church's life. It seemed to me too enormous a task to undertake. But now, in my retirement, I have done so. May God be pleased to use this book to strengthen the faith of our covenantal children, to instill in them a love for Christ's church, and to give them incentive to devote their gifts to the church of which they are a part.

It is my firm belief that the students in our schools ought to learn church history, and that the subject ought to have high priority for all those who love Christ's church. If we are to live responsibly as God's children in the world, we ought to be acquainted with the history of those who have gone before us from the world to their eternal rest. So this book is prepared for use as a textbook and for the general edification and strengthening of God's people everywhere. I have tried to make it as interesting as possible, for the history of the church is like a travelogue filled with adventure that describes the journey of the church through time until the Lord returns.

It is somewhat embarrassing to include in the book many footnotes that call the reader's attention to two of my own books: *Portraits of Faithful Saints* and *Contending for the Faith*. This inclusion of my own books is not intended, at least not in the first place, to promote them. It was suggested that I do this by the teachers of church history in our schools, for these teachers use those two books for collateral reading in the courses they teach.

It is my hope and prayer that the Lord will use what I have written in weakness to the strengthening of the faith of those who love Christ and his church.

Herman Hanko

ACKNOWLEDGMENTS

This book could not have been written without the help of Dan Van Uffelen, a church history teacher at Covenant Christian High School in Walker, Michigan. He not only was kind enough to read the entire manuscript, but he also offered detailed suggestions for improvements that he drew out of his own experience teaching church history in the classroom. He even tested the entire Ancient Church History section in teaching that course so that he could see how it worked out in the actual teaching situation. His help proved invaluable.

Calvin Kalsbeek, a retired church history teacher from Covenant Christian High School, also read the entire manuscript. He tested it for readability and clarity of understanding. His evaluation kept out many words beyond the understanding of high school students, thus making the book more readable. He is also to be thanked for suggesting inclusion of various events and also omission of less than important matters.

Tom De Vries, a retired teacher in our Protestant Reformed schools, also read the entire manuscript and made significant changes that were incorporated into the book.

I recall that many years ago *Time* magazine ran an essay on how to write well. The essay concluded with the words: "Rule 1: Revise. Rule 2: Revise again. Rule 3: Revise again." I have found this to be true. The tedious work in revising is, however, to type the revisions into the original manuscript. I was saved from this task by Shari Bosveld, who did all this work for me. She also took the opportunity to read the entire manuscript at least two times and offer her own insightful suggestions on word usage, sentence construction, and clarity of thought. Without her assistance the task would have taken a much longer time.

Finally, I have to recognize with deep gratitude my wife, Wilma, who never complained about enduring whole summers of my writing without a vacation, and who encouraged me repeatedly to continue the work at those moments when discouragement with the enormity of the task overtook me.

INTRODUCTION

In the house of God, which is the church of the living God,
the pillar and ground of the truth.

—1 Timothy 3:15

CHURCH HISTORY IS FAMILY HISTORY

A growing interest in one's past and a search for one's ancestors has become a favorite pastime. All have ancestors who were born in other lands, and people like to know their roots. This desire is understandable and often proves interesting. But the believer has roots of a quite different kind. His roots go back two thousand years to Pentecost, when the exalted Christ poured out his Holy Spirit on the church. The believer has a spiritual ancestry as well as a physical one.

This spiritual ancestry is composed of a multitude of saints who are all one spiritual people or nation: the church of Christ (1 Pet. 2:9). This church is a family that ultimately traces its history back to the beginning of time. The church is not only a nation, but also a family with a spiritual ancestry. One who belongs to it has many brothers and sisters who are a part of the same household of faith. They are all of the family of God, for God is their father, Jesus Christ is their elder brother, and all believers are brothers and sisters in this family, for they are all sons and daughters of God (2 Cor. 6:18).

What this family has in common, and what makes them one family, is a spiritual birth that brings them into the family of God. This rebirth is regeneration, which God sovereignly performs through Christ and by the Holy Spirit. The birth that unites the members of this family is not a physical birth that enables them to trace their

1

ancestry back through many generations, but the spiritual bond of a common life given through the wonderful and sovereign work of God.

In addition to a spiritual birth, the family also has in common spiritual characteristics, such as a shared goal in life, quite different from the goals of the people of the world. The members of this family have a calling to witness to the truth of God as revealed in the sacred scriptures. They have a common calling to walk in the world as a holy people, reflecting in their lives the holiness of their God who has saved them. They all seek one destination, their heavenly home, to which so many of their brothers and sisters have already gone and at the doors of which angels will be waiting to usher them into their home.

The result of this is that throughout two thousand years of history all the saints have believed the same truth. They are united into one family by this truth, for it is the truth of God revealed in Christ, and it is a truth given to them by faith in Christ. But because that truth is under constant attack in a world of sin, their unity in the truth becomes a war in its defense; for faithfulness to the truth marks their membership in God's family. To deny the truth is to join the enemy. The church militant on earth is at war; the church triumphant in heaven has gained its victory, for faith is the victory that overcomes the world (1 John 5:4).

This family of God is called the "church of God" or the "church of Christ." The church of one generation hands down to the next generation the truth for which it has fought and the weapons with which it has defended its cause. So it has been since Pentecost; so it will continue until the Lord comes again. It is of this history that I write.

CHRIST AND HIS CHURCH: THE CENTER OF ALL HISTORY[1]

Christ is the center of all history. He is the firstborn of every creature; he is the Alpha and the Omega, the beginning and the ending. He is the first in God's counsel—not in order of time, but in principle. And he is the first and the last in history—the revelation of the counsel of God in time. History in the old dispensation pointed ahead to Christ; the new dispensation is the dispensation of the coming of Christ.

But inasmuch as this is true of Christ, it is equally true of the church. Christ and his church are one. There is no Christ apart from and without the church, even as

---

1 Taken from Herman Hanko, "Ancient Church History, AD 100–AD 590" (syllabus, Theological School of the Protestant Reformed Churches, 1977), 2–4.

there is no church apart from Christ. Christ came as the head of his elect church. For this elect number he died, securing redemption; on their behalf he rose again from the dead; these are the ones destined to inherit the everlasting kingdom of righteousness. Hence, even as Christ is the center and focal point of all history, so also this is true of the church—the elect and eternally chosen body of Christ. Thus the church is the goal of all that happens in history.

All this must be interpreted in terms of Christ's sovereign rule over all things in this dispensation. By his conquering death and his victorious resurrection, Christ gained a position of universal rule at God's right hand in heaven. All authority is given unto him. He is the Lord of lords and the King of kings. His rule is, in the strictest sense of the word, universal. He rules over all the brute creation; he rules over angels and devils; he rules over all wicked men, governing in such a way that their affairs are strictly under the sway of his sovereign scepter; he rules over his own elect church. And in all this rule of Christ, the purpose of God is realized—the glory of the only adorable God through the salvation of the elect into everlasting glory.

We must be careful to distinguish properly between the rule of Christ over his elect people and his rule over the wicked. Failure to make this distinction will inevitably result in a destruction of the antithesis and in the error of some form of postmillennialism. The rule of Christ over the wicked and devils is surely a sovereign rule. Christ rules over them in such a way that they serve Christ's purpose in spite of their rebellion and hatred of God and his Christ. They are wicked, desperately intent on destroying the kingdom of Christ and establishing the kingdom of darkness. They take counsel together and plot against the Anointed of the Lord. But Christ rules over them so that, in spite of their hatred and rebellion, they nevertheless accomplish all the purpose of God.

It is different with the elect people of God. Christ rules over them too, but in such a way that their hearts are changed. The elect are called out of the kingdom of darkness into the kingdom of light. They are made citizens of the kingdom of heaven that Christ came to establish. Their wills are bent to the service of Christ. They are made, by the power of sovereign grace, willing subjects of Christ who bow before him and subject themselves to his rule. And presently they shall be taken into Christ's everlasting kingdom when that is perfectly established at the end of the age.

Yet there is a relation between the rule of Christ over the wicked and his rule over his people. Christ rules over the wicked so that they must serve the church. All that the unbelieving do is for the purpose of the realization of the kingdom of heaven. Even Christ's rule in the brute creation and in the realm of the angels must be subservient to the final deliverance of those for whom Christ died. "For all things are yours; and ye are Christ's; and Christ is God's" (1 Cor. 3:21–23). "And we know that all things work together for good to them that love God, to them who are the called according to his purpose" (Rom. 8:28). It is the establishment of Christ's kingdom that is the purpose of all things and the goal of Christ's universal rule: "The kingdoms of this world are become the kingdoms of our Lord, and of his Christ; and he shall reign for ever and ever" (Rev. 11:15).

This principle starting point must control our entire view of church history. Church history is the important history of this world. All other history is subservient to the church. Only when we apply this principle will we come to a proper understanding of the history of the church. We must see Christ's scepter swaying in all the events of time. But we must see that it sways for the realization of Christ's kingdom that the elect of God shall inherit.

THE DEFINITION OF CHURCH HISTORY

Before we begin our journey with Christ and his church through the ages, two important distinctions should be made in order to define church history clearly. The first distinction is that between *church history* and *secular history*; the second is between *church history* and *sacred history*.

Church History Distinct from Secular History

As we have seen, God has ordained that the history of the church takes place in the history of the world. Church history is not a history divorced from secular history, taking place in a realm of its own, independent of and invisible to the wicked world. It is a history interwoven with the history of the nations. Never can the history of the church be separated from the history of the nations. Such an experiment has been tried, for example, in the Anabaptist attempt in Münster shortly after the Reformation; but it ended in immorality and bloodshed. The Lord is emphatic: "Remember the former things of old, for I am God, and there is none else; I am God, and there is none like me; declaring the end from the beginning, and from ancient times the things that are not yet done, saying, My counsel shall stand, and I will do all my pleasure" (Isa. 46:9–10).

Yet church history can be distinguished from secular history: not separated from it, but distinguished from it. The former is the history of the church from God's announcement of the "mother promise" to our fallen parents, by which the church was sovereignly begun; the latter is the history of the nations. The former takes place within and as a part of the latter, but it is distinct, and the two must never be confused.

The secular history of this world, fallen in sin and doomed to everlasting destruction, is the stage on which is enacted the drama of the salvation of the church. It is not of man's devising, nor is man's destiny in his own hands. Man does not determine what happens; God does, for he has eternally ordained it. But God has a purpose also in all that he sovereignly does in secular history. In God's providence, secular history serves church history. God had a purpose with Nebuchadnezzar, Nero, Pelagius, Charles V, Napoleon, Hitler, and every man, woman, and child who ever lived and played a prominent or minor role in secular history. That purpose is ultimately to manifest God's holiness and righteous judgment in the punishment of sin. God is "just, in leaving others in the fall and perdition wherein they have involved themselves."[2]

Into this sad world of sin, suffering, darkness, and awful wickedness, God comes also in his grace and mercy. He, as it were, causes the power of heaven itself, with all its holiness and righteousness, to shine into this world. He does this through the gospel, first preached to Adam and Eve in paradise, and constantly and unendingly preached throughout all history. By that gospel God announces that he has one overriding purpose in all he does: to reveal himself in Jesus Christ as merciful and gracious. By the gospel God gathers a church, the membership of which possesses heavenly life, even though the members are still in this world and are a part of its history. That church is saved by the miracle of Jesus Christ. He came into this world. He suffered at the hands of the world power of his day and those of his own countrymen. He died on a wooden cross planted on Calvary. He rose again by the power of God from Joseph's garden. He ascended into heaven from Mount Olivet just outside Jerusalem. He is now exalted as Lord of lords and King of kings.

Trailing in the wake of the miracle of Christ are all the miracles recorded in scripture: the flood, the victories of Israel in Canaan, the raising of the dead, the healing of the blind, the casting out of demons, and all that the Old Testament saints, the Lord himself, and his apostles performed over the centuries. Those many miracles were but signs of the great miracle of Jesus Christ and the salvation of his church. That central miracle continues and will continue until the end of secular history, the return

---

2   Belgic Confession 16, in *The Confessions and the Church Order of the Protestant Reformed Churches* (Grandville, MI: Protestant Reformed Churches in America, 2005), 41–42.

of our Lord, and the everlasting realization of the kingdom of Christ. The physical miracles that dominated the history of the church have faded away, for the reality to which they pointed, the miraculous work of Christ in salvation, is now an everyday event as Christ saves his elect sinners.

Church history is the story of the great miracle of salvation through the ages.

Church History Distinct from Sacred History

In addition to the distinction between church history and secular history, another important distinction must be made within church history itself. Church history is of two parts. The first part, while a part of the history of the church, is also sacred history or the history of revelation. While all this history took place in this world, God was revealing himself in his purpose of salvation in Jesus Christ. It is the history from paradise the first to the writing of Revelation by the apostle John on Patmos. That history of revelation God preserved for the church of all ages by the divine and infallible inspiration of sacred scripture. That part of church history ended with the closing of the canon of scripture around AD 100.

However, the history of the church continues, not now as the history of revelation, but as the history of the same church, now guided in all her life by scripture. Church history, narrowly defined and in distinction from sacred history, is God's revelation of his sovereign, infinitely wise, merciful, just, and all-embracive counsel regarding Christ's church on earth, from the death of the last apostle to the second coming of the Savior. It is thus a biography of the church—of her development both normal and abnormal; of her life, activity, and tribulations in the world; and of all her physical, intellectual, and ethical forces within the limits above specified. It is this church history that is the focus of this book.

Let it never be forgotten, however, that both sacred history and church history take place on this earth and in the cradle of secular history. It must be so, because God sovereignly controls and directs the whole. Christ saves his church from a fallen human race. Through Christ the creation is redeemed from the curse and saved by Christ's atoning work (Col. 1:20). And God's sovereign rule over the wicked, of which scripture so often speaks, is for the purpose of the salvation of the elect. The reprobate are the scaffolding needed to build the temple of the church. They are the roots, stalk, tassel, husks, and cob, necessary for the kernels of corn, but ending their purpose when the corn is ripe. They are the tares in the field, staying in the field until the harvest (Matt. 13:24–30, 37–43).

In this book I deal with church history, but with church history that takes place in the world of wicked men. I deal therefore with church history in its warfare and peace, in its triumphs and seeming defeats, in its influence in and its struggle with the world about it. I deal with the truth for which the church fought and died, for the enemy of the church is not only the wicked world, but also the false church. In the attacks of the false church lies the greatest danger, for when persecution comes from the false church it comes deceptively, with a mask of friendship but hiding a blood-thirsty heart.

Much of the history of the church is written with the ink of the blood of martyrs who loved not their lives unto death. There were also those great moments when Christ showed in emphatic ways that the church is victorious, not *in spite of* the martyrs' death, but *in* their death, for they entered the gates of glory. The church marched on from victory to victory, under the banner of the cross (Ps. 60:4; Song of Sol. 6:4), led by the captain of their salvation (Heb. 2:10), and armed with the weapons of the word of God (Eph. 6:10–17). "All things work together for good to them that love God, to them who are the called according to his purpose" (Rom. 8:28).

THE IMPORTANCE OF STUDYING CHURCH HISTORY[3]

For many reasons, the study of church history is important for the child of God.

First, and principally, the reason for studying church history is to see the glory and wonder of the works of God. History in general, and church history in particular, is the unfolding of the eternal counsel of God through Jesus Christ. We come to know God through church history as part of his revelation to us. This is in order that we may bow in adoration before him who is worthy of all praise.[4]

Second, as we have already seen, church history is family history. The history of the church is the history of the family to which we belong. It is our history, therefore; and we have the solemn obligation, as members of the church, to know our own history. It is good and necessary that we know our roots.

Third, the history of the church can never be separated from the history of doctrine. The history of the church is the history of the work of the Spirit of truth whom

---

3 Taken and slightly altered from Hanko, "Ancient Church History, AD 100–AD 590," 4–6.

4 This is not the place to enter into a discussion of the relation between God's revelation in scripture and in creation and history. It will be sufficient to point out that there is no possibility of understanding God's revelation in history without standing by faith upon the truth of scripture. Scripture gives us the eyes to see God in history and the knowledge to understand God's truth revealed there. This must be our approach throughout a study of church history.

Christ promised to give to his church. To ignore this history is to despise the work of the Spirit of Christ. Thus, church history serves as a necessary background for the history of doctrine.

Fourth, it is essential to have a thorough acquaintance with the history of the church in order that we may fulfill our own calling in our present time. It has been well said, "The present is the fruit of the past and the germ of the future." To understand our times, we must know the past; to prepare for the future, we must labor in the present. Specifically, we cannot fight the battle of faith today in defense of the truth once delivered to the saints unless we know the battles the church before us has fought and won. The battle never changes materially. The enemy is the same; the weapons with which he fights and with which we fight are identical. To fight successfully means that we have studied the battles of those who are now made perfect. The church lapses into error when she loses the consciousness of her heritage. Further, only when we know the truth as it was developed in ages gone by can we take this heritage of the truth and develop it further. We build on a foundation already laid. We can uncover yet greater riches of the knowledge of God only when we work with the heritage entrusted to our care. A church that loosens herself from the moorings of the past is a church hopelessly adrift in the seas of time, doomed to be smashed to pieces on the shoals of error. Faithfulness requires that we know the fruit of the Spirit of truth.

Finally, we shall someday live in glory with those who have belonged to the same church in which we live and die. They were prepared for their place in the perfected temple of heaven by their lives in their day. Likewise we are prepared for our place by God, fashioned and fitted by the Master Builder. Because all this is true, they with us and we with them shall enjoy perfectly the communion of the saints.

THE EXCITING ADVENTURE OF THE MARVELOUS WORK OF GRACE

The importance of Church History is based upon the firm conviction that Scripture is the infallibly inspired Word of God which is given to the church as the revelation of Jehovah God in the face of our Lord Jesus Christ. It contains the whole mystery of salvation which to believe is to be saved. It is everlastingly sure and fixed and relevant for the Church in every age. The history of the Church and of her doctrine is the history of God, through the preaching of the Scriptures and by the work of the Spirit of Christ in the church, gathering, defending, and preserving His Church until the end as He leads that Church into all truth. The history of the Church is the demonstration of the marvelous work of grace. It is the exciting adventure of the marvelous work of grace. It is the exciting adventure of the realization of the work of Christ in the salvation of the elect. Amid the cries of martyrs who loved not their lives unto death, in the crash of the battles for the defense of the faith, through the triumphs and tragedies of a Church living in every age, one comes face to face with the truth: upon the rock which is Christ God builds His church and the gates of hell cannot prevail against it.

It is necessary to know that truth. When Israel forgot the wonders which God performed for the nation, Israel went apostate. When the Church does not know her heritage, the Church loses her heritage and joins Laodicea in being spit from the mouth of Christ. A Church which has no appreciation for the blood of martyrs will not be faithful until death. A Church which does not understand the subtleties of Satan in his fierce attacks against the truth will be easy prey for every wind of doctrine. A Church which does not appreciate and give thanks to God for the work of the Spirit of Truth in leading the Church into all truths will be a Church that despises the truth and sells her heritage for a mess of worldly pottage. A Church which will not learn from the mistakes of the past is doomed to repeat them. But a Church which lives out of her past is a Church vibrant with life and power in this present age to fulfill her calling before God.

—Herman Hanko, "Church Historical Studies," *The Standard Bearer* 57, no. 2 (October 15, 1980): 36

The Ancient Church
(AD 30-590)

PART 1: THE APOSTOLIC PERIOD (AD 30–100)

PART 2: THE POST-APOSTOLIC PERIOD (AD 100–313)

PART 3: THE NICENE AND POST-NICENE PERIOD (AD 313–590)

Part One

The Apostolic Period

(AD 30–100)

INTRODUCTION TO THE APOSTOLIC PERIOD

orty days after his death on the cross and just before his ascension to heaven, the resurrected Lord Jesus Christ told his disciples, "Behold, I send the promise of my Father upon you: but tarry ye in the city of Jerusalem, until ye be endued with power from on high" (Luke 24:49). With these words, the Lord reminded the disciples of his promise to send to his church the Comforter, the Holy Spirit, who would guide the church into all truth (John 16:13). Ten days later, on the Jewish holy day of Pentecost, that promise was fulfilled; and the New Testament church was founded.

The year was likely AD 30, and Jerusalem was packed with devout pilgrims from throughout the Roman world who were there to celebrate the Old Testament Feast of Weeks, a Jewish harvest festival called "Pentecost" (which means "fiftieth") because it was celebrated fifty days (seven weeks) after the Feast of Firstfruits. The disciples of Jesus were there too, waiting for the fulfillment of Christ's promise at his ascension. As 120 disciples met together, God accomplished a tremendous work in church history: he poured out his Holy Spirit upon the church, a wonder accompanied by the sound of a mighty wind, by the appearance of cloven tongues as of fire, and by speaking in tongues. When the apostle Peter preached the gospel of Jesus Christ at the temple that day, three thousand people believed and "the Lord added to the church daily such as should be saved" (Acts 2:47).

Understanding the significance of what Christ accomplished at Pentecost is of supreme importance for the child of God and for the student of church history. At Pentecost, God blessed his New Testament church with the gift of the Holy Spirit. That day made it plain that the Old Testament types and shadows were fulfilled in Jesus Christ, who makes all things new. As men from every nation heard the good news in their own languages, Pentecost demonstrated that the gospel is not just for the Jews, but also for the Gentiles. This event marked the beginning of the rapid expansion of the church as the gospel spread to every major city throughout the Roman Empire.

In addition, Pentecost made it abundantly clear that the Lord had placed a handful of men in a special office in order to lead the New Testament church in its infancy. These men were the apostles, the "sent ones," who were commissioned, equipped, and empowered by God to lead the early church and to lay the foundation of the church by writing the New Testament scriptures. Their apostolic office existed for just seventy years, from the day of Pentecost, when they were filled with the Holy Spirit, through the death of the apostle John, the last living apostle. For this reason, we call this crucial era in church history the Apostolic Period (AD 30–100).

These years are indeed special ones for the church. Much of what we know about the early history of the church is revealed in sacred scripture. These years witnessed the leadership of the apostles, special signs and wonders, the very first synod in church history, the writing of every New Testament book, the rapid spread of the gospel throughout the world, the first outbreaks of persecution against the church, and the shocking destruction of the Jewish temple and the city of Jerusalem by the Romans.

A proper understanding of church history requires an appreciation for God's work during these crucial years—years in which the cornerstone and the foundation of the church were laid, and in which the trumpet blast of sovereign grace through Jesus Christ rang loudly in the world.

Timeline of the Apostolic Period

30	The death, resurrection, and ascension of Jesus Christ; the outpouring of the Holy Spirit at Pentecost.
34	Stephen, one of seven early deacons, is stoned, becoming the first Christian martyr; Paul is converted.
40	The disciples of Jesus Christ are first called *Christians* in the city of Antioch in Syria.
44	James, the son of Zebedee and the first apostle to be martyred, is beheaded by Herod Agrippa I.
45	The Gentile church in Antioch sends famine relief to the Jewish church in Jerusalem.
47	The apostle Paul embarks on his first missionary journey, traveling to Cyprus and then Asia Minor.
48	The Jerusalem Council, the first synod in church history, settles whether Gentiles must be circumcised.
50	The apostle Paul begins his second missionary journey, traveling to Asia Minor, Macedonia, and Greece.
53	The apostle Paul begins his third missionary journey, traveling to Asia Minor, Macedonia, and Greece.
58	Arrested in Jerusalem for starting a riot, the apostle Paul is imprisoned in Caesarea for two years.
60	The apostle Paul appeals to Emperor Nero, is taken to Rome, and lives there under house arrest.
64	Emperor Nero initiates the first Roman persecution; the apostles Peter and Paul are soon martyred.
70	The fall of Jerusalem; the Romans stop the Jewish revolt, raze the city, and destroy the temple.
75	Christians are expelled from Jewish synagogues; the rift between Jews and Christians widens.
90	Emperor Domitian persecutes Jews and Christians for refusing to offer incense to the emperor.
95	The apostle John writes Revelation on the island of Patmos, completing the canon of scripture.
96	The apostolic father Clement of Rome writes *1 Clement*, one of the oldest non-canonical epistles.
97	Timothy, a disciple of the apostle Paul, is killed by a mob while opposing a pagan festival in Ephesus.
100	The apostle John, the last of the apostles, dies; the apostolic father Clement of Rome is martyred.

Map of the Apostolic Period

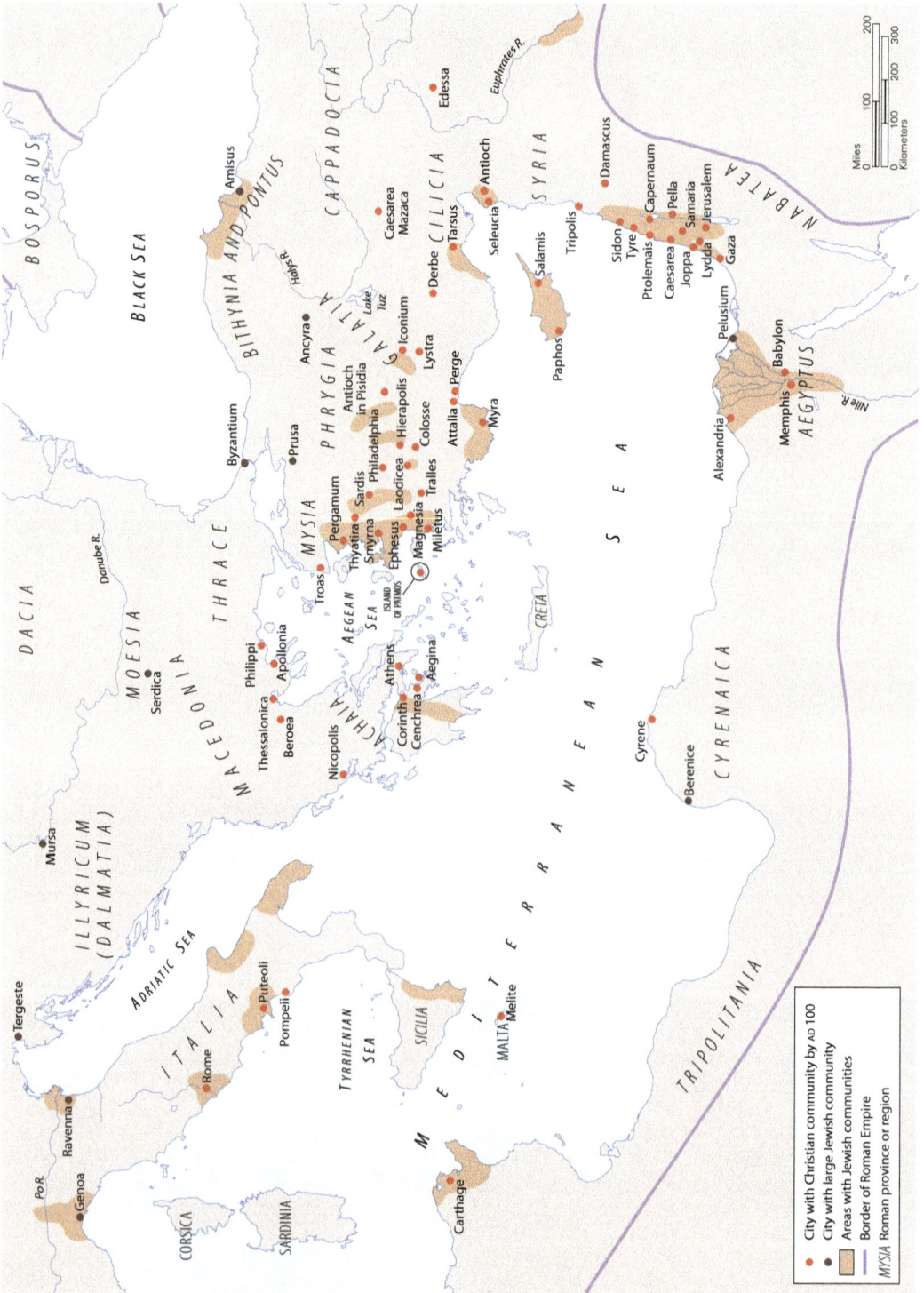

Distribution of Christianity by AD 100. Tim Dowley, *Atlas of Christian History* (Minneapolis, MN: Fortress Press, 2016), 24–25. Used with permission from 1517 Media.

CHAPTER 1: **THE CORNERSTONE OF THE CHURCH**

Now therefore ye are no more strangers and foreigners, but fellow citizens with the saints, and of the household of God; and are built upon the foundation of the apostles and prophets, Jesus Christ himself being the chief corner stone; in whom all the building fitly framed together groweth unto an holy temple in the Lord: in whom ye also are builded together for an habitation of God through the Spirit.

—Ephesians 2:19–22

THE FULLNESS OF TIME

When the apostle Paul was telling the saints in the Galatian churches what God had done for their salvation, he said, "But when the fulness of the time was come, God sent forth his Son" (Gal. 4:4).

What did Paul mean that Christ came at the fullness of time? The expression is a figure. He pictures the time of the history of the world as a cup, the size of which is determined by God. Gradually that cup was being filled as the moments and years of history passed. But a moment came when the cup was filled. That was the moment when Christ came into the world. Because the cup is filled, Christ's coming is the end of history.

It does not seem that way to us, for two thousand and more years have gone by since the coming of Christ into the world, and two thousand years is a long time. But God does not look at time in the same way we do, and he does not use time in the same way we use it. He created time when he began the work of creation, and he uses time also for his own glory. Because time is a creature, the mere passing of moments means nothing to him. He tells us that "one day is with the Lord as a thousand years, and a thousand years as one day" (2 Pet. 3:8). We must try to understand time from God's viewpoint.

19

The four thousand years before the coming of Jesus were years in which God made everything on this earth ready for his Son's arrival. Everything had to be ready, not only in the history of the world, but also in the history of the church, the nation of Israel. Making all things ready meant that God had to teach his people what the coming of Christ meant. He did that by revealing increasing amounts of information about the work that Christ would do to defeat the devil and his work. He did this by dividing the history of the Old Testament into dispensations, or periods of time. God marked the end of one dispensation and the beginning of a new one by specific works that gave his people the additional information God wanted them to have.[1]

After the fall of Adam and Eve in paradise, God almost immediately gave these two sinful humans the promise that he would send the seed of the woman to crush the head of the serpent and his poisonous brood: "And I will put enmity between thee and the woman, and between thy seed and her seed; it shall bruise thy head, and thou shalt bruise his heel" (Gen. 3:15). Adam and Eve fell into sin, but they fell into the arms of Christ. Although God's promise included all that he would do to save his people, God revealed only a little bit of that promise to Adam and Eve. Gradually, through the four thousand years before Christ came, God revealed more and more of his promise.

The revelation of God's promise in the Old Testament was like the full blossoming of a rosebud. When a rose first appears on the bush, it is only a small bud, although the whole rose is in the bud. But over the course of a few days, the rose gradually grows and unfolds until it is fully opened and all the beauty of the flower is displayed. So it was with God's promise. The "bud" was shown to Adam and Eve in paradise; the full bloom was revealed in Christ's work.

God revealed the truths of his work of salvation in a very simple way. In Galatians 4:1–3, Paul compares the Old Testament church with a child. A child cannot understand things very well, and the church in the Old Testament could not understand things very well either. The church had a childish understanding because God had not yet poured out his Spirit on his church as he did on Pentecost. So God made his truth known to the saints through pictures, or types.

Because a child cannot understand very well a book of Reformed dogmatics, he needs pictures to help him understand. God gave Israel a picture book that would help his people understand his works. Some of these pictures were the tabernacle and later the temple, all the sacrifices made in the tabernacle and temple, and all the feast

---

1   Matthew speaks of three of these dispensations in Matthew 1:17, each dispensation limited to fourteen generations.

days. God also gave the people pictures in mighty miracles that he performed: the flood, the passage through the Red Sea on dry ground, the manna from heaven, water from a rock, and the defeat of Israel's enemies when the sun and moon stood still. All these pictures made the believing children of Israel understand better the promise of Christ and increased their longing for Christ to come. These believers knew that God was showing them only pictures, but the pictures were so beautiful that they wanted to see the real work of God in Christ. If you had never been to Yellowstone National Park but saw pictures of the park, you would want to go see it for yourself, because you know that the park is far better than the pictures, even though the pictures are very beautiful. So it was with the Old Testament people of God.

THE OLD TESTAMENT DISPENSATIONS

Although the cornerstone of the church was not laid until Christ's death and resurrection, the people in the Old Testament were also part of the church built on the cornerstone and, in fact, built on the same cornerstone and foundation as the church of the new dispensation.

Baptists and dispensationalists deny that the saints in the Old Testament were part of the church. But this denial is a serious mistake. Stephen calls the nation of Israel "the church" in his speech before the Sanhedrin (Acts 7:38). The cornerstone of the church in the Old Testament was also Christ, and he was given to the church by promise.

The six dispensations of the Old Testament are the following.

Dispensation 1: From the Fall to the Flood

The first dispensation began with the announcement of the promise of Christ to Adam and Eve after they had fallen into sin in paradise, and it ended with the worldwide flood. God revealed that his promise would be fulfilled in the seed of the woman (Gen. 3:15). That is, his promise would be someone born in the generations of Adam and Eve who would destroy the devil's power. This seed of the woman is Jesus Christ.

A dove is sent forth from the Ark

Dispensation 2: From the Flood to Abraham

The second dispensation began when God sent the great flood on a world that had become ripe for judgment, while at the same time saving Noah and his family in the ark. He revealed by the flood that when his promise would be fulfilled, God would destroy the wicked world that had become as wicked as it could possibly be, but he would save his church from the world, of which baptism would later be a sign (1 Pet. 3:20–21). The flood also revealed that salvation would include the covenant that God would make with the whole creation, so that the creation that was under the curse would also be saved and made new. God gave the rainbow as a sign of this promise (Gen. 9:8–17).

Dispensation 3: From Abraham to the Exodus

The third dispensation began with the call of Abraham out of Ur of the Chaldees and ended with the exodus of Israel from Egypt. It was a dispensation in which God revealed a number of things about his promise. He revealed that the content of the

Abraham journeys into the land of Canaan

promise was a covenant that would be a personal relationship between God and his people in which God and his people would be friends. He revealed that his covenant would be established by God alone without man's help, permission, or agreement (Gen. 15). God revealed that his covenant would be established with his people and their generations (17:7), but that these generations would be gathered from both Jews and Gentiles (vv. 5–6). This covenant, God said, would

be made with his people only, because he would send the Messiah, the seed of the woman (Gen. 3:15; Gal. 3:16). God told Abraham that part of the treasures of that covenant would be the land of Canaan for his possession, which was a picture of heaven. Such a covenant also included a prophecy from God that these people would have to be slaves in the land of Egypt (Gen. 15:14), a picture of the slavery of sin from

Moses comes down from Mount Sinai

which Christ saves his church. This was a very important dispensation.

Dispensation 4: From the Exodus to the Conquest

The fourth dispensation began with the deliverance of the Israelites from Egypt by signs and wonders, and it ended with the inheritance of the land of Canaan, under the leadership of Moses and Joshua. It too was a dispensation in which God revealed much concerning his promise. He revealed that the inheritance of Canaan was only a picture of the real inheritance, which was a new heavens and a new earth (Heb. 11:10, 13–16). He also reminded his people that before he would take them to heaven, they would have to be in this world for a long time; that this world is like a desert, without spiritual food and spiritual water; and that he would take care of them by protecting them from many enemies and by providing them with the spiritual food and water they needed (1 Cor. 10:1–4). God also showed them that there would always be wicked among them who would greatly distress them (vv. 5–14). He told them that they would be under the law that came to them from Sinai, but that the Messiah would save them by fulfilling the demands of the law for his people, for they could not keep the law by their own power. God would make it possible for them to keep the law (Gal. 3:23–25; Heb. 8:10–12). He also said that the covenant he would establish with them would be given to them by a mighty warrior named Joshua who would fight for them and defeat all their enemies. The name *Joshua* is Hebrew for Jesus.

The sun stands still for Joshua

Dispensation 5: From the Conquest to David

The fifth dispensation started with the conquest of the land of Canaan under Joshua and lasted until the reign of David. During this period, which included the time of the judges and the rule of Saul, God showed Israel that they could never inherit the real promised land of heaven without a king. Yet the king who would make it possible for them to inherit heaven would not be a king of their choice, like Saul—who was a king like the other nations had—but a king God would give, who really is our Lord Jesus Christ, pictured in David (Ps. 89:19–37).

Dispensation 6: From David to the Captivity

The sixth dispensation extended from the reign of David and Solomon through the Babylonian captivity. It made clear that God's covenant with his people would be in the form of a kingdom, in which Christ would be king. It would be a kingdom of righteousness and peace in which all sin would be taken away. It would be a kingdom of great heavenly riches as in Solomon's days, but it would be ruled by one much wiser than Solomon could ever be. And it would be a kingdom in which God would be acknowledged as worthy of all praise and glory.

Although God did not reveal anything more during this dispensation that began with David's rule, he did show his people that all the types and shadows of the Old

The prophet Amos

Testament were not the real blessedness of the covenant. The types and shadows disappeared, one by one, until they all were gone and God's people found themselves in Babylon, where they could no longer sing the songs of Zion (Ps. 137).

After four hundred years when silence settled over the whole land of Canaan and God did not speak to his people anymore, the fullness of time had come. There was nothing more for God to say. He had described in detail what his promise included. It was a treasure chest of wonderful blessings. But God had shown too that all that his people tried to do on their own ended in disaster, and so God himself had to fulfill his promise. This he did when he sent forth his Son.

THE NEW TESTAMENT DISPENSATION

At the end of all these years of Old Testament types, Christ came as the fulfillment of all that God had promised. With our Lord's birth the new dispensation began. It is the dispensation of the coming of Christ and the fulfillment of our Lord's promise: "Lo, I am with you always, even unto the end of the world" (Matt. 28:20).

This dispensation is the dispensation of the coming of Christ because he comes to his church by his word and Spirit; he comes by his Spirit to lead the church into all truth (John 16:13); he comes when we die in order to take us to heaven (vv. 14:1–4); he comes upon the clouds of heaven at the end of time to finish his work (Matt. 24:30).

Christ's coming is the end of all these dispensations, but it is also the end of the world. That Christ's coming is the end of the world is difficult for us to see, for Christ was born of Mary in Bethlehem over two thousand years ago. How then can Christ's birth be considered the end of the world?[2]

The concept is hard for us to understand because we are so tied up by the chains of time that we cannot think of things from God's point of view. God does not look at time as the passing of minutes, hours, days, and years, but he looks at it entirely as a means to accomplish his own purpose to glorify himself in Christ. God looks at time from the viewpoint of what he does in time.

Peter gives us an idea of how God looks at time when he says, "But, beloved, be

---

2 The word "end," used in this sense, refers to a purpose that is accomplished. The end of a war is the accomplishment of the defeat of the enemy.

not ignorant of this one thing, that one day is with the Lord as a thousand years, and a thousand years as one day" (2 Pet. 3:8). In God's works the mere passing of one day or of a thousand years means nothing; the important thing is what happens in time. What difference does it make to God whether what he does takes a day (the creation of the rainbow) or a year (the time Noah and his family were in the ark) or forty years (the time Israel was in the wilderness) or four thousand years (the time it took for God to teach his people everything they had to know about his covenant) or more than two thousand years (to bring the world to an end through the coming of Christ)?

The prophets spoke of the "day of the LORD" as the day of the coming of Christ (Joel 2:1–2, 28–32; Acts 2:16–21). But although it became evident that the day of the coming of Christ would be a period of many, many years, the prophets spoke of it as a "day." They did this because, regardless of whatever length of time it took for Christ to come and to finish his work, the "day" of the Lord was the climax and fulfillment of all God had said he would do.

THE COMING OF CHRIST

The coming of Christ in the New Testament dispensation is the laying of the cornerstone of the church (Eph. 2:19–22). The church is a temple, and Christ is the cornerstone.

In ancient times the cornerstone was an extremely important part of a building. The foundation began with the cornerstone; therefore, builders spent a great deal of time looking for the proper one and preparing it. The cornerstone had to have an outside angle of ninety degrees and a level, flat top. If the cornerstone was right, the walls attached to it were square, and the walls were level if the top of the stone was level. So Christ, the first in God's counsel in the building of his church, determines the shape and perfection of the church.

The Bible speaks of the one coming of Christ the cornerstone in many different ways. These ways include the birth of Christ in Bethlehem, the outpouring of the Holy Spirit at Pentecost, the death of believers in every age, and the coming of Christ at the end of time.

The Birth of Christ

Christ came when he was born of the virgin Mary in Bethlehem. That coming included all the work that Christ did here on earth in his incarnation. He grew up, began his public ministry, preached and worked miracles, gave himself up to be a captive of the Jews, suffered and died on the cross for the sins of his people, rose again from Joseph's grave, and went back to glory. All that was the coming of Christ (John 1:11). The purpose of this part of Christ's coming was specifically to crush the head of Satan by smashing his power, which he did on the cross.

God's works are always marvelous. So it was with the laying of the cornerstone. The cornerstone was laid by means of its rejection by those who claimed to be builders of God's house. But in so doing, they rejected the only cornerstone on which the house could be built. God used their very rejection (the cross) to lay the cornerstone (Isa. 28:16; Matt. 21:42; Acts 4:11; 1 Pet. 2:7–8).

The Outpouring of the Spirit

What happened on Pentecost was also the coming of Christ. In his sermon to his disciples on the very eve of his crucifixion, Christ told his disciples that he would not leave them comfortless but would come to them (John 14:16–18, 28). Christ comes from heaven to his church when he sends his Spirit to the church, for he is with the church by means of his word and Spirit.

The Death of Believers

Furthermore, Jesus speaks of the death of believers as his coming. In John 14:1–4, he tells the church that after his death and resurrection he is going away to prepare a place for them in his Father's house. When that place is ready for each saint, Christ will come again to take his saint to glory. Christ himself has prepared each saint for his place. The saint is ready to go home at the same time that his place is ready in the Father's house. There Christ's people will be with him. Death is a part of the gathering of the church. Christ does not gather his church to make his church to live in the world forever. He comes to lead his saints into the heavenly land of rest. In every respect, the moment of death for a believer is the end of the world for him.

The End of Time

The coming of Christ at the end of time is final. He comes in judgment to destroy all the wicked and Satan and his devils. He comes to take his whole church to glory, for then all God's people will have been born and saved. God's purpose with the whole creation and all history will be accomplished, and there is no reason why the world should continue. It would be like coming to the end of a book but trying to continue to read. There is no more to read. The world comes to an end. There is no more to be done.

THE LAYING OF THE CORNERSTONE

The work that our Lord performed is therefore the cornerstone for the entire Old Testament and the New Testament church. The cornerstone of the church was laid by Christ's suffering and death. He bore the curse of sin, which was rightfully ours; he went to hell in our place; he was obedient to his God in all respects, even when hell burned him with its hottest fires; and he fulfilled the law by his obedience. In this way he made it possible for us to be saved, for we do not have to do anything to atone for our sins and deliver ourselves from them. The church could now be built on a solid foundation.

Our Lord arose from the dead in power. He did not come from the grave by means of the door through which his body had been carried; but he broke a new door from the grave that opens in heaven. Throughout all history, the grave was the door to hell. But it could not be a door to hell for Christ, for he had already been to hell and had broken hell's power. He broke out of the grave through a new door to heaven that he had made through his work. That door becomes the door to heaven for all those for whom he died.

Now Christ is exalted in the highest heavens. All authority in heaven and on earth is given to him. He holds the reins of the universe and of the heavenly creation in his hands. God has given him the power to do all the things that God had determined in his counsel to do. Our Lord from heaven saves his church and takes his church into heaven with him. He also rules over all things so that "all things work together for good, to them that love God and are called according to his purpose" (Rom. 8:28).

So is the cornerstone laid on which the foundation and the temple of the church is built.

4. To whom coming, as unto a living stone, disallowed indeed of men, but chosen of God, and precious,
5. Ye also, as lively stones, are built up a spiritual house, an holy priesthood, to offer up spiritual sacrifices, acceptable to God by Jesus Christ.
6. Wherefore also it is contained in the scripture, Behold, I lay in Sion a chief corner stone, elect, precious: and he that believeth on him shall not be confounded.

7. Unto you therefore which believe he is precious: but unto them which be disobedient, the stone which the builders disallowed, the same is made the head of the corner,

8. And a stone of stumbling, and a rock of offence, even to them which stumble at the word, being disobedient: whereunto also they were appointed.

9. But ye are a chosen generation, a royal priesthood, an holy nation, a peculiar people: that ye should shew forth the praises of him who hath called you out of darkness into his marvellous light. (1 Pet. 2:4–9)

CHAPTER 2: **THE FOUNDATION OF THE APOSTLES**

And he gave some, apostles; and some, prophets; and some, evangelists;
and some, pastors and teachers; for the perfecting of the saints,
for the work of the ministry, for the edifying of the body of Christ.

—Ephesians 4:11–12

SACRED APOSTOLIC HISTORY

I have deliberately begun the story of Christ and his church through the ages with the apostles. Church historians have debated the question whether actual church history begins in 4 BC (the approximate date of the birth of Christ), AD 27 (when Christ began his public ministry), AD 30 (the death of Christ and the outpouring of the Holy Spirit at Pentecost), or AD 100 (the death of the apostle John and the end of the apostolic period). The discussion is somewhat beside the point, for if one sets aside the error of the dispensationalists, who make a sharp distinction between the old and new dispensations, a case can be made for beginning the history of the church with the announcement of God to our fallen parents that he would send the seed of the woman to crush the head of the serpent (Gen. 3:15). The Old Testament saints are one church along with the saints of the entire new dispensation.

It is, however, necessary and important to make a distinction between the sacred history of the Apostolic Period (AD 30–100) and the history of the new dispensational church (AD 100–present). The period from the mother promise at the beginning of history to AD 100 is that part of history in which God revealed his mighty work of salvation. This period is called *historia revelationis* (the history of revelation) or *historia sacra* (sacred history). The Apostolic Period is part of the sacred history of God's revelation of himself in Jesus Christ.

The age of sacred history finished near the end of the first century with the apostle John's writing of Revelation, the last book of the Bible. The charismatic movement wrongly claims that new revelation continues today in tongue-speaking, prophecies, and miracles. It is an error that approaches the sin against the Holy Spirit. The truth is that when God finished his work of revelation at the end of the Apostolic Period, church history—insofar as it is distinguished from sacred history—began.

The fact remains, however, that I have begun our travels with Christ and his church with a discussion of the sacred history of the Apostolic Period given to us in the New Testament. There is good reason for this.

Christ, from his position at God's right hand, continues to work and to teach throughout the entire new dispensation. But first our Lord teaches the foundation of the entire history of the new dispensation church. That is, he lays down the principles of his word in gathering, defending, and preserving his church until he comes again. He gives the church these principles in order that the church may know why and how he does what he does in his work of saving the church. Referring to the church institute, our Lord makes clear how he gathers, defends, and preserves his church so that in our work in the church we may know what he has done and what we are to do. All this instruction is found in the New Testament books of the Bible.

Especially in our modern age, theologians and leaders in the church consider the principles of church life as outlined in the New Testament to be only *descriptions* of the work of the apostles. They teach that the foundation that Christ gave to the church in her doctrine, worship, and government are not binding on us. So they ordain women into office, condone homosexuality, deny the towering truth of justification by faith alone, and ignore the sovereign rule of Christ in gathering his elect by his power.

However, the New Testament scriptures are not a manual of rules and regulations. God's revelation of himself in sacred history is revelation *in history*. These principles are to be found in the outpouring of the Spirit on Pentecost, in the work of the apostles as described in Acts, and in the letters of the inspired writers to the churches, which address problems and errors in the church, as well as her calling and labors. The principles, as they always do, arise out of the organic life of the church.

Hence, we begin this journey with the foundation of the new dispensation church, a foundation built by divine revelation and in history. Our concern in the pages that follow is how the church observes these principles.

THE FOUNDATION OF THE CHURCH

After Luke was used by God to write the third gospel, he also became God's instrument to write the book of Acts. Luke began Acts with the words, "The former treatise have I made, O Theophilus, of all that Jesus began both to do and teach, until the day in which he was taken up" (Acts 1:1–2). Luke's former treatise was his gospel narrative in which he recorded what Jesus *began* to do and teach until his ascension. In the book of Acts, Luke tells us what the ascended Lord *continued* to do and teach from heaven.

In other words, the gospels tell us how the cornerstone of the church was laid; Acts tells us how the foundation of the apostles was laid. The apostle Paul writes, "Now therefore ye are no more strangers and foreigners, but fellowcitizens with the saints, and of the household of God. And are built upon the foundation of the apostles and prophets, Jesus Christ himself being the chief corner stone" (Eph. 2:19–20).

The foundation of the church is the teaching of the apostles, the New Testament scriptures. It is true that Ephesians 2:20 speaks also of the prophets, but that is because the apostles and the prophets said the same things. The distinction is that the prophets spoke in the Old Testament language of types and shadows, while the apostles made clear what the prophets had said and how it applied to the dispensation of the coming of Christ. The old saying is true: "The new is in the old contained; the old is in the new explained."

THE OFFICE OF APOSTLE

Christ, from his position at God's right hand as the King of the church, gave to his disciples the special office of apostle. The term *apostle* means "sent one"; an apostle was one who had the unique qualification that he was commissioned and sent by the risen Christ to lay the foundation of the church (Eph. 2:20). The apostolic office, therefore, was special for several reasons.

First, the apostles held all three special offices that later appeared in the New Testament church: the

The apostles preach the gospel

offices of minister, elder, and deacon. Fairly early in the history of the apostolic period these three offices developed organically from the office of apostle.

Second, the apostles were inspired in their preaching and teaching. For example, the apostle Peter's sermon on Pentecost and his two speeches before the Sanhedrin were inspired by God (Acts 2:14–40; 4:8–12; 5:29–32). Whatever speeches of the apostles are recorded for us in Acts, they too are inspired.

Third, the apostles performed miracles to accompany their preaching. These miracles were many, varied, and of great power. The apostles healed the sick, cast out devils, and raised from the dead. But these miracles always demonstrated in vivid deeds what the gospel was doing to a man spiritually. Because the scriptures had not yet been completely written, the hearers of the gospel had little standard by which to judge whether the preaching was actually of God. The miracles, always accompanying the preaching, demonstrated the truth of the gospel (Acts 8:6–7; 2 Cor. 12:12; Heb. 2:3–4). When the scriptures were completed, the apostolic office ended and the miracles ceased to be performed.

WHO WERE THE APOSTLES?

The apostles ("sent ones") were thirteen men who were chosen by the Lord Jesus Christ to be witnesses of his resurrection. They were commissioned by Jesus Christ and equipped by the Holy Spirit to lead the early church, to preach the gospel throughout the world, and to write the New Testament scriptures, thereby laying the foundation of the church.

The individuals who held this unique church office are identified by name in Acts 1 and 9.

Peter (also called Simon, the brother of Andrew)

Andrew (the brother of Peter)

James (the brother of John, the son of Zebedee)

John (the brother of James, the son of Zebedee)

Philip (not the deacon and evangelist)

Bartholomew (also called Nathanael)

Thomas (also called Didymus)

Matthew (also called Levi)

James (the Less, the son of Alphaeus)

Simon (the Zealot)

Judas (not Iscariot, also called Jude and Thaddaeus)

Matthias (replacing Judas Iscariot by lot)

Paul (also called Saul)

LAYING THE FOUNDATION: THE WRITING OF SCRIPTURE

The apostles were inspired by God to write the New Testament scriptures. The apostles themselves in their own persons were not the foundation of the new dispensational church; their infallibly inspired writings are that foundation. The writing of the New Testament scriptures was the laying of the foundation of the New Testament church. Where the scriptures are purely preached, there the temple of God is built. A church that preaches partly the scriptures and partly the words of men is a church sliding off the foundation. And a church that does not preach the scriptures at all is a sandcastle without a foundation.

More must be said about the writing of the scriptures.

The twenty-seven books of the New Testament were not written very early. The church went for at least two decades after Pentecost without even a part of the written New Testament. It had, of course, the Old Testament scriptures. When the Bereans searched the scriptures to see whether what the apostle Paul taught was true (Acts 17:11), they were searching the Old Testament scriptures.

The apostle Paul writes an epistle

The four gospel accounts were written for different reasons. Matthew was written to help the churches in their "home missionary" work among the Jews, to prove that Jesus Christ was indeed the promised Messiah who had come to fulfill the Old Testament. This purpose is the reason why, in Matthew, so many references to these scriptures are found. In Matthew 1 and 2 alone there are three references to and five direct quotations from the Old Testament. The references are the genealogies of Christ found in Matthew 1, the appearance of the star (Num. 24:17), and the gifts of the wise men (Ps. 72:10–11). The quotations are found in Matthew 1:23 and Matthew 2:6, 15, 17–18, and 23.

Mark was written so that the church could prove to the Gentiles that Jesus was a king of great authority. This gospel account also shows the church how extremely busy the Lord was in his earthly ministry (Mark 1:32–39). To read the whole gospel at once and to absorb all that is described of the Lord's works almost leaves one breathless. It is proof of what the disciples realized at the first cleansing of the temple: "The zeal of thine house hath eaten me up" (John 2:17).

Luke was written to prove that Jesus Christ was like us in all things, except for sin. He was truly a man such as we are. He was the Son of Man who came to seek and to save those who are lost (Luke 19:10) and the Shepherd who goes out to find the lost sheep (15:4).

John tells us why he wrote his gospel narrative: "But these are written, that ye might believe that Jesus is the Christ, the Son of God; and that believing ye might have life through his name" (John 20:31). John therefore shows in unmistakable language that Jesus is true God of true God.

All the books of the New Testament canon were written for specific purposes. The apostles did not sit in their studies and receive the Spirit who inspired them to write these books. The apostles wrote what they wrote because of circumstances in the churches that compelled them to write. All the books are addressed to specific problems or needs that arose in the churches. But God also created the circumstances that required a given book to be written.

The last book written, Revelation, also the last in our Bible, was written by the apostle John while he was banished to the island of Patmos during the reign of the Roman emperor Domitian around AD 95. So the entire New Testament was written over a period of about fifty years.

By the end of the first century, the canon of scripture was completed and the foundation of the entire church was laid. This foundation included the doctrine of the church, the principles of public worship and of church government, and the calling of the church in the world. Early on, the church recognized the same books that are in our Bibles as being God's word to them. The gospels and the epistles were copied many times and widely circulated among the churches. We can easily imagine how all the churches in western Asia Minor, for example, would want a copy of Paul's letter to the Colossians. This desire for what the church knew to be inspired scripture was the reason for the early multiplication of documents of the New Testament Bible.

LAYING THE FOUNDATION OF DOCTRINE

In the inspired scriptures, given to the church through the apostles, God gave the church of all ages its doctrinal foundation, the truth that the church was commanded to maintain, confess, and develop (Acts 2:42). Everything the church must know and teach is found in the scriptures alone, including everything the church must know about God, man, Christ, salvation, the church, and the last things. In the scriptures, the church has the revelation of the gospel of Jesus Christ—the good news that the church is saved by God's sovereign grace alone by faith alone through Jesus Christ alone and apart from man's works. The apostolic truth of sovereign grace is worth emphasizing here, for this truth is always attacked by heretics in every age; and this is the truth that the true church in every age confesses and defends.

SOVEREIGN GRACE:
THE ONE REAL ISSUE IN THE HISTORY OF THE CHURCH

The issue of salvation by sovereign grace has always been the one real issue in the history of the church when the church was called to fight against false doctrine.

This was already the issue in the apostolic era when Paul, in his battles against the Judaizers in Galatia and Rome, fought tenaciously against any kind of salvation by works.

Sovereign grace was the issue at Nicaea in AD 325 when the truth of the divinity of Christ was given creedal formulation. Athanasius, the great defender of the truth, made that clear when he argued passionately for Christ's divinity on the ground that if Christ were not "very God of very God" we could not be saved. Salvation, he said, is of God alone.

Sovereign grace was the issue when Augustine waged battle with the Pelagian and Semi-Pelagian heresies brought into the church in the fifth century. Augustine not only defended salvation by sovereign grace, but insisted that sovereign grace could be maintained only on the basis of sovereign predestination, that is, on the basis of sovereign election and sovereign reprobation. Yet, Semi-Pelagianism became the official teaching of Rome. That Rome adopted Semi-Pelagianism is not surprising, for Rome was intent on preserving the doctrine of human merit, and sovereign grace destroys human merit.

Though the truths of sovereign grace were hidden beneath many layers of Rome's errors concerning the merit of good works, God restored His truth to the church through the work of the Reformers. Luther insisted that "justification by faith alone without works" was the hinge on which the whole church turned. And that doctrine, written in large letters, was the theme of the entire reformatory work of the sixteenth century.

This was the issue at Dordrecht (Dordt) when Arminianism went down in defeat at the greatest assembly of Reformed theologians in post-Reformation times.

And this is the issue in the history of the Protestant Reformed Churches (PRC). Sovereign grace. Nothing else.

—Herman Hanko, *For Thy Truth's Sake*
(Grandville, MI: Reformed Free Publishing Association, 2000), 3–4.

LAYING THE FOUNDATION OF GOVERNMENT

The scriptures also contain the foundation of church government. These principles are not given in a mechanical way so that the New Testament scriptures contain lessons in church government; rather, they are given as the apostles addressed themselves, in their letters, to the problems they confronted in their missionary work.

Just as in the old dispensation God gave Israel prophets, priests, and kings, so also in the new dispensation God gave his church prophets in ministers, priests in deacons, and kings in elders. The apostles instituted the office of deacon early when the need arose in the church (Acts 6:1–6). Paul ordained elders in every city (14:23). He trained ministers and ordained them (1 Tim. 3; 4:14; 2 Tim. 2:1–2). So the role of those who hold these special offices in the church was defined.

The office of ministers is to be found, for example, in Colossians 4:17, "Take heed to the ministry which thou hast received in the Lord, that thou fulfil it"; in Paul's instructions to Titus in the book that carries his name; and in Paul's letters to Timothy, a minister in the church of Ephesus, in 1 and 2 Timothy, but especially in 2 Timothy 4:2, "Preach the word; be instant in season, out of season; reprove, rebuke, exhort with all longsuffering and doctrine." Paul expands further on this in his own descriptions of his ministry to the elders of Ephesus in Acts 20:24–35.

The work of elders is clearly defined in several passages. In addition, passages such as 1 Peter 5:1–4 and Hebrews 4:7, 13–17 instruct us regarding the attitude that members of the church ought to have toward their officebearers.

The work of the deacons is described at the time of the institution of the office in Acts 6.

The Bible even tells us about the need for the censure of the wicked in the church. Jesus speaks of censure in Matthew 16:18–19. Paul speaks of censure in 1 Corinthians 5:4–5 and Titus 3:10–11. Even the need for broader ecclesiastical assemblies is demonstrated and described in the account of the great Jerusalem synod, discussed in detail in Acts 15.

LAYING THE FOUNDATION OF WORSHIP

The foundation was laid as well for the worship of the church. Jesus had already, early in his ministry, given an important qualification for all worship that was acceptable to God: "God is a Spirit: and they that worship him must worship him in spirit and in truth" (John 4:24).

The practices of the apostles in their work in the churches were the way in which the Spirit told the whole church what elements must be included in the worship of God.

The apostles worshiped on the first day of the week and set a pattern for the New Testament church. The worship of the church must be on the first day of the week because Christ arose on the first day of the week and because his resurrection makes our worship possible (Acts 20:7; 1 Cor. 16:2).

Preaching, according to the practice of the apostles, was to be the most important element in the worship

Paul preaches to the Thessalonians

of God. Wherever Paul went on his missionary journeys he preached, first in the synagogues and then wherever he could find a place to meet. The Lord himself laid down the example, for wherever he went he entered the synagogues and opened the scriptures. Yet the Lord preached anywhere and everywhere, teaching the church that the place in which the church meets is not the most important part of worship.

Singing was to be a part of the worship of God too. Paul writes of this to the churches in Ephesus and in Colosse (Eph. 5:18–20; Col. 3:16). Singing was a carry-over from the Old Testament. In the worship of God in the temple, there was much singing. In the Old Testament it seemed to be done mostly by the Levites, probably because the Holy Spirit had not yet been poured out. We do read, however, of Israel singing at the time of the successful passage through the Red Sea (Ex. 15:1). The psalms were written for the purpose of the worship of God. That purpose is a powerful incentive to sing psalms in the worship services of the church today.

Prayers also were to be a part of worship. Paul specifically commands Timothy that he must pray for all in authority (1 Tim. 2:1–3). In that passage Paul assumes that Timothy leads the congregation in prayer and specifically addresses himself to one thing for which Timothy must pray. Worship without prayer is almost impossible to imagine. Worship is covenantal fellowship with God. At the center of covenantal fellowship is conversation. In worship God speaks to his people, and his people in the holy conversation of prayer speak to him.

Collections are specifically commanded to be a part of worship. Paul refers to collections in 2 Corinthians 9:1–8 and mentions them as part of the worship in 1 Corinthians 16:1–2. These collections were for the poor in the church of Jerusalem, but Paul also speaks of the need for churches to support the work of the ministry.

Presumably he means that the churches do this through collections (1 Cor. 9:9–17; 2 Cor. 8:10–24; Gal. 6:6).

Christ, through the apostles, laid the foundation for the entire life of the church. He laid this foundation through their inspired writings and in the areas of doctrine, worship, and government. Thus the purpose of the apostles' presence in the church was attained. The church was now ready to embark on her long and perilous journey through time, little realizing that that journey would last over two thousand years.

CHAPTER 3: **THE SPREAD OF THE GOSPEL**

Go ye therefore, and teach all nations, baptizing them in the name of
the Father, and of the Son, and of the Holy Ghost.

—MATTHEW 28:19

THE IMPORTANCE OF PENTECOST

At the time of our Lord's ascension from Mount Olivet, outside Jerusalem, he told his disciples: "But ye shall receive power, after that the Holy Ghost is come upon you: and ye shall be witnesses unto me both in Jerusalem, and in all Judaea, and in Samaria, and unto the uttermost part of the earth" (Acts 1:8). It was our Lord's last command spoken before he went to heaven.

Not only did these words of the Lord give the apostles and the church their marching orders, but the Lord indicated also the order of the spread of the gospel: Jerusalem, Judea, Samaria, and the uttermost parts of the earth. The apostles followed this pattern.

Throughout the entire Old Testament, from the time of Abraham to Pentecost, the gospel had been limited to Jews only. A few Gentiles were saved, including the widow of Zarephath, Naaman the leper from Syria, and the Ninevites who repented at the preaching of Jonah. These were saved without becoming Jews. They were saved as individuals and were not saved in their generations as God had promised Abraham (Gen. 17:7). They were prophetic of another day coming.

That God limited salvation to the Jews does not mean that Gentiles never joined the nation of Israel. We need think only of the multitude of Egyptians who went with Israel out of Egypt (Ex. 12:38), of Rahab (Heb. 11:31; James 2:25) and Ruth (Ruth 1), of the Gibeonites who made peace with Israel in Canaan (Josh. 9:3–27), and of Uriah the Hittite (2 Sam. 11), Araunah the Jebusite (24:18–25), and a host of others. But all these Gentiles could only be saved by becoming Jews. They had to be incorporated into the Jewish nation by the rite of circumcision and by adopting the Jewish religion. The hour of the Gentiles was not yet (Luke 4:25–27).

Pentecost changed all that. By pouring out the Spirit of Christ on the church, God made the church confront its calling to bring the gospel to all nations. The three signs that accompanied this outpouring demonstrated in a graphic way the work of the Spirit of Christ, whom Christ gave to his church.

Paul preaches at Pentecost

First, the sound of a rushing mighty wind was a sign of the irresistible power of the Spirit of Christ, who was sent by Christ to gather his church. Nothing in heaven or on earth could prevent the work from being accomplished.

The second sign of the tongues as of fire demonstrated how the Spirit would perform his work: by destroying all that was of sin and bringing about a new creature purged from sin. Just as fire burns away dross and purifies gold, so does the fire of God's judgment destroy all that is wicked, and in the way of judgment, it purifies the redeemed church and the whole creation.

The third sign of the outpouring of the Spirit was the miracle of speaking in other tongues. When the 120 disciples of Christ upon whom the Spirit was poured out confronted the many people who gathered in the street, they spoke in the native languages of the people. Each one heard the explanation of what had happened in his own language. Jerusalem was full of proselytes and Jews from all over the Mediterranean basin, and these people spoke both the Aramaic of Jerusalem and also the languages spoken in the provinces from which they came (Acts 2:8–11). In this way God showed the early church and the people who were converted under Peter's preaching on Pentecost that with the dawn of the new dispensation, God would save Gentiles as well as Jews; that he would save Gentiles not by making them Jews, but by keeping them Cretians, Egyptians, Cappadocians, Phrygians, Dutchmen, Irish, Singaporeans, and all the rest. They would be saved not by becoming Jews through circumcision, but as natives of the foreign lands in which they were born and lived with their national, racial, linguistic, and cultural characteristics.

The significance of Pentecost is as great as the birth of Christ, his death on the cross, and his resurrection and exaltation. Christ from heaven poured out on his church the Spirit whom the Father had given him. In this way Christ fulfilled his promise, "Lo, I am with you always, even unto the end of the world" (Matt. 28:20). Pentecost meant that the old dispensation, the dispensation of types and shadows, had passed away, pushed aside by the reality of the work of Christ, to whom all the types pointed.

With the outpouring of the Spirit, the spiritual understanding of the apostles and of the church was much greater than it ever could have been in the old dispensation. At the time of the ascension of the Lord, the disciples were still thinking in terms of an earthly kingdom that Christ would establish (Acts 1:6). But after the Spirit was given, Peter preached a sermon in which he showed that he suddenly understood the entire work of Christ from Christ's birth to the end of time (2:14–40).

Finally, the gift of the Spirit made it clear that all God's people are prophets, priests, and kings (Acts 2:17–18). Pentecost was the climax of Christ's work on earth and the beginning of his work at God's right hand.

THE GOSPEL TO THE GENTILES

A word must be said about the place of the Jews in the first century. The early church was established within the confines of the Jewish nation. Jesus Christ was born a Jew and performed his entire earthly labors within the boundaries of Jewry. Only through his cross and resurrection did Christ become the catholic Christ.

Nevertheless, the early church was composed almost exclusively of Jews; and the early work of the apostles was limited almost exclusively to their kinsmen. But the Jews were spread over the whole known world. The Jews had fixed abodes in every part and corner of the empire. For the most part, they remained faithful to their Jewish faith. In their distant homes they had established their synagogues and carried Jewish culture to every land. All of this had bearing on the part they played in the spread of the gospel of Christ.

The early church had a difficult time breaking loose from the Old Testament rules. After over a thousand years of salvation only for Jews, the early church had difficulty understanding that Gentiles could also be saved as Gentiles! To enter a new dispensation in which Gentiles were saved as Gentiles meant that the church had to leave behind the temple, its sacrifices and ceremonies, the Old Testament feast days, and all the civil and ceremonial laws that had become a part of being a Jew.

Until late in the first century the church struggled with whether or not new converts had to be circumcised. The first synod was held in Jerusalem to discuss this very problem (Acts 15:1–35). The epistles of Paul to the Romans and the Galatians dealt with this question. The controversy shifted from Jerusalem to Antioch in Syria and caused division there (Gal. 2:11–14). It was still troubling the church when Paul was in Jerusalem at the end of his third missionary journey and had nearly finished his life's work (Acts 21:21–26).

God gradually led the church to understand the great doctrine of a truly catholic church. A catholic church is a universal church in which every elect child of God is saved while keeping his racial, national, and personal characteristics. How long it took the church to learn this! The change was finally accomplished by Christ's sovereign rule over all things, bringing about several events that tore the church away from its narrow Jewish identity and making it universal.

Peter preaches to the family of Cornelius

First, God's salvation of proselytes was a half-step in the direction of a catholic church. Proselytes were actually Gentiles, but Gentiles who had adopted the Jewish religion. Many were present at Jerusalem from other lands when the Holy Spirit came to the church at Pentecost (Acts 2:10). The presence of proselytes in the church enabled the members of the church to begin thinking in terms of a catholic church. Among the three thousand believers at Pentecost were many proselytes who were saved and received the Spirit, and who then returned to their own countries. Cornelius, a Roman centurion, was a proselyte. It took a vision to Cornelius and to Peter to persuade Peter to go to Cornelius's house (Acts 10). Upon his return to Jerusalem, Peter had to justify his eating with the Gentiles (11:1–18). The church was beginning to see that it must bring the gospel to the Gentiles.

Another way in which the church was led to go to the Gentiles was God's work of bringing persecution to the church in Jerusalem, for it forced many to leave the city and flee to other parts of the known world of that day, where they brought the gospel (Acts 8:1–4).

At the time of the persecution in Jerusalem, God brought the gospel to Samaria through the work of Philip, a deacon and evangelist (Acts 8:5), even though Samaritans were not full-blooded Jews. It was as if God gradually nudged the church out of Jerusalem and Judea to that area just north of Judea where the Samaritans lived.

The continued persecution of the church in Jerusalem forced the church to move the center of its work out of Jerusalem to Antioch in Syria. God did this because Antioch was a Gentile city and Jerusalem was not suited to be the calling church of missionaries to the Gentiles in far-off lands. A Gentile church could better do missionary work among Gentiles, and Jerusalem was continuously embroiled in controversies over the role of the Old Testament law in salvation (Acts 11:1–18; 15:30; 21:20–27; Gal. 2:1–15). In the book of Acts, Jerusalem fades into the background and Antioch becomes the center of the church's work. Jerusalem had served its purpose as the picture of the church of the new dispensation, and so it not only faded into the background but was destroyed by the armies of Rome under Titus in AD 70.

PAUL'S MISSIONARY WORK

The way was now opened for the gospel, under the pressure of the work of the Spirit, to break out of the narrow confines of Jewry, leaving behind all the dead trappings of Judaism, and to travel westward until it reached the Atlantic Ocean. Paul, made an apostle by Christ, was specifically called by God to the work of foreign missions.

The apostle Paul was the chief instrument in the work of the Spirit to bring the gospel to the Gentiles. He had been born a Jew in the Asian city of Tarsus, a city in Cilicia on the northeast corner of the Mediterranean Sea. Birth in that city gave Paul Roman citizenship, something that aided him greatly in his work as a missionary to the Gentiles (Acts 16:34–40; 22:24–30). Over the course of three missionary journeys and a final voyage to Rome, Paul brought the gospel of Jesus Christ to the Gentiles of the Roman world.

As the apostle Paul and other early missionaries performed their labors, the Holy Spirit taught the church various principles of mission work and of the establishment of churches. These principles, observed by the apostles, remain authoritative for the entire new dispensation church.

First, the missionary work of the apostles was directed by the Holy Spirit through a calling church. The Holy Spirit worked in the church of Antioch through prophets who chose and sent Paul and Barnabas (Acts 13:1–4). From the role that the Holy Spirit played in directing the apostle on his second missionary journey (16:6–7), we may conclude that the Spirit also directed them to the areas in which Christ wanted them to labor. The exalted Christ, through his Spirit, gathers his church. He knows where his elect are and where he wants a church to be established. The church does its work in obedience to Christ, through missionaries who are ordained men sent by a calling church.

Second, the apostolic missionaries went out sometimes two by two, but more frequently in small groups. This principle of two by two is also authoritative for the church throughout the new dispensation. Paul never went alone. On the first missionary journey of Paul and Barnabas, John Mark went along, until he returned to Jerusalem when Paul and Barnabas arrived in Asia Minor. Paul and Silas went together on the second missionary journey, the beginning of which is described in Acts 18:23. We are told that several accompanied Paul on his travels (20:4). Further, we know that Luke went with him because he wrote the book of Acts, and those passages that describe the events of the trip use the first person plural (v. 6). We also know that Timothy went with Paul on some of his journeys and that Paul gave Timothy seminary training (2 Tim. 2:2). Paul also speaks in this same passage of "witnesses," implying that there were others in the company who heard Paul's instruction to Timothy.

Third, the apostles ordained elders in the cities where churches were established (Acts 14:23). Paul visited with the elders of the church in Ephesus on the seashore (20:17–38). In Philippians 1:1, specific mention is made of elders and deacons. Peter specifically defines the work of elders in 1 Peter 5:1–4. In several places the members of the church are admonished to submit to the rule of the elders (Heb. 13:7, 17; 1 Thess. 5:12–13). Further, it is clear that Paul made a point to see that the churches were supplied with pastors as much as possible. Timothy was the pastor of the church of Ephesus, and Titus was pastor of the church in Crete. By the time John wrote to the seven churches of Asia Minor, each church had its own "angel," or pastor.

Fourth, the missionary work of the apostles teaches us that the gospel moved steadily westward. It went from Jerusalem north to Samaria and Antioch in Syria; from there it went westward to Asia Minor, then to Greece, and then to Italy. The book of Acts begins in Jerusalem and ends in Rome. Although no record is found in scripture of missionary work in Spain, in the farthest western part of Europe, Paul's desire to visit Spain leads one to conclude that a church had been established there (Rom. 15:28).

Finally, the apostles established centers for further missionary work. The book of Acts speaks only of the main centers of the work of the apostles and the churches established in them. But these were centers for the gospel to be preached in surrounding areas as well (Acts 19:10).[1] It is likely that six of the seven churches to which the Lord addressed letters through John (Rev. 2–3) were churches established during or shortly after Paul's work in Ephesus. This practice of establishing centers of further

---

1 The reference to Asia in this passage is to the westernmost province of Asia Minor, also called Asia.

PAUL'S MISSIONARY JOURNEYS

Paul's first journey
Paul's second journey
Paul's third journey
Paul's journey to Rome
◉ City addressed in an Epistle
• Other city

© 1990 World Bible Publishers, Inc.

200 Miles
Kilometers

Black Sea

GALATIAN PONTUS

COMMAGENE

SYRIA

Aleppo • Euphrates
Seleucia Pieria
Damascus • Sea of Galilee
PHOENICIA ABILENE
Tyre • Ptolemais Jordan
Caesarea
JUDEA Jerusalem Dead Sea
ARABIA

CAPPADOCIA
Caesarea (Mazaca)
Halys
GALATIA
Ancyra (Ankara)
Lake Tuz
Gordion
Iconium Derbe
Antioch in Pisidia
PISIDIA Lystra
Tarsus
CILICIA
Seleucia Tracheotis
PAMPHYLIA
Perga Attalia
LYCIA Patara

Issus
Antioch
Salamis
Cyprus Paphos

BITHYNIA AND PONTUS
Byzantium Chalcedon
Nicaea
Sea of Marmara
Sangarius
ASIA
MYSIA
Pergamum Thyatira
Sardis Philadelphia
PHRYGIA
Smyrna LYDIA
Ephesus Laodicea Colossae
Miletus

THRACE
Philippi Neapolis
Amphipolis Apollonia
MACEDONIA
Thessalonica
Berea
EPIRUS
Delphi
Athens ACHAIA
Corinth Cenchreae
Sparta

Mediterranean Sea
Rhodes Scarpanto
Crete
Cyclades
Cerigo
Aegean Sea
Lemnos
Troas Assos Mitylene
Zante Cephalonia Corfu *Ionian Sea*
Strymon

ITALIA
Rome Puteoli
Rhegium Syracuse Sicily
Sardinia
Malta
Cyrene
MACEDONIA Philippi Thessalonica
ASIA Ephesus Colossae Cnidus
Fair Havens Lasea Crete
GALATIA CAPPADOCIA CILICIA
SYRIA Sidon
Myra Cyprus Caesarea
Corinth Rhegium
Ionian Sea *Aegean Sea* *Mediterranean Sea*
300 Miles Kilometers

mission work took root during the history of the apostolic church and the years following. Important centers were established at this time: Antioch, Ephesus, and Rome are examples. From these centers, the gospel radiated in all directions. Even in the post-apostolic age, the distinction between city churches and country churches showed that the practice was carried out throughout the empire. It became a major reason for the rapid spread of the gospel. City churches sent out evangelists and missionaries to bring the gospel to areas nearby.

At the end of the Apostolic Period, the gospel had been brought to the entire known world of that day. The apostles, especially Paul, had carried out the mandate of the Lord, and the stage was set for the expansion of the gospel beyond the reaches of the Mediterranean basin.

GODLESS ROME USED TO ADVANCE THE CAUSE OF THE CHURCH

Admittedly, Greek culture attained an extremely high level of intellectual and aesthetic advance; and Roman civilization was surely noted for its tremendous advances in jurisprudence. But we must remember that this is precisely the world Paul is describing in Romans 1:18ff. God makes himself known to the heathen through the things which are made. But he does this in order to reveal his wrath from heaven upon those who are without excuse. The heathen, in all their religion, culture, and intellectual advance are always and only changing "the glory of the incorruptible God into an image made like to corruptible man, and to birds, and four-footed beasts, and creeping things." They "shew the work of the law written in their hearts, their conscience also bearing witness, and their thoughts the mean while accusing or else excusing one another" (Romans 2:15). But they worship the creature rather than the Creator and sink deeper into the morass of sin. Yet their evil is never one of ignorance; it is always conscious rebellion against God. They know better; but they are depraved, devoid of the image which they have lost. And the result is that their noblest productions are mere idols. They always manifest hatred against God in deliberately destroying his glory. When they show an outward conformity to the law, this is not because they desire to conform their lives to God's

Caesar Augustus

holy demands; this is rather because they see that some external conformity to God's law is necessary to preserve their civilization from anarchy and chaos. Paul's description of the heathen in Romans 1 is God's sentence upon a heathen world at its very best.

All this does not mean, however, that God had not sovereignly prepared the heathen world for the advance of the church and for the history of the church in the new dispensation.

The awful sin of the heathen world gives sharp emphasis to the truth that wicked man fills the cup of iniquity in his obstinate rebellion against God. And, in this way, man's sin underscores the tremendous power of the gospel of the cross to save the elect church from the raging blackness of depravity.

But, in a positive way, God was making the history of the world serve the purpose of his church. The Graeco-Roman world was one universal empire uniting the whole known world into one political whole. The result was that there was peace throughout the world; there was easy travel and communication in every part of the empire; there was a common language—the Greek "koine," understood and spoken everywhere. And all this was highly conducive to the travel of the apostles, the spread of the gospel, the growth and fellowship of the church. It is difficult to conceive of the early church spreading so rapidly throughout the entire known world under different political and social conditions than those existing in the Roman empire of the first century. God used godless Rome to advance the cause of the church.

—Herman Hanko, "Ancient Church History," 8–9.

THE EXPANSION OF THE CHURCH

Although the scriptures record the missionary work primarily of the apostle Paul, other work was also being done. The other apostles carried the gospel to the far-flung reaches of the world. Early tradition says that Peter brought the gospel to Britain and Gaul, the doorway beyond the Alps to the rest of Europe. Traditions tell us that Andrew preached in Scythia, Asia Minor, and Greece; that John ministered in Ephesus; that Philip labored in Hierapolis; and that Matthew may have gone to Ethiopia, Parthia, Persia, and Macedonia. Bartholomew may have labored in Armenia, James the Less in Syria, Thaddaeus in Edessa, and Simon the Zealot in Persia. Another old tradition says that Thomas brought the gospel as far as India, where a church was early established.[2]

Other old church traditions speak of work done in Egypt by John Mark, Paul's companion on part of his first missionary journey. Mark is said to have established a

2 Walton, *Chronological and Background Charts*, chart 1.

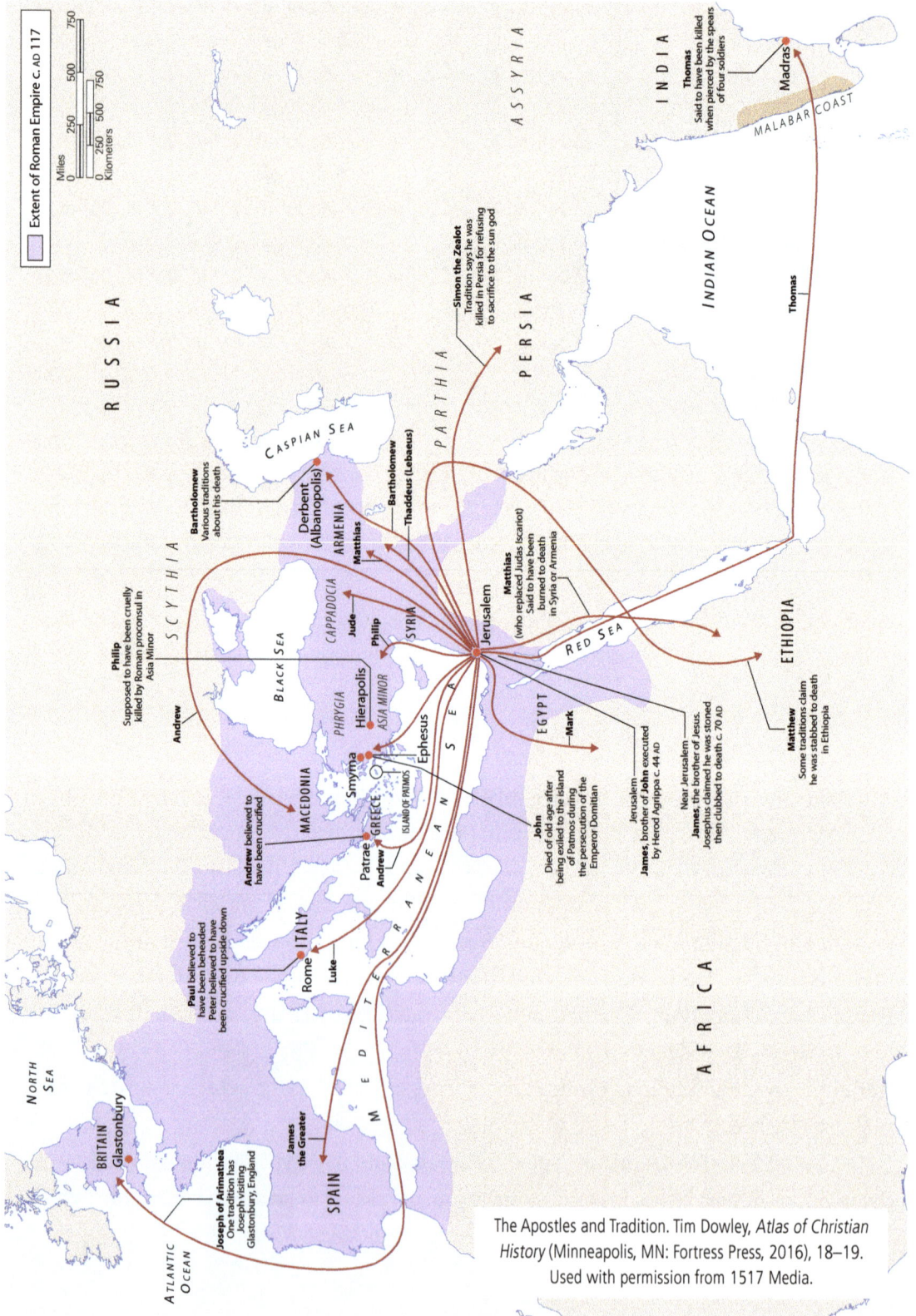

The Apostles and Tradition. Tim Dowley, *Atlas of Christian History* (Minneapolis, MN: Fortress Press, 2016), 18–19. Used with permission from 1517 Media.

church in Alexandria, which became also a center of missionary labor and in which city a major theological school was started. It is no surprise that a church was established there very early. We know too that from the time of the captivity of Judah (Jer. 42–43), a large Jewish community was established in Egypt. In that Jewish community, a Greek translation of the Hebrew scriptures had been made by a group of seventy Jewish scholars. Because it was prepared by seventy Jews, it was called the Septuagint (a name derived from the Latin word for "seventy"). It was an excellent translation, and the men whom God used to write the New Testament scriptures quoted from it extensively in their writings. The Septuagint was a powerful tool in the hands of the church when it brought the gospel to a Greek-speaking world.

Philip baptizes the Ethiopian eunuch

The gospel, especially in the immediate post-apostolic era, was brought beyond Egypt to the whole of North Africa. One wonders what role was played by the return of the Ethiopian eunuch to his place in the court of Candace, queen of Ethiopia. The church in Ethiopia itself claims to be very, very old.

In addition to the work of missionaries, one of the most powerful means God used to spread the gospel was the witness of those converted to Christianity. This witnessing took place through women testifying of their faith to other women gathered by riverbanks to wash their clothes, through merchants in marketplaces speaking of their faith to their customers, and through soldiers in the Roman army discussing scripture with fellow soldiers. However, the most effective witness was the antithetical life of the Christian. Their home lives that were transformed by the gospel, their godly families, their refusal to participate in the dramas and gladiatorial contests in the arenas, their kindness toward their servants and the emancipation of their slaves, their care of the poor, their love for their infant children, their steadfastness in persecution—all these and more made an indelible impression on their neighbors. "Actions speak louder than words," says the proverb. God spoke more loudly through the Christian living of the saints than through any words they may have spoken.[3]

Even the Roman legions were instrumental in the spread of the gospel. In God's judgment on the apostate nation of Israel, he sent Roman armies to destroy Jerusalem

---

3 Michael Green, *Evangelism in the Early Church* (Grand Rapids, MI: Wm. B. Eerdmans Publishing Co., 1979). See especially chapter 8.

in AD 70, burning the Jewish temple, killing much of the Jewish population, and ending the Jewish nation. Jerusalem and Mount Zion were forgotten; the church had become universal. Church historian Philip Hughes writes: "The Roman soldiery had in very grim fashion crowned the work of St. Paul. But for all that Jerusalem was no more, razed to the very ground as Our Lord had prophesied, with only the camp of the Tenth Legion to mark where it had stood.[4]

THE DESTRUCTION OF JERUSALEM, AD 70

The Jewish-Roman War (AD 66–73) began during the reign of Emperor Nero when Jews rebelled against a daily sacrifice to the emperor and the plunder of silver from the temple. After the Jews defeated the Roman garrison in Judea, Nero dispatched his general and the future emperor Vespasian with an army of sixty thousand to put down the rebellion. Vespasian's son, Titus, besieged the city of Jerusalem with a wall and a ditch and crucified anyone trying to escape. In AD 70, the Romans breached the city walls, slaughtered the starving inhabitants, burned the temple to the ground, and utterly destroyed the city. The Jewish-Roman War ended at the mountain fortress of Masada, where Jewish defenders committed suicide to avoid capture by the Romans.

The results of the Jewish-Roman War were devastating for the Jews and effectively brought an end to the Jewish nation until modern times. The Romans slaughtered the Jews, enslaved them, and scattered them throughout the empire. They destroyed the temple, abolished the Jewish sacrificial system, and carted the temple treasures to Rome. For good measure, they also annihilated every synagogue in Palestine.

The Bible speaks prophetically of this event and reveals that the destruction of Jerusalem by Roman armies was God's judgment on a people who had completely

The siege of Jerusalem

The Arch of Titus

---

4 Philip Hughes, *A History of the Church: An Introductory Study*, 2 vols. (London: Sheed & Ward, 1936), 1:72.

rejected the Lord Jesus Christ. During his earthly ministry, Jesus wept over the city of Jerusalem because it had rejected the visitation of the Lord (Luke 19:41–44) and foretold these awful events as a vivid sign of the end of the world (21:20–24).

In God's providence, the destruction of Jerusalem had an immediate impact upon the church. First, it widened the gulf between the Jews and the Christians. Because the early church had fled Jerusalem before its destruction, the Jews later refused to let Christians use their synagogues. Second, although the apostolic church had been centered in Jerusalem for several decades after Pentecost, the early church was forced through the destruction of Jerusalem to carry the gospel of Jesus Christ farther into Gentile lands.

During the Apostolic Period, the church spread throughout the entire known world, to the ends of the earth. This is the explanation for the apparently abrupt ending of the book of Acts. There was no place in the Roman Empire where the church had not been established. In Palestine, Syria, Asia Minor, Greece, Italy, Spain, and North Africa the elect had been gathered and the church established. Wherever it had been established, it quickly became firmly rooted and a center for additional evangelistic work.

From the outpouring of the Holy Spirit on Pentecost to the destruction of Jerusalem by the Romans, the Lord revealed that the gospel would go forth to the Gentiles. The apostle Paul summed up his work with these words: "For I am not ashamed of the gospel of Christ: for it is the power of God unto salvation to every one that believeth; to the Jew first, and also to the Greek" (Rom. 1:16).

Part Two

The Post-Apostolic Period

(AD 100–313)

INTRODUCTION TO THE POST-APOSTOLIC PERIOD

When the Lord Jesus Christ took the aged apostle John to glory around the year AD 100, he ushered in a new era in the history of his church. John, traditionally believed to be the youngest of the apostles, had outlived the others and was the only apostle not to die a martyr's death. While John was banished to the island of Patmos shortly before his death, the Holy Spirit moved him to write Revelation, the last book of holy scripture. But now the last apostle was taken from the church militant on earth to the church triumphant in heaven. With his death, the office of apostle came to an end, the special miracles ceased, and the canon of scripture was closed. The members of the church that remained on earth must have wondered what this would mean. Who would lead them in the days ahead? Were they now on their own?

But the Lord is always present with his church. After he ascended to heaven in his glorified body and called his last apostle home, he did not leave his church to make her own way in the world. He had promised his church, "Lo, I am with you always, even unto the end of the world" (Matt. 28:20). Christ remains with his church through the ages in two related ways. First, he is with his people by his Spirit in their hearts. He describes his Spirit as the Comforter and the Spirit of truth, who guides the church into all truth (John 14–16). But Christ is also with his church by his word, the completed canon of scripture, which is entrusted to her care. The Spirit, ever present with the church, makes his presence known through the word, by which he puts the church into constant fellowship with her ascended Lord.

The infant church of the Post-Apostolic Period (AD 100–313) needed the fellowship of Christ by his word and Spirit, for during this crucial period of church history, Satan ferociously and relentlessly attacked the church with persecution from without and heresy from within.

The most striking characteristic of this era is persecution at the hands of the Roman Empire. For nearly 250 years, from the maniacal brutality of Emperor Nero to the systematic cruelty of Emperor Diocletian, the church endured wave after wave of state-sponsored terror. But through it all, Christ was with his church, causing her to flourish and expand throughout the sprawling Roman Empire and beyond.

In addition to persecution, heresy plagued the church during this period. The writings of the apostles are filled with warnings against dangerous wolves who enter the flock of Christ and seek to destroy it with false doctrine (Acts 20:29). If persecution cannot destroy the church, the devil resorts to false doctrine, because a loss of the truth is the end of the church. During this age, the truth of the gospel was ridiculed by pagan intellectuals and twisted by pernicious false teachers. But the Spirit of truth was present with the church in this battle too, guiding the church to search the scriptures and develop her understanding of the truth in her warfare against gnosticism, Marcionism, and Montanism. The devil meant it for evil, but God meant it for good (Gen. 50:20).

The rapidly expanding post-apostolic church was characterized by exceptional unity throughout these adversities. For good reason, the church began to refer to herself as "catholic" (universal). This formative era in church history witnessed the definition and defense of the canon of scripture; the writing of the first Christian creed; the bold defense of the faith by early apologists; the development of the church's doctrine, worship, and government; and the explosive spread of the gospel throughout the world. This period also contained many valuable lessons for the church of today, the most important of which may be that the Lord Jesus Christ is always present with his church by his word and Spirit, using all things for her good.

Timeline of the Post-Apostolic Period

100	The apostle John, the last of the apostles, dies; the apostolic father Clement of Rome is martyred.
107	The apostolic father Ignatius of Antioch is martyred in Rome, likely fed to wild beasts in the Coliseum.
130	Justin Martyr is converted through the witness of an old man who shares the scriptures with him.
140	The gnostic Valentinus writes *Gospel of Truth*; he is at the peak of his influence for the next twenty years.
145	The Old Roman Symbol, a precursor to the Apostles' Creed, is first used in the church of Rome.
150	The gnostic Marcion compiles the first New Testament canon of scripture to fit his heretical agenda.
154	The Quartodeciman Controversy over the celebration of Easter on the Passover or on Sunday begins.
155	Justin Martyr writes *First Apology*, describing early Christian worship; Polycarp of Smyrna is martyred.
165	The apologist Justin Martyr is beheaded in Rome during the reign of the emperor Marcus Aurelius.
172	The heretic Montanus of Phrygia begins the charismatic, ascetic, and apocalyptic Montanist movement.
177	The martyrs of Lyons die; among them are the bishop Pothinus and the courageous slave girl Blandina.
185	Irenaeus of Lyons writes *Against Heresies*, a detailed attack on gnosticism and statement of orthodoxy.
188	Clement of Alexandria writes three works synthesizing Christian doctrine and Greek philosophy.
197	Tertullian of Carthage writes *Apology*, defending Christianity and appealing to the empire for toleration.
200	Irenaeus of Lyons, the chief apologist against gnosticism, dies, possibly martyred for his faith.
203	Origen of Alexandria becomes the head of the Alexandrian School; Perpetua is martyred in Carthage.
248	Origen of Alexandria writes the famous apology *Against Celsus*; Cyprian is elected bishop of Carthage.
250	Emperor Decius requires emperor worship and orders the first empire-wide persecution of Christians.
251	The Novatian Schism over the forgiveness of apostates begins just after the Decian Persecution is over.
258	Emperor Valerian issues an edict to arrest and punish Christian clergy; Cyprian of Carthage is martyred.
268	The Council of Antioch deposes heretic Paul of Samosata for teaching the error of Monarchianism.
270	Anthony of Egypt takes up a life of solitude in the desert, making asceticism increasingly popular.
303	Emperor Diocletian begins the "Great Persecution," the most extensive Roman persecution to date.
312	Constantine is converted and victorious at the Battle of the Milvian Bridge; the Donatist Schism begins.
313	Emperor Constantine issues the Edict of Milan, legalizing Christianity and tolerating all religions.

Map of the Post-Apostolic Period

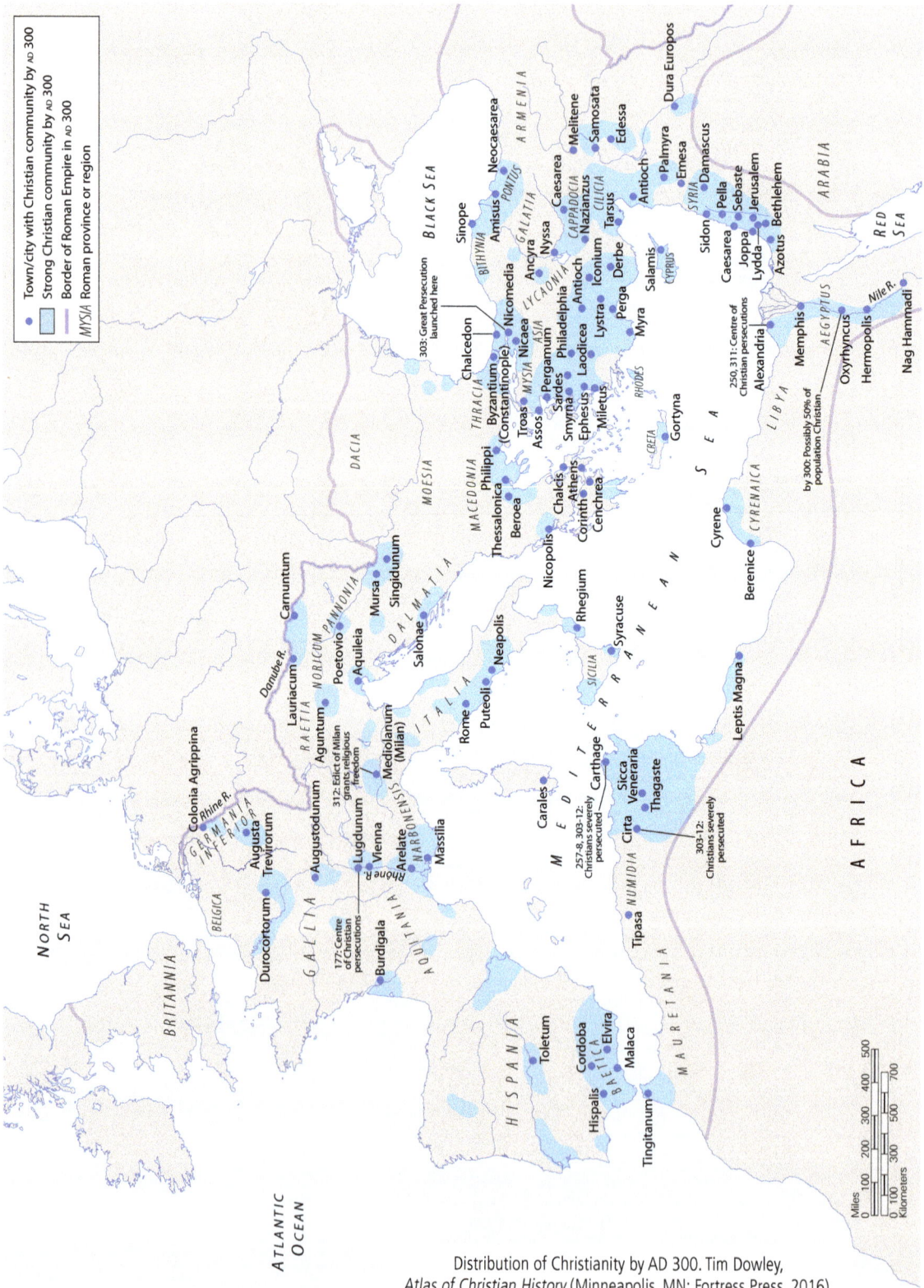

Legend:
- Town/city with Christian community by AD 300
- Strong Christian community by AD 300
- Border of Roman Empire in AD 300
- *MYSIA* Roman province or region

303: Great Persecution launched here

250, 311: Centre of Christian persecutions

by 300: Possibly 50% of population Christian

257–8, 303–12: Christians severely persecuted

303–12: Christians severely persecuted

177: Centre of Christian persecutions

312: Edict of Milan grants religious freedom

Distribution of Christianity by AD 300. Tim Dowley,
Atlas of Christian History (Minneapolis, MN: Fortress Press, 2016),
24–25. Used with permission from 1517 Media.

CHAPTER 4: **THE PERSECUTION OF THE CHURCH**

And when they had preached the gospel to that city, and had taught many,
they returned again…confirming the souls of the disciples, and exhorting them
to continue in the faith, and that we must through much tribulation
enter into the kingdom of God.

—ACTS 14:21–22

PERSECUTION IN THE APOSTOLIC CHURCH

During the first three centuries of the church of Christ, persecution was its most outstanding characteristic as far as its life in the world was concerned. The persecution began almost as soon as the church was established, and it continued somewhat sporadically until the rule of Constantine the Great at the beginning of the fourth century.

Such persecution began shortly after Pentecost. Jesus's words were almost immediately fulfilled: "In the world ye shall have tribulation: but be of good cheer; I have overcome the world" (John 16:33).

In Acts 4 Luke records the beginning of persecution. The apostles Peter and John had healed a man lame from birth at the gate of the temple. The people present expressed their astonishment at the miracle, for the man who had never walked was now running, leaping, and jumping around in his exuberance. Peter took the opportunity to explain to the people that the miracle had been done by the exalted Lord Jesus Christ, who, though crucified, had risen and was now in heaven. This preaching of Peter was enough to bring the temple police, who, at the command of the Jewish rulers, arrested Peter and John. After a night in prison, they were summoned before the Sanhedrin, the Jewish high council. Peter again boldly gave testimony to their faith in the risen Lord. After warning them not to preach in the name of Jesus and threatening them with many dire punishments if they disobeyed, the Sanhedrin released them.

But the apostles paid no attention to the command of their rulers, which required disobedience to their Lord in heaven; they preached again openly and publicly. This led to their second arrest and a whipping with thirty-nine strokes.[1] Obeying the command of their Lord to rejoice in persecution (Matt. 5:12), they joined with the church in praising God (Acts 4:23–30).

This event was the beginning of persecution, which continued with the martyrdom of Stephen, one of the first seven deacons, and became common practice in Jerusalem and Judea (Acts 7; 8:1–4). After the death of Stephen, Saul (later called Paul) was the Sanhedrin's appointed leader in their persecution of Christians. Paul spoke more than once of how deeply he regretted his actions of persecuting the church of Christ (Acts 8:1–3; 9:1–2; 1 Cor. 15:9). Persecution continued when Herod Agrippa, the king of Judea, killed the apostle James and imprisoned Peter with a view to putting him to death (Acts 12:1–5). Later, Paul was repeatedly persecuted on his missionary journeys (2 Cor. 11:23–33).

The martyrdom of Stephen

PERSECUTION BY THE JEWS

The persecution of the church in the earliest years was carried on almost exclusively by the Jews. When Paul began his missionary journeys, he preached first in the synagogues. When the reprobate Jews rejected the gospel, they turned in fury against the apostles and the members of the church (Acts 14:2, 19–20; 17:5–8).

When the church spread throughout the Roman Empire and some Jews were brought to faith in Christ, their fellow Jews often persecuted the Christian Jews. The persecution was usually not the infliction of physical pain, but the persecution of loss of jobs, of mockery and derision, of ostracism,

Paul addresses the crowd after his arrest

---

1 The Jewish law required no more than forty strokes for various offenses, but the Jews, wary of breaking the law, limited the number to thirty-nine (see also 2 Cor. 11:24).

and of being made the objects of cruel charges. Several of the New Testament books indicate that this kind of persecution was common throughout the empire. First Peter was written especially to churches that were enduring persecution.

So it is throughout the history of the church; persecution of the faithful always comes most severely from the false church. The church of Jesus's day crucified Christ. It was so in the Apostolic Period; it is so today.

There were, of course, exceptions: Paul was nearly killed in Ephesus in the riot sparked by Demetrius, the Diana-worshiping silversmith (Acts 19:24–31); Paul and Silas were imprisoned by the Romans in Philippi (16:19–24); and the Roman emperor Nero persecuted the church in Rome already in AD 64. But the unbelieving Jews were the main agents of persecution in the church's early history.

REASONS FOR PERSECUTION

When the unbelieving Jews persecuted their fellow Jews, the reason was, undoubtedly, their guilty consciences. The Jews themselves admitted this when the Sanhedrin angrily charged John and Peter: "[Ye] intend to bring this man's blood upon us" (Acts 5:28). The wicked, especially those who belong to the church, always know what the truth is. They do not reject the truth out of ignorance; they reject it because they hate it. And hating it, they hate those who preach it. Hence there is always persecution, and it often begins with the false church.

However, as the gospel entered every nook and cranny of the Roman Empire, the heathen became more and more involved in the persecution of the church. At last it became, under some Roman emperors, official government policy.

The Roman Empire had, in its conquest of the whole world, adopted a policy of toleration of all native religions. This policy was instrumental in establishing the so-called *Pax Romana*, the Roman Peace, which brought peace to all parts of the empire.

However, this rule of toleration had two exceptions. The first was that no cult or religion was tolerated that was hostile to the empire. The second was that no cult or religion was tolerated that claimed it alone represented the true religion. It is not surprising, then, that the emperors and the local governors in the Roman Empire soon took notice of Christianity. Christians claimed that the God whom they worshiped was the only true God and that those who worshiped any other gods were idolaters who would go to hell. The wicked world and the false church do not really care at all what religion a person confesses and before what idols one bows; however, to claim that one worships the only true God and that idol worship is not only vain and futile, but is *sinful*, is to incur the wrath of the wicked. So it has always been in the history of the world; so it is now; so it will be in the time of antichrist.

Why do the world and the false church refuse to tolerate the true religion, while they are ready to tolerate any departure from the truth? The reason is that Christianity itself is an intolerant religion. It claims to be the only true religion, because it is not an invention of men but is directly given by God to his people in the inspired scriptures. All other religions, Christianity rightly claims, are inventions of man and are therefore false (Gal. 1:8–9). Everyone who believes the truth must insist on this.

The religion of the final antichristian kingdom will be based on the same policy as that of Rome, for the Roman Empire was part of the development of the antichristian world power. All religions will be tolerated, except that one religion that claims to be and is the only true religion. *Toleration* is the password of the antichristian kingdom.

It was inevitable, therefore, that sooner or later post-apostolic Christianity would come into conflict with the Roman Empire. The empire was pagan, and many emperors claimed divinity. By 250, the Emperor Decius (r. 249–51) made emperor worship mandatory, requiring every Roman citizen to offer incense to the emperor and to recite the words "Caesar is lord." He insisted that, along with their worship of all kinds of idols, people also worship the emperor. Christians, living under the rule of Christ their king, were not opposed to the state, but they did refuse to worship the emperor. This refusal was interpreted as hostility to the state.

In addition to the church's refusal to worship the emperor, she was persecuted for other reasons. Christianity was often a threat to prosperous businesses, especially those that made money by selling miniature idols or the trappings that went along with idol worship (Acts 19:24–29). Businessmen sometimes instigated persecution, as they did in Philippi on Paul's second missionary journey (16:19). Pagan priests saw their lucrative businesses in the temples of heathen idols destroyed as many forsook the temples to join themselves to the congregations of believers.

The antithetical lives of the Christians were also causes of persecution. Christianity disrupted family life when God brought only some in a family to faith in Christ. The Christians' refusal to participate in gladiatorial combats was a condemnation of these means of entertainment. The Christians' care of the poor and sick and their kindness toward slaves and adoption of abandoned infants (a common practice in the empire) were also a silent condemnation of the cruelty of life under Roman rule.

Christians were also persecuted because they refused to worship the pantheon of Roman gods. The Roman Empire claimed, with all its gods, to be religious. As a consequence, Christians were often called *atheists* (those who claim that there is no god) because they refused to worship the pagan gods and to worship Caesar himself when he claimed divinity.

Even Christian religious practices, such as love feasts and the Lord's supper, were often maliciously interpreted as immoral and cannibalistic.

In addition to all this, the Romans were deeply superstitious and often blamed the Christians for catastrophes, floods, earthquakes, and the inroads

The martyrdom of Ignatius

of barbarians from the north into the empire. These judgments of God quickly brought people into the streets shouting, "The Christians to the lions!" Even as late as the early fifth century, Augustine found it necessary to defend Christianity against the charge that the barbarian invasions were due to the fact that the Christians had forsaken the old religions of the Romans.

GOD'S PURPOSE IN PERSECUTION

God is sovereign in all that happens in the world. The persecution of the church, though a wicked act on the part of the world, also comes through God's will. Therefore, it is necessary to ask the question, "Why does God want his people to suffer persecution?"

Christ told his disciples that just as the wicked persecuted him, so also would the wicked persecute his people (John 15:18–19). The saints must be persecuted just as Christ was persecuted because they belong to him. When the wicked persecute Christ's people, they persecute Christ himself even though he is in heaven, for Christ and his people are one. This is why Jesus said to Saul at his conversion on the Damascus road, "Saul, Saul, why persecutest thou me?" (Acts 9:4).

Persecution is also necessary for the salvation of the saints, because persecution purifies them (1 Pet. 1:6–7). Only through much persecution are we able to enter the kingdom (Acts 14:22; Rom. 8:17). We can easily see this when we think of how attached we become to earthly possessions. If God takes them away from us through persecution, we are freed from our longing to own more of the things of this world, and we are more inclined to lay up treasures in heaven (Matt. 6:19–21). The church is always at the peak of its spiritual strength in times of persecution. Then the church has nothing but her Lord and Master. In other words, God uses persecution to strengthen and purify the faith of his people.

As was true of the early church, God uses persecution in one place to spread the

The Christian martyrs' last prayer

gospel to other places (Acts 8:1–4). Unable to stay in their home villages and cities, God's people flee to other places where persecution is less severe. When they find new places to live, they bring the gospel to those places.

God even has his purpose with the wicked in their persecution of the saints. The wicked become ripe for judgment when they persecute the church. The Bible compares the judgment of the wicked to a harvest (Rev. 14:14–20). They become ripe for judgment because they have committed every sin that wicked men can possibly commit. In persecuting the church, they have committed the worst possible sin. The church is the bride of Christ. Christ does not sit idly by when his bride is tortured, abused, and killed. When God sends the wicked to hell, everyone, including persecutors themselves, will confess that they have received what was justly coming to them.

PERSECUTION BY THE ROMANS

The attitude of the Christians toward persecution in the Roman Empire was one of humble submission to the Lord's will. The apostles rejoiced that they were counted worthy to suffer for Christ's sake (Acts 5:41). Most of the Christians followed this example. They were willing to suffer for Christ's sake, and in fact, their steadfastness and calm composure while being gnawed by lions was itself a means God used to bring others to the faith. The church father Tertullian of Carthage (c. 160–225) put it this way: "The blood of the martyrs is the seed of the church."

Roman persecution was not carried out in all parts of the empire throughout the entire period and without cessation. It was often limited to provinces here and there, and it was very sporadic. Roman persecution came in waves during the first three centuries of the church, beginning with Emperor Nero's persecution in the city of Rome in AD 64 and culminating with Emperor Diocletian's empire-wide persecution from 303 to 311. But there were times of quiet when the church enjoyed a respite from suffering. Some parts of the empire were untouched by persecution at a time when this was the lot of the people of God elsewhere. Eusebius of Caesarea (c. 260–340), the early church historian, says that in times of peace the church tended to become worldly, and God sent persecution to wash the church of its sin.

ROMAN PERSECUTION OF CHRISTIANS[2]			
Dates	Emperor	Nature and Extent	Notable Martyrs
64	Nero	Took place in Rome and vicinity only. Christians were made scapegoats for burning Rome. Sadistic measures included burning Christians alive to illuminate Nero's gardens.	Paul Peter
c. 90–96	Domitian	Capricious, sporadic, centered in Rome and Asia Minor. Christians persecuted for refusal to offer incense to genius of emperor.	Clement of Rome John (exiled to Patmos)
98–117	Trajan	Sporadically enforced. Christians were lumped with other groups whose patriotism was considered suspect. Christians were to be executed when found, but not sought out.	Ignatius Symeon Zozimus Rufus
117–138	Hadrian	Sporadically enforced. Continued policies of Trajan. Any who brought false witness against Christians were to be punished.	Telesphorus
138–161	Antoninus Pius	Sporadically enforced. Continued policies of Trajan and Hadrian.	Polycarp
161–180	Marcus Aurelius	Emperor was a Stoic who opposed Christianity on philosophical grounds. Christians blamed for natural disasters.	Justin Martyr Pothinus Blandina
202–211	Septimius Severus	Conversion to Christianity forbidden.	Leonidas Irenaeus Perpetua
235–236	Maximinus the Thracian	Christian clergy ordered executed. Christians opposed because they had supported emperor's predecessor, whom he had assassinated.	Ursula Hippolytus
249–251	Decius	First empire-wide persecution. Offering of incense to genius of emperor demanded. Enthusiastic return to paganism required utter extermination of Christianity. Led to rise of Novatianism.	Fabianus Alexander of Jerusalem
257–260	Valerian	Christians' property confiscated. Christians' right of assembly prohibited.	Origen Cyprian Sixtus II
274	Aurelian	Required sun worship as official state religion, but died before it could be implemented.	
303–311	Diocletian Galerius	Worst persecution of all. Churches destroyed, Bibles burned, civil rights of Christians suspended, sacrifice to gods required. Led to rise of Donatism.	Mauritius Alban

---

2 Walton, *Chronological and Background Charts*, chart 20.

The persecution of Nero

The methods of persecution were very cruel. The apostle Paul was beheaded in Rome, and the apostle Peter was crucified—upside down at his own request, for he was not worthy, he said, to die as the Lord died. After blaming the Christians for a terrible fire that destroyed much of Rome, the emperor Nero crucified Christians in his garden and burned them alive. The crosses on which they hung gave light to him and those with him as they dined in the palace gardens. Ignatius (c. 35–107), the bishop of Antioch, was devoured by beasts in the Coliseum. Polycarp (c. 69–155), the bishop of Smyrna, was burned alive at the stake. Justin Martyr (c. 100–165), the philosopher-apologist, and Cyprian (c. 200–258), the bishop of Carthage, were both beheaded. Christians were fed to wild animals in the arenas of big cities for the entertainment of the spectators. Some were tied to the horns of mad bulls to be tossed around and gored. Some were worked to death in the mines.

By God's grace, the church was preserved through these tribulations. He hears the cries and the prayers of his people. The story is told concerning the martyrs of Sebaste that forty Christian soldiers under a centurion were sentenced to death by freezing. They were put in the middle of a frozen lake, naked and hungry, during the dead of winter. The unbelieving soldiers gathered in a circle around them, warming themselves by huge fires, eating and drinking, but also urging the freezing Christians to abandon their faith and come where they could be warm and could eat. The suffering soldiers prayed for each other that they might be faithful, although one soldier, unable to bear the torture, left the dying men and joined those who were warm and filled. One from their ranks had denied his Christ. The faithful prayed that he might repent and join them again. He didn't, but another soldier, moved deeply by the willingness of the faithful soldiers to suffer for their faith, stripped off his clothing and joined them in their misery. This was God's way of answering their prayer.

In some instances, Christians eagerly sought out persecution and martyrdom. But inviting persecution is not our calling. Surely the saints are called to endure persecution and be thankful that they are counted worthy to suffer for Christ's sake. However, they must not invite death but rather fulfill their calling upon earth, committing their way to their heavenly Father. Christ himself commands his church to flee when persecution breaks out against them.

Felicitas, a Christian slave girl in Carthage, North Africa, gave birth to a baby in prison. When she screamed at the pain of delivery, her jailers mocked her and said that her pain would be a lot worse when she was fed to the wild animals. She responded, "What I am suffering now, I suffer by myself. But then another will be inside me who will suffer for me, just as I shall be suffering for him."[3] She was a representative for all those who went to their deaths praying for their tormentors and singing the psalms of the church. They are now robed in white before Christ's throne (Rev. 20:4).

THE GREAT PERSECUTION

The fierce Roman persecution of the church came to a climax under the rule of the emperor Diocletian (r. 284–305) and came to an end with his successor, Constantine the Great (r. 306–337).

Diocletian was the last of the pagan emperors and the only one to abdicate voluntarily his position as emperor. Born from parents in the lower class, he achieved great success in the Roman legions. Because of his skill in strategy and his courage in battle, he rose through the ranks and gained the favor of his fellow soldiers. When the emperor Carus died, the soldiers made Diocletian emperor. Although he had one challenger, Diocletian defeated him in battle and assumed the role of emperor.

Not only did Diocletian excel in battle, but he was also a gifted administrator. He combined these gifts with his continued presence at the head of Rome's armies in

Polycarp of Smyrna (c. 69–155)

A personal friend of the apostle John, Polycarp served the church of Smyrna as a faithful pastor for many years. A greatly respected apostolic father, he tried to settle an early debate over the date of Easter; battled the infamous heretic Marcion; wrote warm, pastoral letters to the churches (his letter to the Philippians still exists); and died a martyr's death by fire in the crowded arena of Smyrna. Commanded to deny Christ, Polycarp declared, "For eighty-six years I have served him, and he never did me any wrong. How can I blaspheme my king who has saved me?" To learn more, read "Polycarp: Martyr of Christ," chapter 1 of Herman Hanko's *Portraits of Faithful Saints*.

---

3   Herbert Musurillo, ed., *The Acts of the Christian Martyrs* (Oxford: Oxford University Press, 1972), 123–24.

their battles on the frontier, and he led the armies to a series of victories that secured the frontier. He also reorganized the government to make his rule more effective. He formed a tetrarchy (a rule of four), dividing the empire into four parts and making three other men sub-emperors: Galerius in the East to rule with him and Maximian and Constantius (the father of Constantine) in the West. Diocletian's efforts at more efficient administration were successful.

The story of Diocletian's determination to destroy Christianity is a reflection of the paganism of the empire. In the winter, while enjoying the mild climate of Nicomedia, Diocletian consulted with Galerius concerning the problem of Christianity. Diocletian, the less murderous of the two, was content to prohibit Christians from serving in the armed forces and in government. Galerius, however, argued for the total extermination of the church. The two men decided to consult the oracle of Apollo. The answer, vague and ambiguous as always, said that the enemies on earth were hindering Apollo's advice. Diocletian and Galerius interpreted this to mean that the Christians were enemies who were obstructing the gods. The result was an all-out, empire-wide effort to exterminate Christianity: confiscate its buildings, burn its books, and force Christians to renounce Christ or die.

This last Roman persecution, which lasted for eight long years (303–311), was also the worst. Eusebius of Caesarea, who lived at the time, called it "The Great Persecution." Describing the persecution in vivid detail in his *Church History*, he wrote:

> I myself saw some of these mass executions by decapitation or fire, a slaughter that dulled the murderous axe until it wore out and broke in pieces, while the executioners grew so tired they had to work in shifts. But I also observed a marvelous eagerness and a divine power and enthusiasm in those who placed their faith in Christ: as soon as the first was sentenced, others would jump up on the tribunal in front of the judge and confess themselves Christians. Heedless of torture in its terrifying forms but boldly proclaiming their devotion to the God of the universe, they received the final sentence of death with joy, laughter, and gladness, singing hymns of thanksgiving to God until their last breath.[4]

Meanwhile, the emperor Diocletian became increasingly ill. Under pressure from his co-emperor Galerius, he resigned and turned the empire over to Galerius, who

---

4   Paul L. Maier, trans., *Eusebius: The Church History* (Grand Rapids, MI: Kregel Publications, 1999), 298.

continued the policy of persecution with a vengeance. The Christians suffered under Galerius until he wearied of the bloodshed, discontinued his policies, and finally issued a grudging declaration of tolerance on his deathbed in 311.

The period of state-sponsored persecution of Christians was over. Under Constantine the church would become what was in reality a state church, that is, a church favored and promoted by the emperor. But the blood of the martyrs continues to speak. The illustrious pages of the past, written with the ink of martyr's blood, are able to steel the souls of the faithful to the very end. And the story of God's grace is a story of untold comfort, able to encourage God's people in every century.

CHAPTER 5: **THE DEFENSE OF THE FAITH**

*It was needful for me to write unto you, and exhort you that ye should
earnestly contend for the faith which was once delivered unto the saints.*

—JUDE 3

HERESY IN THE APOSTOLIC CHURCH

From the beginning of its history, the New Testament church was called to defend
the truth of the word of God against heresies that arose both within the church
and outside the church. Already during the Apostolic Period, the apostles found it
necessary to address several heresies threatening the church.

Paul wrote the epistles to the Romans and the Galatians to counteract the Judaistic heresy that salvation came through both the work of Christ and the keeping of the
Old Testament law. The book of Colossians and the first epistle of John were written
because gnosticism, a dangerous heresy that threatened the early church, was already
beginning to have some influence within the church.

Peter, especially in his second epistle, warns against "false prophets also among
the people, even as there shall be false teachers among you, who privily shall bring in
damnable heresies, even denying the Lord that bought them, and bring upon themselves swift destruction" (2 Pet. 2:1). In chapter 3 of the same epistle, he warns against
those who deny Christ's second coming, who are "scoffers, walking after their own
lusts" (3:3–4).

John warns the church in his first epistle to "try the spirits," for they are not all of
God; some deny "that Jesus Christ is come in the flesh." These are of antichrist (1 John
4:1–3). In his second epistle, he rejoices greatly when he finds people who walk in the
truth (v. 4) and warns, "For many deceivers are entered into the world, who confess

not that Jesus Christ is come in the flesh. This is a deceiver, and an antichrist" (v. 7).

Jude intended to write concerning the "common salvation" but changed his mind and wrote instead an exhortation that the church "should earnestly contend for the faith which was once delivered unto the saints" (Jude 3). The reason why Jude changed his mind was that "there are certain men crept in unawares, who were before of old ordained to this condemnation, ungodly men, turning the grace of God into lasciviousness, and denying the only Lord God, and our Lord Jesus Christ" (v. 4).

Heresies were present in the apostolic church; and they have continued until the present.

WHAT HERESY IS

In the time of the apostles, heresies were teachings in the church that disagreed with the doctrines that the apostles taught. To accomplish their ends, heretics had to deny the authority of the apostles. This denial of apostolic authority is the reason why heretics in the Galatian and Corinthian churches attempted to persuade church members that Paul was not an apostle at all. Such attempts prompted Paul to defend his apostleship in Galatians 1:11–24, Galatians 2:1–14, and 2 Corinthians 11. When the apostolic age came to an end, heresies multiplied.

Not all wrong teachings in the early church were necessarily heresies. First, remember that the church was a theological infant for the first centuries, and leaders in the church did not have a clear understanding of all the truths of scripture. The church fathers themselves, struggling to understand the truth more fully and trying to find ways to express the truth more clearly, often made mistakes in their teachings. If these mistakes were taught today, they would be considered heresies; but early in the life of the church this was not so.

Second, men who taught doctrines contrary to scripture raised difficult problems. In the search for understanding, wrong solutions were proposed. This was the case with Apollinaris of Laodicea (c. 310–90), who, attempting to solve the problem of the relation between the human and the divine natures of Christ, made a mistake. His motive was not evil, but his solution denied a fundamental truth concerning Christ. He was not at that point a heretic. We will meet him again.

Third, sometimes church fathers who had been converted from paganism did not immediately abandon all their pagan learning. This was the case with Justin Martyr (c. 100–165), who taught ideas from pagan philosophy that, though contrary to scripture, he considered true. But he was not a heretic and, in fact, died a martyr's death.

Yet the people of God, though having only a kindergarten knowledge of the truth, could sense something wrong with what some men in the early church were saying. Perhaps they could not point directly to those scriptures that were being contradicted, and perhaps they could not clearly state why a given teaching was wrong, but the people of God generally knew what was biblical and what was not.

Christ has promised to send to his church the Spirit of truth, who would guide the church into all truth (John 14:16–18, 26; 15:26–27; 16:7–14). As the church struggled to understand the truth more fully, the Spirit of truth led them into an understanding of the teachings of the scriptures. When the church made official decisions about these doctrines, they, just like our own confessions, became the doctrines of the church. At that point, anyone who taught contrary to what the church had decided was the teaching of scripture was branded a heretic if he could not prove from scripture that the church was wrong and that he was right. Heresy is therefore distinguished from orthodoxy in this way: *orthodoxy* is a teaching within the church of a doctrine that is in agreement with scripture and what the church has declared to be the teaching of scripture; *heresy* is a teaching within the church of a doctrine that is contrary to scripture and to what the church has officially declared to be the teaching of scripture. Yet scripture is always the standard of truth, even of doctrines adopted by the church.

WHAT HERESY IS NOT

The members of the church are, after all, though saints in Jesus Christ, also sinners as long as they are in this world. Sometimes in their study of Scripture they make mistakes in their understanding of God's word and begin to teach ideas that are not in harmony with Scripture.

There are several instances of such mistakes made by men in the past. Indeed, sometimes men taught wrong ideas that were even generally accepted in the church but that were proven wrong by later men of God who understood the scriptures more perfectly. These mistakes are not really heresies.

An instance of this is Augustine's view of the sacraments. While Augustine was completely in harmony with scripture in most of his teachings, especially when it came to his teachings on the doctrines of sovereign grace, he erred in viewing the sacrament of baptism as having itself the power of regeneration. This view was accepted by the church until the time of the Reformation.

But heresy is different. One does not necessarily teach heresy when he sets forth a view born out of a less than full understanding of the truth. But once the church of which he is a part has shown a man that his view is wrong, that it is not in harmony with the teaching of Scripture, and that he should not, therefore, teach it—if he continues to teach it nonetheless, at that point he becomes a heretic.

Or if the church has already established a certain doctrine as being the teaching of scripture, and if some man comes along and begins to teach something contrary to what the church has established as the truth of God's word, that man teaches heresy.

Heresy is, therefore, a teaching within the church of a doctrine contrary to what the church has officially declared to be the truth of the word of God.

—Herman Hanko, *Contending for the Faith*, 1–2.

Seldom do heretics teach what they do because they are persuaded that what they teach is really biblical. Paul points out that the Judaizers in the Galatian churches were not interested in the truth, but rather sought to gain positions of leadership in the church. Heretics love to have the preeminence as Diotrephes did (3 John 9). Paul also accuses the Judaizers of being afraid of persecution and of teaching what the Jews taught because they did not want to suffer the offense of the cross (Gal. 5:11; 6:12–13). Heretics know the truth, but either they do not want it, or they are so conceited that they are willing to sacrifice the truth on the altar of their own pride. Even when the church shows them that they teach contrary to scripture, they cling to their false doctrine.

THE REASONS FOR HERESY

We may ask the question, "What is the explanation for heresy in the church?"

First, as we have already seen, the church after the Apostolic Period was struggling to develop the rich doctrines of scripture. As the church discovered the truth in the sacred writings, she had to develop it into her own confession. The church did not yet understand the truth clearly. The result was that, as men of God engaged in theological pursuit, they sometimes fell into error. They did not consciously desire to destroy the truth. They simply did not have a clear conception of it, sometimes producing an innocent misapprehension of the word of God. But this was not usually the reason for heresy in the church.

Second, the reason for heresy lies in the depraved heart of unbelieving man. The truth has enemies *outside* the church who hate God and who are determined to obliterate the truth; and *within* the church there are hypocrites who have no love of God in their hearts. Although God saves all his elect people, and although many of these elect people are children of believers, God has not promised that every child of believers is saved. God did not promise this in the days of Israel and Judah; God does not do so now. Some of the children of believers grow up without the grace of God and, though in the church, are not true believers. Paul speaks of this in Acts 20:29. Peter describes these church members as men who once confessed that they were Christ's possession, purchased with the blood of Christ shed on Calvary, but now have denied the Lord who bought them (2 Pet. 2:1). These consciously try to destroy the truth, and their motives are legion. Such heretics are particularly troublesome, for they are often men who had been faithful pastors and teachers in the church. Perhaps they had many relatives and friends whom they helped in times of sorrow and suffering. It is difficult for some to see that personal relationships are not the test of truth.

Third, the reason for heresy is found in Satan himself as he works through wicked men. Satan hates Christ, and he hates the church because the church is Christ's bride. He is always unbending in his determination to destroy the church of Christ. Satan has different weapons in his arsenal to accomplish this end. Sometimes he uses the instrument of persecution. Other times he makes use of false doctrine, for he knows that if the church loses her confession of the truth, she will also cease to represent the cause of God in the world. Satan knows, perhaps better than we do, that false doctrine can and will destroy the church. So Satan works in the hearts of men to promote false teachings that are contrary to scripture, and thus to lead the church into confessing doctrines that God hates.

Finally, and most importantly, the reason for heresy in the church rests upon the premise of God's absolute and sovereign rule over all things. We believe and confess that God is always sovereign: sovereign over all things; sovereign over his church, but also sovereign over all the powers of darkness and hell. Wicked men and Satan himself are also under God's control; heresy enters the church by God's sovereign will. Heresy is also in the hands of the Lord, guided by his irresistible and providential rule. In this we find one of the most striking features of church history. God uses heresy within the church for the good of his saints.

GOD'S PURPOSE IN HERESY

What good purpose can there be in a church torn to pieces by heresy? God has his own purpose, and his purpose is good: good for his glory and good for his church. Chiefly, heresy is the goad to prod the church to develop the truth that has been confessed by the church of the past, so that the riches of scripture may be brought out more fully. The church must grow in grace, and it grows in grace as it grows in the knowledge of the truth. When heresy rears its ugly head, the church is forced, in self-defense, to turn again to God's word to find the truth over against the erroneous doctrines that appear. As a result, the body of the truth grows and the confession of believers is enriched—a confession of God, whom to know is life eternal.

This was the case with the Christological controversies that gave us the great creeds of Nicaea-Constantinople (325/381) and Chalcedon (451). The Reformation too, in its defense of the truth of sovereign grace against the works-righteousness of the Roman Catholic Church, produced a great number of wonderful creeds. The doctrines of particular grace, as taught in the Protestant Reformed Churches, were forged in large measure in the controversies that arose with those who taught common grace. And the beautiful doctrine of an unconditional covenant of grace became our heritage through the bitterness of the struggle with conditional theology in the late 1940s and early 1950s.

God uses heresy to prod the church to perform her calling to defend and develop the truth. Throughout the entire history of the church, the truth is not developed in the ivory tower of theological contemplation far removed from the noise of combat. It is rather hammered out on the anvil raised on the battlefield of the ages in order that it may serve as weapons of defense in the wars of the saints. From the smoke and dust of spiritual conflict rises the glorious structure of the truth of God in Christ, which serves as a bulwark of the church throughout the ages.

THE APOLOGISTS

Throughout the entire Post-Apostolic Period, paganism constituted a threat to Christianity. Although the heathen in the Roman Empire were frequently the instigators of persecution, some heathen launched intellectual attacks against the faith of God's people. In general, their efforts were geared to defend polytheism (the worship of many gods) and to charge Christianity with atheism (the worship of no god) because Christians repudiated the gods of Greece and Rome. When the Caesars claimed divinity and the Christians refused to worship them, these Roman intellectuals charged Christians with treason.

These pagan intellectual attacks against the church were not strictly heresies, for heresies arise within the church and are corruptions of particular doctrines officially adopted by the church. But these attacks did show the members of the church the need to defend their faith.

Celsus, a second-century Greek philosopher, was a well-known critic of the church. In a book entitled *True Discourse*, he attacked Christianity as one of the many cults that filled the empire, differing from other cults only in its emphasis on morality and prescription of strange rules of behavior for its members. Celsus also repudiated the possibility of miracles, scorned the truth of the birth of Jesus Christ from a virgin mother, and said that Christianity, insofar as it rested its case on miracles, thrived on the deception of common and ignorant folk. Celsus and his writings are known today only through the work of Origen (c. 185–254), the eccentric Alexandrian church father and theologian, who answered these attacks many years later in his book *Against Celsus*. He quoted extensively from Celsus's writings and thus preserved for posterity the vicious attacks launched by this enemy of Christianity.

Lucian of Samosata, another well-known second-century critic of Christianity, used ridicule to make Christianity look foolish in the eyes of his contemporaries. He was the perfect man for this because, although he had been trained to be a rhetorician, he earned his living by making speeches and giving humorous soliloquies. He thought highly of himself as a traveling jokester and even offered his services to those who were pleading a case in court. He thought his witty and persuasive writings and speeches would convince any judge of the position he was defending. Lucian had no interest in religion or theology and turned his ridicule on Christians. He ridiculed the monotheism of the Christian beliefs, the miracles of which Christianity spoke, and the morality that Christianity practiced and promoted. His ridicule of the truth is the same as the ridicule of evolutionists today who mock the truth of creation.

Lucian of Samosata

The first defenders of the faith against these early attacks are known as the *apologists*. Later ages gave them this name because their main purpose was to defend Christianity against the attacks of their accusers. *Apology* means "a defense of one's position" (1 Pet. 3:15, where the word "answer" is properly translated *apology*). An apologist, then, is a defender of the faith. The apologists wrote to answer the accusations of their critics and to teach the Christian faith to their readers. Answering the charges of pagans and Jews outside the church and of heretics within the church, they carefully explained and defended the doctrines and teachings of the church.

THE ARGUMENTS OF THE APOLOGISTS [1]	
Jewish Arguments vs. Christianity	**Responses of Apologists**
Christianity is a deviant form of Judaism.	The Jewish law is by nature temporary and points to the New Covenant.
The humble carpenter who died on a cross does not correspond to the Messiah prophesied in the Old Testament.	The Old Testament predicted both the sufferings and the glory of the Messiah.
The deity of Christ contradicts the unity of God.	The Old Testament indicates a plurality of persons within the unity of the Godhead.
Apologists' Arguments Against Judaism	
Old Testament prophecy is fulfilled in Christ. Old Testament types point to Christ. The destruction of Jerusalem showed God's condemnation of Judaism and vindication of Christianity.	
Pagan Arguments vs. Christianity	**Responses of Apologists**
The doctrine of the resurrection is absurd.	There were eyewitnesses in the Gospels. The effect on the disciples was profound. There are analogies in natural cycles (e.g., seasons).
There are contradictions in the Scriptures.	Harmonies like Tatian's Diatessaron answer contradictions.
Atheism is widely held.	Even Plato favored an unseen god.
Christianity is the worship of a criminal.	Jesus' trial violated both Jewish and Roman law.
Christianity is a novelty.	Christianity had been in preparation for all eternity. Moses antedated pagan philosophers.
Christianity evidences a lack of patriotism.	Christians obey all laws that do not violate conscience.
Christians practice incest and cannibalism.	Observe the lifestyles of Christians, particularly the examples of the martyrs; practices of "holy kiss," Lord's Supper.
Christianity leads to the destruction of society.	Natural calamities are really the true God's judgment against false worship.
Apologists' Arguments Against Paganism	
Pagan philosophers plagiarized, stealing their best ideas from Moses and the prophets. Polytheism is a philosophical absurdity and a moral disaster. Pagan philosophers contradict one another and even themselves.	
Apologists' Arguments For Christianity	
All truth found in pagan philosophers anticipates Christianity and is brought together by it. Miracles performed by Christ, the apostles, and other Christians prove the truth of Christianity. The spread of Christianity despite overwhelming obstacles shows it to be true. Christianity alone is suited to meet the deepest needs of human beings.	

---

1   Chart taken from Walton, *Chronological and Background Charts*, chart 15.

Justin Martyr
(c. 100–165)

The first and most famous apologist, Justin Martyr was a gifted philosopher who after his conversion started a Christian school in Rome and defended the faith against enemies within and without the church. He wrote against educated pagans (e.g., *First Apology*), against unbelieving Jews (e.g., *Dialogue with Trypho the Jew*), and against seductive heretics (e.g., *Against Marcion*). After addressing his *Second Apology* to the emperor Marcus Aurelius, he was arrested by the Roman prefect Rusticus and martyred for his Christian faith. To learn more, read "Justin Martyr: Convert from Heathendom," chapter 2 of Herman Hanko's *Portraits of Faithful Saints*.

JUSTIN AND IRENAEUS

Among the most famous of these early apologists were Justin Martyr (c. 100–165), Irenaeus of Lyons (c. 130–202), Tertullian of Carthage (c. 160–225), Origen of Alexandria (c. 185–254), and Lactantius (c. 240–320). In addition to these major apologists, God raised up a host of others during the early years of the church, including Quadratus, Aristides, Tatian, Athenagoras, Theophilus, Melito, and Hegesippus. We will take a closer look at just two of these apologists: Justin Martyr, the first and most famous apologist, and Irenaeus of Lyon, the greatest of the apologists. While Justin Martyr defended the faith primarily against pagan attacks from without the church, Irenaeus of Lyons defended the faith against heretical attacks from within.

Justin Martyr (c. 100–165) gave far too much significance to pagan philosophers, but he nevertheless died a martyr (hence his name) because of his commitment to Christianity. Justin Martyr traveled a long road to his destination within the church. It may have been the early workings of the Holy Spirit that sent him on a search through philosophical schools. He found the Stoics unable to explain to him the nature of God. He joined the Peripatetics (traveling salesmen who taught philosophy for money) but lost patience with their overeagerness to collect their fees. He tried the Pythagoreans,[2] but he was required to learn astronomy, music, and mathematics prior to studying philosophy, which he did not want to do.

---

2 Any student who has had to master plane geometry will recognize this philosophical school as the discoverer of the Pythagorean theorem. This school taught that the basic structure of the universe was numbers, and its adherents were as a result skilled mathematicians.

Justin was converted through the teaching of an old and simple Christian, perhaps on the shore near Ephesus, where Paul met with the elders of the church (Acts 20:16–17) and where Justin discussed with this aged saint the doctrine of God. However, Justin never freed himself from his philosophical leanings. He justified this synthesis of worldly philosophy and Christian theology by speaking of the presence of the Logos in heathen philosophers that made their philosophy compatible with the Christian doctrine of Christ. Amazingly, the same idea is still taught today by the proponents of common grace. It is also taught by Philip Schaff in his magisterial *History of the Christian Church*.[3]

Justin Martyr set up a school in Rome to teach Christianity, he engaged others in public debate, and he wrote several apologies. He was eventually condemned by Roman rulers and died for his faith when he was beheaded.

Irenaeus of Lyons (c. 130–202), a Latin-speaking theologian from Gaul (modern France), was most famous for his apology *Against Heresies*, in which he exposed the foolishness and wickedness of heretical gnostic thought. Irenaeus was an outstanding early Christian believer whose influence was great and who was more responsible than any other man for the defeat of the deadly gnostic heresy. While the exact dates of his birth and death are unknown, he lived during the second century. It is possible that he was born in Smyrna (Rev. 2:8–11), a church faithful in persecution.

Irenaeus of Lyons

If Smyrna was his birthplace, he may have known Polycarp, the minister of Smyrna, for Irenaeus was born into a Christian family. He apparently moved to the city of Lyons in Gaul, where he became a priest. As a citizen of a Latin-speaking country, he penned his major writings in Latin. While he was traveling to Rome to carry a letter warning the bishop of Rome of the spread of the error of Montanism, a terrible massacre took place in Lyons. Upon his return, Irenaeus took the place of the martyred bishop Pothinus and spent the rest of his ministry ably defending the faith against a wide range of heresies within the church, including gnosticism, Marcionism, and Montanism.

STRENGTHS AND WEAKNESSES

Most of the apologists were converted heathens, and the goal in their defense of the faith was to convince their former acquaintances of the truth of Christianity. Some

---

3   Philip Schaff, *History of the Christian Church* (Grand Rapids, MI: William B. Eerdmans Publishing Co., 1946), 1:75–76.

apologists defended the church against the slanders raised against Christians, writing in the (usually vain) hope that Christianity would be tolerated and persecution would be abandoned if only Christianity were understood.

Sometimes the apologists did not fully appreciate the fundamental and total difference between pagan religions and the Christian faith. They considered their work to be useful as a bridge between pagan philosophy and Christianity, which made it easier for the heathen to cross into Christianity. So they were sometimes content with pointing out what was good in paganism while explaining why Christianity was superior. They pointed out that even some Greek and Roman philosophers denied polytheism and that the heathen gods were human, stupid, and prone to every vice known to man. They showed that the vices of the gods led to immorality among their worshipers, while indeed Christianity was morally superior, for the moral life of Christians was conducive to the betterment of society, while pagan immorality led to moral decay and the decline of society.

Despite all their weaknesses, God used these apologists as the means to defend Christianity when it was in its most vulnerable state. The apologists were called to defend Christianity against slander and false doctrine; to soften, if possible, the hatred of the world; and to strengthen the faithful in their confession. They demonstrated to the Jews that the Old Testament clearly points ahead to Christ and that Christ is the one who has fulfilled it. Against the heathen errors of the day, the apologists used various devices. They engaged in a rational defense of the faith and attacked the vices of paganism and the contradictions in its philosophy. They pointed to the prophecies and their fulfillment as proof of the divine origin of their religion. They appealed to miracles, to the heroic martyrdom of the saints, and to the continuous growth of Christianity in the face of opposition as proof that their faith was not the work of men. They argued that Christianity, because it addressed all the needs of men, was a religion eminently suitable to the needs of a wicked world. In a word, the apologists were bold to "earnestly contend for the faith which was once delivered unto the saints" (Jude 3).

CHAPTER 6: **THE EARLIEST HERESIES**

After my departing shall grievous wolves enter in among you,
not sparing the flock.

—ACTS 20:29

This chapter examines three of the earliest and most important heresies with which the early church found it necessary to contend: Ebionism, an ancient form of works-righteousness; gnosticism, an ancient form of rationalism; and Montanism, an ancient form of mysticism.

Ancient heresies have a way of creeping back into the church from time to time. Throughout its long history, the church has often found it necessary to confront various forms of works-righteousness (the teaching that human effort merits with God), rationalism (the teaching that human reason is the ultimate authority), and mysticism (the teaching that human emotion is the ultimate authority). Because this is true of the church today too, we do well to study the spiritual warfare of early church history, to learn from the history of heresy, and to give thanks to God for preserving his church in her confession of the truth of sovereign grace and her conviction that God's word is the sole authority of faith and life.

THE HERESY OF EBIONISM

The first heresy the early church encountered was Ebionism, a Judaizing heresy that denied Christ's fulfillment of the law and that taught that the keeping of the law was necessary for salvation. Ebionism was a direct assault on the doctrine of sovereign grace.

From the beginning of the New Testament church at Pentecost, unconverted Jews bitterly resented and hated Christians. They were a great grief to the church and a grave threat to the continued existence of the church.[1] As we noted, two epistles (Romans and Galatians) were written in defense of the faith against Judaism.

With the destruction of Jerusalem and the scattering of the Jewish nation, Judaism developed into Ebionism. This name comes from a Hebrew root that means "poor" and was more than likely given to the Ebionites because of their material poverty.[2] They were found predominantly in Palestine, east of the Jordan, and in Syria, with a center in Pella, to which place of safety many fled when the Roman legions marched into Palestine in AD 70. After the destruction of Jerusalem, the Ebionites clung to their Judaistic heresies and spread to Asia Minor.

Although the Ebionites claimed to be Christians, they separated from the Christian church. Not surprisingly, they emphasized the need for circumcision and the observance of the ceremonial laws of the Old Testament. They taught that Christ was a mere man born of Joseph and Mary, but that he possessed the spirit of an angel. They accepted only the New Testament books of Matthew, James, and Peter and called Paul an apostate. Various Ebionites differed on the question of whether Christ was the Messiah. Many later became gnostic in their religion.[3] Over the years the movement died out.

One author writes:

The waning and disappearance of the groups of Christians who sought to remain within Judaism made it clear that the radical newness of the Gospel was not to be obscured by reducing Christianity to a Jewish sect. Christianity was now unmistakably a separate religion, having rootage in Judaism and honouring the Jewish scriptures, but interpreting them as preparing for the basic and revolutionary novelty of Jesus and the Gospel.[4]

Yet in spite of its rejection of the truth of salvation by grace alone and its condemnation by the early church, the error of the Ebionites continues to raise its head in all those who claim to be justified by faith and works.

---

1   For an interesting history of the Jews from AD 70 (the date of the destruction of Jerusalem) and Jewish Christianity, see F. F. Bruce, *The Spreading Flame: The Rise and Progress of Christianity from its First Beginnings to the Conversion of the English* (Grand Rapids, MI: Wm. Eerdmans Publishing Co., 1964), 261–82.
2   Augustus Neander, *General History of the Christian Religion and Church: From the German of Dr. Augustus Neander*, trans. Joseph Torrey (Edinburgh: T & T Clark, 1847), 1:345–46.
3   Neander, *General History*, 1:349.
4   Kenneth Scott Latourette, *A History of Christianity: Volume 1: to A.D. 1500*, rev. ed. (New York: Harper & Row Publishers, 1975), 1:122.

THE HERESY OF GNOSTICISM

A second heresy that appeared very early in church history was gnosticism. The term *gnosticism* comes from the Greek word for knowledge, *gnosis.* Gnosticism is a type of rationalism that teaches that salvation comes through a mysterious knowledge known only to a few enlightened ones. Paul wrote about what seems to be an early form of gnosticism in Colossians 2:18–23, and John warns against the gnostic heresy in his first epistle.

Gnosticism rose early and posed a serious threat to the church, reaching the height of its influence from 135 to 160. It was finally defeated after a long and bitter battle by the sharp and insistent attacks of the church father and apologist Irenaeus of Lyons. As we noted in the last chapter, Irenaeus's book *Against Heresies* was particularly effective as a defense of the faith. After gnosticism's influence had waned, its adherents formed a separate church that survived into the fifth century.

Gnosticism was not brought into the church by one man, nor did it constitute a sect or an organized group that was officially condemned by the church. It was more like a general system of thought that differed widely from one place to the next and that never was much else than a movement. It was like the New Age movement in our time in its relation to the church.[5]

One historian describes gnosticism this way: "In its relation to Christianity it is a subject of bewildering complexity."[6] Another describes gnosticism as "a stealing of some Christian rags to cover heathen nakedness."[7] Gnosticism was basically a synthesis religion that attempted to unite the best elements of the philosophy of neo-platonism, Eastern mystery religions, Judaism, and Christianity into a unified body of doctrine that would be suitable for all men. In a certain sense of the word, it was an ecumenical attempt to unite all religions into one acceptable system. It was the price the church paid for finding in pagan philosophy elements of truth and goodness, an idea promoted by some of the early apologists.

A brief survey of gnosticism's teachings will demonstrate what a complicated system of thought it really was.

Gnosticism had little to say about God, for he was considered the great eternal Unknowable. From this unknowable, unnamed, cold, impersonal, and spiritual being

---

5   The New Age movement is a synthesis of Christianity with pagan religions, especially mystical religions. (In various forms it is found in many churches today.)

6   Hughes, *A History of the Church*, 1:170.

7   Louis Berkhof, *The History of Christian Doctrines* (Grand Rapids, MI: Baker Book House, 1975), 47.

proceeded a long chain of emanating *aeons*, divine creatures each proceeding from another, each weaker than its parent. The gnostics taught that one aeon finally came who "while powerful enough to create [the world] is silly enough not to see that creation is wrong."[8] This divine creature was called the *demiurge*, sometimes identified with the Logos (Word) spoken of in John 1, but more often as the God of the Old Testament, angry, vindictive, and filled with the desire to punish.

All gnostics were dualists who spoke of two worlds, a good spiritual world and an evil physical world. The creation, composed of matter, was believed to be inherently evil. The church father Irenaeus says in his description of what the gnostics believed that "the thirtieth and last of the aeons, wisdom, fell from the perfection of the pleroma[9] through an excess of passion, finally giving birth to a shapeless mass. And hence they declare [that] material substance had its beginning from (her) [wisdom's] ignorance and grief, and fear and bewilderment."[10]

The gnostics believed that man, as part of the creation, was evil as well. However, within man was a spark of divinity that, if freed from the physical body and the physical world, would flow back to God to be eventually absorbed into the divine being.

Salvation came by *gnosis*, a secret knowledge possessed by only a few elite, *spiritual* people. Much of mankind was composed of *psychical* people, who were on the way to attaining gnosis because they showed some life of the soul. The remainder were *material* people, the majority of the world's population, who were wholly bound up in the material world.

Because the material world was inherently evil, gnosis was the power by which a man could escape the evil world, including his material body, and return to union with God to be absorbed into the godhead. (Its appeal was somewhat the same as that of the Masonic Lodge today.) Secret ceremonies, rituals, rights for the initiated, and appeals to the teachings of Christ made gnosticism convincing to many. It claimed to open the doors of heaven. The ethics of the gnostics extended from a rigid asceticism to a vicious licentiousness, depending on the character of each gnostic group.

Because gnosticism was a movement, not a heresy promoted by just one man

---

8   Charles Bigg, quoted by Charles Williams, *The Descent of the Dove: A History of the Holy Spirit in the Church* (New York: Meridian Books, 1956), 23.

9   The creatures emanating from God were sometimes called *pleroma*, the Greek word for fullness.

10 The quotation is from Jaroslav Pelikan, *The Emergence of the Catholic Tradition (100–600)* (Chicago: University of Chicago Press, 1971), 87. The quotation within is from Irenaeus, *Against Heresies*.

or by a few men who worked together, it had many different proponents who differed widely from each other in their views. The most important gnostic teachers were Simon Magus, Cerinthus, Basilides, Saturninus, Marcion, Valentinus, and Tatian. Their differences were so great that they represented different kinds of gnosticism, and they often spread their views through their writings, which included such titles as the *Gospel of Thomas*, the *Gospel of Philip*, the *Gospel of Mary*, the *Apocryphon of John*, and the *Apocalypse of Adam*.

In general, gnostic teachers were divided into three main groups, defined by what views were emphasized in their system. Jewish gnosticism emphasized the teachings of Ebionism. Heathen gnosticism emphasized pagan philosophy. Christian gnosticism emphasized some elements of Christianity, especially the doctrine of Christ.

> ## Valentinus
> ### (c. 100–160)
>
> Valentinus was the most popular and successful of the gnostic teachers. After studying in Alexandria, he started a gnostic school in Rome and may have written an influential gnostic book called *Gospel of Truth*. Valentinus gained a significant following in Europe, the Middle East, and North Africa. Consequently, the great apologist Irenaeus of Lyons defended the faith against Valentinus's false teachings in his masterpiece apology *Against Heresies*. To learn more about Valentinus and gnosticism, read "Gnosticism: Synthesis Religion," chapter 2 of Herman Hanko's *Contending for the Faith*.

To these so-called Christian gnostics, Christ was a good spirit sent from the unknowable, unnamed God to bring secret, saving knowledge to mankind. They taught that Christ could not have had a human nature, for that would have meant that Christ's human nature was inherently evil. This dilemma gave rise to another heresy, docetism, which denied the reality of Christ's human nature, teaching instead that Christ was a wraith or a ghost who possessed what only *seemed* to be a human nature. The term *docetism* comes from a Greek word that means "to seem."

The heresy of gnosticism served a good purpose under God's all-wise rule of his church. It forced the church to consider the relationship between pagan and mystical thought on the one hand and the Christian faith on the other. As I mentioned, some of the early apologists were of the opinion that elements of pagan thought could be incorporated into the Christian religion. This is a common error even in our day. For example, when I was going to college, my professors often spoke of the beauty and truth of Greek and Roman philosophy from which the church could learn much. Such truth could be found in pagan philosophy because the grace of God was operative also among the heathen and certain truths were, as a result, taught by the pagans.

Pelagius, a couple of centuries after gnosticism had reached the height of its influence, taught that many pagans of outstanding ability were saved because of the amount of truth they discovered. Roman Catholic Scholasticism attempted to forge a union between Aristotle and Christ, between Aristotelian philosophy and the Christian faith. Arminianism argued that the natural light of the unbeliever made him more susceptible to the gospel. Common grace teaches that much good, also in thinking and ideas, can come from wicked men, so that the joyful marriage of Athens and Jerusalem was to be blessed. The problem is an age-old one.

When the church freed itself from the gnostic heresy, it did so by underscoring the unique character of the Christian religion. The unique character of the Christian faith was to be found not only in the life the people of God lived, but also in the faith they confessed. Gnosticism, with its emphasis on knowledge, forced the church to give intellectual substance to its faith. One church historian writes that gnosticism "represented a fundamental distortion of Christian doctrine at each of these points, and the church had to resist it. But it also represented a serious effort to come to terms with issues of Christian doctrine from which no theologian, be he orthodox or heretical, could escape."[11]

The church began to see that the Christian faith is antithetical at every point to all pagan religions. There are no similarities at all. Paganism was not only false, but a corruption of the knowledge of God made known in creation—a deliberate and wicked changing of the truth of God into idols (Rom. 1:18–32). The antithesis between pagan philosophy and the truth of the scriptures was an absolute antithesis between light and darkness, for all human philosophy has its origin in sinful man's mind, while the truth of God revealed in Jesus Christ has its origin in divine revelation. It was a point of immense importance that controlled the development of the Christian faith through all the ages.

THE APOSTLES' CREED

The Apostles' Creed, in its earliest and simplest form, was probably written in the mid-second century, during the peak of gnostic influence within the church. The creed clearly presents the orthodox truths of Christianity over against the heretical tenets of gnostic thought. In its earliest form, the creed was called the Old Roman Symbol or

---

11 Pelikan, *Emergence of the Catholic Tradition*, 97.

the Old Roman Creed. Although the apostles did not write it, the creed captures the central truths of scripture as taught by the apostles and was used to prepare catechumens for baptism. The Apostles' Creed likely reached its present form, found below, by the end of the fifth century. It has been the confession of the church for nearly two thousand years.

I. I believe in God the Father, Almighty, Maker of heaven and earth:

II. And in Jesus Christ, his only begotten Son, our Lord:

III. Who was conceived by the Holy Ghost, born of the Virgin Mary:

IV. Suffered under Pontius Pilate; was crucified, dead, and buried: he descended into hell:

V. The third day he rose again from the dead:

VI. He ascended into heaven, and sitteth at the right hand of God the Father Almighty:

VII. From thence he shall come to judge the quick and the dead:

VIII. I believe in the Holy Ghost:

IX. I believe an holy catholic church: the communion of saints:

X. The forgiveness of sins:

XI. The resurrection of the body:

XII. And the life everlasting. Amen.

THE HERESY OF MONTANISM

With the rise of Montanism, a third important early heresy, came the beginning of mysticism and Pentecostalism. The church suffered greatly from the heresy of Montanism. The rise of this heresy was due to the worldliness that had crept into the church in times when the people of God were free from persecution.

The church of Christ is usually, if not always, spiritually strongest in times of persecution, for her place in the world and her share of the world's goods are small. In times of freedom from persecution, the church, weak and prone to sin, begins to covet the things of the world, because life in the world is comfortable. The church as a result is in danger of becoming worldly and spiritually weak.

Yet in times of spiritual lethargy and worldliness, some rebel against the weakness of the church and seek a deeper and inner religion that is the opposite of the outward and formal worship so displeasing to God. Frequently the result is mysticism and a religion of feeling. This was Montanism.

Montanus of Phrygia, the second-century father of Montanism, began a movement of mystical religion that has been present in the church through all the centuries since his day; for example it is present today in the charismatic movement. It substitutes for the knowledge of the truth a purely subjective feeling of well-being without much, if any, intellectual content. One historian describes the beginning of the movement in these words: "Montanus, a recent convert, began to experience ecstasies, in the midst of which, to the accompaniment of bizarre gesticulations and long drawn out howlings, prophecy poured forth from him and new revelations."[12]

Montanus of Phrygia (Second Century)

A former pagan priest from Phrygia in Asia Minor, Montanus converted to Christianity and founded an ancient heresy called Montanism. Accompanied by two prophetesses, Montanus claimed new revelations from the Holy Spirit, the ability to perform miracles (including tongue-speaking and healings), and a special knowledge of the end of the world. His heresy became quite popular, spreading throughout Asia Minor and then to Rome and North Africa, where it ensnared even the great church father Tertullian. Montanus was, in fact, the first charismatic, and the early church condemned his views at a number of early synods. To learn more about Montanus and Montanism, read "Montanus: First Charismatic," chapter 3 of Herman Hanko's *Contending for the Faith*.

Montanus, shortly after his conversion from paganism to Christianity, began prophesying. He quickly acquired two female companions, Priscilla and Maximilla, who claimed identical prophetic gifts. These two women gained even greater popularity than Montanus himself, and their teachings spread through Phrygia, a province of Asia Minor.

Montanus claimed that the Holy Spirit had appeared to him and had given him a new, extra-scriptural revelation about the last days. The faithful, at Montanus's command, were summoned to the city of Pepuza in Phrygia of Asia Minor, there to await the return of Christ. Beginning around the mid-second century, the heresy spread to North Africa and Rome.

The Montanists divided history into three dispensations: the dispensation of the Father, the dispensation of the Son, and the latest dispensation of the Holy Spirit. Montanus claimed that revelation continued beyond the age of the apostles and that he spoke for the Holy Spirit, producing new revelations in addition to the scriptures. The Montanists taught that all Christians were preachers, although carnal Christians ought to refrain from the practice of preaching. They taught that Christ was to return at any moment and people ought to sell their possessions, abandon the world, and wait for Christ.

The heresy was a protest against worldliness, spiritual laxity, and the rise of hierarchical church government. It was very ascetic and was characterized by sobriety and gloominess. It condemned all jewelry, it insisted on virgins wearing veils, and it

---

12 Hughes, *A History of the Church*, 1:119.

made periods of fasting a requirement. It was suspicious of marriage, and it promoted wild religious frenzy and Holy Spirit–inspired ecstasy. It was severe in the exercise of the keys of the kingdom.

In addition to these views, the Montanists also spoke of a two-level Christianity, the lower level consisting of ordinary saints, and the higher level of Spirit-filled people who experienced supernatural ecstasies. It was highly distrustful of the instituted church and the sacraments, and it claimed that true Christianity came to expression in special gifts of prophecy, tongue-speaking, and miracles.

Sadly, Tertullian of Carthage (c. 160–225), the church father and apologist who played such an important role in the formation of the doctrine of the Trinity, joined the Montanist sect, for he himself was something of an ascetic and was troubled by the worldliness and lack of genuine piety in the church.

The church, alarmed by the popularity of the movement, held several provincial synods that condemned the movement and were instrumental in quashing it. Montanism was condemned for its doctrine of ongoing revelation (in addition to the scriptures) and its mystical and subjective character, which tended to reduce religion to subjective feelings. But the heresy was only the first of a long line of similar movements that repeatedly appeared in the church. It is true that outward religion, worship of God by lip service only, worldliness, and carnality are constant threats to the welfare of the church. But the cure of these ills is not to make religion a matter of the feelings; it is rather the lively preaching of the word and the exercise of Christian discipline.

There will be opportunity to discuss this erroneous view in later history, for the error is frequently taught by mystics. But for the present it is sufficient to remind ourselves that God created man with a soul. The faculties of the soul are mind and will. An important part of man's will is his emotions. Man fell, and the depravity of sin destroyed the spiritual good of man in body and soul, including mind and will. Salvation is God's work of grace to save the whole man, both body and soul, both mind and will with its emotions. True religion is to *know* the truth with our minds, for "Ye shall know the truth, and the truth shall make you free" (John 8:32); but true religion is also sorrow for sin, joy in the Lord, mercy and compassion, love and kindness—all profoundly emotional.

The church had to learn that salvation means "that I with body and soul, both in life and death, am not my own, but belong unto my faithful Savior Jesus Christ."[13]

---

13 Heidelberg Catechism A 1, in *Confessions and Church Order*, 83.

THE PENDULUM OF CHURCH HISTORY

There is a kind of a pendulum that swings in the church from one extreme to the other. It swings between rationalism, which makes man's reason the final arbiter of truth, and mysticism, which makes feelings the final arbiter of truth. Both have in common that they abandon or add to the Scriptures as the sole authority of faith and life. The one puts reason in Scripture's place; the other puts feelings there.

Reason and feelings are opposed to each other, and this opposition makes the pendulum swing. Weary of the coldness of rationalism, the pendulum swings in the direction of mysticism; then, frightened at last by the quagmire of the shifting sands of mysticism, the pendulum swings wildly back toward rationalism. Both are reactions; both are wrong.

The great lesson to be learned by it all is simply *sola Scriptura*, the one great principle of the Reformation.

—Herman Hanko, *Contending for the Faith*, 22.

CHAPTER 7: **THE FORMATION OF THE CANON**

All scripture is given by inspiration of God, and is profitable for doctrine, for reproof,
for correction, for instruction in righteousness: that the man of God may be perfect,
thoroughly furnished unto all good works.

—2 TIMOTHY 3:16–17

EARLY CONCEPTIONS OF THE CANON

The scriptures are the word of God in which is found the truth of God as God makes himself known in Christ. It was therefore important for the early church to establish which books were of God, because no possible development or defense of the truth could be made until this was done. God in his wisdom led the church to set the canon of scripture—the authoritative list of books that belong in the Bible—very early in her history, for scripture was to be the foundation of all the other truths the church would later confess.

There was never any serious question in the church about which books belonged to the Old Testament. The Jews themselves had fixed the Old Testament canon by naming the inspired books and rejecting the apocryphal books. They had done this at the meeting of the Council of Jamnia in the year 90 BC. To this canon Jesus referred when he spoke of the scriptures and called them the law and the prophets (Matt. 5:17). The Old Testament canon had been fixed by the time the church began its task. Because Jesus accepted this canon, we may be sure it contained all the inspired Old Testament books that are now in our Bibles.[1]

---

1   Church historians are increasingly inclined to believe that no such meeting as the Council of Jamnia was ever held. Whether or not that is correct, the fact remains that our Lord referred to a specific and defined canon when, in appealing to the Old Testament scriptures, he spoke of them as "the law and the prophets."

If one consults the writings of the early church, it becomes evident that from the beginning the church accepted the canon as we now know it. The apostles understood that the Old Testament scriptures were infallibly inspired, for Peter writes that the prophets searched their own writings carefully that they might learn as much as they could of God's work in sending the Messiah (1 Pet. 1:10–11). If the prophets searched their own writings to know more about the coming of Christ, they knew that God had inspired them. One does not otherwise search his own writings to learn from them. The same was true of the New Testament writers. They were conscious of their own inspiration as apostles.

Certain other books were written by the apostles that were never considered canonical. It is more than likely that Paul wrote an additional letter to the Corinthians not included in the canon (1 Cor. 5:9); and Paul himself mentions a letter he wrote to the Laodiceans (Col. 4:16). These books, as well as other non-canonical books in both the old and new dispensations, although mentioned in the Old Testament, were not infallibly inspired and therefore were not included in the canon.

By the end of the first century, the four gospel narratives were circulated together. The same was true of Paul's writings: a *Corpus Paulorum* (body of Paul's writings) was copied and distributed widely. Every church wanted a copy, for it, along with the gospels, was accepted as a collection of divinely inspired writings. First Peter, 1 John, and Revelation were accepted early as well, and no doubts were raised about them. Because Luke wrote both the third gospel narrative and the book of Acts, Acts also was readily accepted as part of the sacred writings.

Questions were sometimes raised concerning 2 Peter and 2 and 3 John, but in the accepted canon, they were frequently included with 1 Peter and 1 John respectively. James and Jude presented problems, because they were not written by apostles, and apostolic authorship was considered the mark of canonicity. James and Jude were written by half-brothers of Jesus. Yet the majority of the church accepted them as inspired writings. Because there was no doubt that the apostle John had written Revelation, this book also was accepted as canonical.

In its early post-apostolic life, the church, perhaps somewhat naively, simply accepted the canonical books as such and made no official decision as to which books were canonical and which books were not.

MARCION'S ATTACK ON THE CANON

God used the heretic Marcion of Sinope (c. 85–160) to compel the church to define the canon officially.

Marcion was the son of a bishop in Sinope, Pontus. It seems as if Asia Minor, of which Pontus was a part, was a hotbed of heresy, beginning with the Galatians, against whom Paul wrote his epistle. As a successful ship owner, Marcion left his homeland and moved to Rome, where he began to teach his heresies. In the end he was excommunicated in Rome for wrong teachings concerning scripture. He had given a large sum of money to the church in Rome, which gift was returned to him.

Sinope, Asia Minor

---

2 Belgic Confession 4, in *Confessions and Church Order*, 25.
3 Belgic Confession 5, in *Confessions and Church Order*, 25.

After his excommunication, Marcion founded a church separate from the apostolic church and had considerable influence on many who flocked to him and joined his movement. His sect spread throughout the Mediterranean world as far east as Syria and Palestine. Although Marcion died in 160, his church survived until the sixth century, a strong testimony to his influence.

Marcion was not, strictly speaking, a gnostic. He was not a metaphysical philosopher who appreciated pagan philosophy and attempted to integrate it with the Christian faith. Like the gnostics, he rejected the material world as evil; but unlike the gnostics, he emphasized a careful study of the apostle Paul, as opposed to any secret knowledge. Marcion articulated his ideas in his main work, *Antithesis*.

Marcion's main problem was that he did not understand the relationship of the Old and New Testaments. He had problems reconciling the law and the gospel. The former, in his opinion, belonged to the old dispensation and the latter to the new. After a very superficial study, he said that the God of the Old Testament was a Jewish God opposed to the God of the New. The former was cruel, vindictive, demanding perfection, and quick to destroy. The God of the New Testament was kind, merciful, gracious, and abundantly willing to save.

To defend such a strange view, Marcion and his followers were compelled to butcher the scriptures. They rejected the Old Testament in its entirety and were willing to accept only some of the New Testament: only ten epistles of Paul and the gospel according to Luke. To make matters worse, Marcion mutilated the gospel of Luke by removing elements he found distasteful and keeping those parts more to his liking. This determination concerning the New Testament was senseless and purely arbitrary; it revealed that Marcion was not interested in truth at all and cared nothing for God's holiness and justice but was determined only to promote himself.

Marcion was a heretic much like the higher critics today, of whom we must be aware. To a greater or lesser degree, these critics put so much emphasis on the men whom God used to write the scriptures that they minimize or deny God's authorship. The result is that these higher critics claim to find mistakes in scripture. They say that incorrect views of the world (such as a flat earth) were included by the men who authored the scriptures. They also find grammatical errors, geographical errors, and other numerical errors. If higher critics do not like a particular doctrine in scripture, they put that part of scripture aside as the mistaken notion of the writer and of no contemporary value. If a given doctrine of scripture is not to their liking (such as the silence of women in the church) and does not happen to agree with their preconceived ideas (such as evolutionism), they are quick to assign it to the realm of legend, myth, or parable. Critics are also quick to examine the canonicity of every book by criteria they themselves invent; and they feel perfectly free to question whether a given book belongs to any kind of sacred writing. By doing this, the foundation of the Christian faith is destroyed.

THE SETTLING OF THE CANON

Marcion's attack on the canon of scripture goaded the church to set down officially the books that belong to the canon of sacred scripture. This was done only gradually and without a great deal of fanfare, chiefly because the church itself, with the exception of Marcion and his followers, generally agreed on the canon.

The earliest writing concerning the books properly belonging to the canon is a pastoral letter sent out by Athanasius (c. 296–373), the bishop of Alexandria. The Roman bishop's determination of the proper day for the celebration of Easter (on the first Sunday after the first full moon following the vernal equinox) required some knowledge of astronomy. Because Egypt had a reputation for the science and knowledge

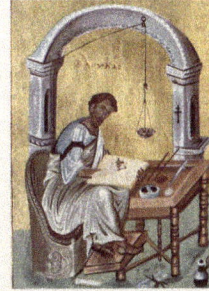

Marcion of Sinope
(c. 85–160)

A wealthy and well-traveled ship owner from the town of Sinope on the coast of the Black Sea, Marcion settled in Rome and joined the church there, giving money to charity and gaining wide popularity. Influenced by gnosticism, Marcion soon developed his own heresy of dualism and Paul-worship and became the first to define the New Testament canon. Although his mutilated canon was a blasphemous assault on scripture, he unwittingly drove the church to define the canon and defend the truth of God's word. To learn more about Marcion and Marcionism, read "Marcion: First Bible Critic," chapter 1 of Herman Hanko's *Contending for the Faith*.[4]

of astronomy, the church of Alexandria was assigned the task of determining when Easter would be celebrated and informing all the churches of the proper date. Athanasius was accustomed to sending a pastoral letter along with information concerning the date. In one such pastoral letter, Athanasius listed the twenty-seven books that properly belong to the New Testament canon: that list is identical with the church's doctrine of the canon as we hold it today. The letter was sent in 367.

---

4 Picture taken from https://postbarthian.com/wp-content/uploads/2015/01/640px-Byzantinischer _Maler_des_10._Jahrhunderts_001.jpg, (accessed November 3, 2020).

The canon was officially fixed at the Synod of Rome in 382, at the Synod of Hippo in 393, and finally at the Synod of Carthage in 397. The church, seemingly as an after-thought, added the Old Testament Apocrypha (a handful of non-canonical books written between the Old and New Testaments) to the canon, but in a somewhat hesitant way.

THE DEVELOPMENT OF THE NEW TESTAMENT CANON [5]					
Period	Characteristics	Approx-imate Dates	Significant Sources	Books Received	Books Questioned
APOSTOLIC FATHERS	No serious debate, no official pronouncements	100–140	Quotations in Apostolic Fathers	Four Gospels Pauline Epistles (unspecified corpus)	None
GNOSTIC OPPOSITION	Reaction against gnostic truncation of canon (esp. writings of Marcion)	140–220	Quotations in Church Fathers Muratorian Canon (c. 180) Gospel of Truth (gnostic)	Four Gospels, Acts 13 Pauline Epistles 1 Peter 1 John Jude Revelation	Hebrews, James 2 Peter 2–3 John Shepherd, Didache, Apocalypse of Peter
FINAL SOLIDIFI-CATION	General agreement by end of 4th century	220–400	Origen	Four Gospels, Acts 13 Pauline Epistles 1 Peter 1 John Revelation	Hebrews, James 2 Peter 2–3 John Jude Shepherd, Didache
			Eusebius	Four Gospels, Acts 14 Pauline Epistles 1 Peter 1 John	James 2 Peter 2–3 John Jude, Revelation Shepherd, Didache
			Athanasius (Paschal letter of 367—final acceptance in the East)	Present Canon	
			Synod of Rome (382—final acceptance in the West)	Present Canon	
			Synod of Carthage (397—acceptance by entire church)	Present Canon	

5   Chart taken from Walton, *Chronological and Background Charts*, chart 17.

What were the criteria for determining which books are canonical and which books are not? The Belgic Confession lists the apocryphal books that are not to be included in the canon and says that they are to be rejected because "they are far from having such power and efficacy as that we may from their testimony confirm any point of faith or of the Christian religion; much less detract from the authority of the other sacred books."[6]

Further, the Belgic Confession gives the source of the dignity and authority of holy scripture:

> We receive all these books, and these only, as holy and canonical, for the regulation, foundation, and confirmation of our faith; believing, without any doubt, all things contained in them, not so much because the church receives and approves them as such, but more especially because the Holy Ghost witnesseth in our hearts that they are from God, whereof they carry the evidence in themselves. For the very blind are able to perceive that the things foretold in them are fulfilling.[7]

By these criteria the fathers who wrote and adopted the Belgic Confession meant that the Holy Spirit is the Spirit promised by Christ in John 14–16, who leads the church into all truth. The Holy Spirit never testifies in the hearts of believers, however, apart from the objective testimony of the scriptures themselves. This testimony of the scriptures is powerful and compelling and is sealed on our hearts by the testimony of Christ's Spirit. One reads the scriptures and is compelled by their own testimony that they are divine.

It is quite different with the apocryphal books. One need only read them, and he will come to the same conclusion as the Belgic Confession: "The church may read and take instruction from [them] so far as they agree with the canonical books."[8] Such is easily done. As one reads, one says to himself, "This is interesting reading. This gives us some information about some inter-testamentary history. But it is not any more inspired than a good history book. It does not read like the Bible and is not from God."

So the foundation of the New Testament church, the canon of scripture, was firmly set in place and agreed upon by all the true church. The history of Marcion is a remarkable instance of how God used a raving heretic to produce in the church a most important truth. God's scriptures are the rule of faith and life. God's word is the fountain from which all truth flows as a mighty stream. To lose the scriptures is to lose Christ.

---

6   Belgic Confession 6, in *Confessions and Church Order*, 26.
7   Belgic Confession 5, in *Confessions and Church Order*, 25.
8   Belgic Confession 6, in *Confessions and Church Order*, 26.

CHAPTER 8: **THE ORGANIZATION OF THE CHURCH**

Let all things be done decently and in order.

—1 Corinthians 14:40

THE THREE SPECIAL OFFICES

Although the total number of Christians in the Roman Empire did not exceed ten percent of the population,[1] the church exercised an influence far beyond its size. This influence was partly due to the close and effective organization of the congregations and of the church as a whole.

The apostles had laid the foundation for the organization of the church by instituting in each congregation the three special offices of minister, elder, and deacon. The work of each office was also clearly defined by the apostles, and for the most part the early church followed what the apostles had taught.

The ministers of the churches faithfully preached the scriptures. Because in the early part of this period no seminary existed to train prospective ministers for the work, the quality of preaching differed widely. However, by the end of this period, two noteworthy seminaries were established, one based in Alexandria, Egypt, and the other in Antioch, Syria.

---

1 Some historians estimate the number to be far higher, one even saying that over 50 percent of the population was Christian. In Rodney Stark, *The Rise of Christianity: A Sociologist Reconsiders History* (Princeton, NJ: Princeton University Press, 1996), a chart on page 7 estimates that in the Roman Empire prior to AD 100, the number of Christians was about 7,500. By AD 150, it was about 41,000. In AD 200, the number was about 220,000. In the middle of the third century (AD 250) the number was 1.17 million, and in AD 300 the number had grown to 6.3 million. At the end of Constantine's reign the number had reached about 34 million, or 56.5 percent of the population. Stark writes, "Hence 40 percent per decade…seems the most plausible estimate of the rate at which Christianity actually grew during the first several centuries," 6. These figures seem to me to be very much too high.

ANCIENT SEMINARIES IN THE EAST

Two early seminaries were established in the Eastern church. The one was in Alexandria, Egypt. The city of Alexandria had been built by Alexander the Great, who gave the city his own name. It was a major port in the Nile Delta and a center of trade between the various countries surrounding the Mediterranean Sea. But it was also the chief junction between the Orient and the Mediterranean basin, and its marketplaces were filled with a babble of different languages and the hustle and bustle of markets, warehouses, and excited, noisy businessmen. Here in this city one could find a ferment of ideas, including Oriental mysticism and Greek philosophy. Because of a large Jewish population in Egypt, the teachings of Judaism were also part of the seething mass of ideas discussed in the open markets.

The School of Alexandria was founded around 180 as a school for catechetical instruction. The catechists were usually well-educated laymen, and the school soon developed into a seminary for the training of bishops. Its influence extended throughout the churches. It was influenced by Greek philosophy, especially Platonism and Stoicism. It was highly speculative and not always orthodox.

Although the Alexandrian school was founded by a converted Stoic philosopher named Pantaenus (died c. 200), the first great leader of the school was Clement of Alexandria (c. 150–215), who was born in a pagan home but was converted to Christianity. His education in the Christian religion came through extensive travels and long talks with leading Christians in the cities he visited. He finally arrived in Alexandria and was further educated by Pantaenus. Appointed to succeed Pantaenus as a teacher in this important school, Clement promoted the ideas of Greek philosophy, particularly Platonism. He even spoke of philosophy as a schoolmaster to bring Greeks to Christ, since the Jews had the law as their schoolmaster (Gal. 3:24).

But the school's leading theologian was Clement's pupil and successor, Origen (c. 185–254). Origen was highly ascetic and mutilated himself for the cause of Christ. Although he was brilliant and original in his thinking, he was also given to speculation and heretical notions. Origen affected subsequent theology profoundly. He traveled widely, was ordained in Palestine, worked in Caesarea during his later years, and died a martyr's death. Origen's work covers the fields of exegesis, textual criticism, commentaries on scripture, apologetics, theology, and philosophy. He was the first to write a systematic theology. He tried to bring Platonic and Stoic philosophy into harmony with scripture through allegorical interpretation.

The lighthouse of Alexandria

But this approach to hermeneutics (the interpretation of Scripture) was opposed by another seminary in the East, the School of Antioch, which was destined to have great influence in the churches. The School of Antioch grew out of the first sending church in new dispensational history. It was not a highly organized school, such as the one in Alexandria, but was more or less a theological gathering.[2] The school's founder was Lucian of Antioch (c. 240–312), whom the later heretic Arius claimed as his teacher.

However, the Antiochian school placed a lot of emphasis on proper hermeneutical practices in the interpretation of scripture. It taught the grammatical-historical method of exegesis, the method still used today in orthodox churches. It put emphasis on the fact that the text of scripture had to be interpreted by careful attention to grammar and by interpreting the text in the light of its historical setting.

—Adapted from Herman Hanko, "Ancient Church History," 41.

Each church was under the rule of a body of men called *presbyters* (elders) or *episcopoi* (bishops). The names come from 1 Timothy 4:14 ("laying on of the hands of the presbytery") and Philippians 1:1 ("with the bishops and deacons"). *Presbyter* means "old one," implying that the elders in the congregation ought to be chosen from among the older men, for they are the wiser men because of their experiences in life. *Episcopos* literally means "one who watches over others; an overseer."

The deacons served well in the early church, for there was much work for them. In the gathering of his church, God often brings the poor and despised to faith in Christ (1 Cor. 1:26–29). The church through its deacons took care of the many widows and orphans. And many who were imprisoned during times of persecution were regularly visited and their families provided for. The deacons often enlisted the aid of deaconesses, women who were not installed into office but who assisted the deacons in their work. The rules of modesty demanded that women visit the widows and women in prisons and hospitals. Deacons summoned godly women to help them in this aspect of their work.[3]

These three special offices in the church were filled by men chosen by the congregation. Clement of Rome, a first-century bishop, writes, "That they [the offices] should be filled, according to the judgment of approved men, *with the consent of the whole community* [the congregation]."[4] These practices are identical to the practices Reformed churches follow today.

---

2 Schaff, *History of the Christian Church*, 2:816.

3 There is no justification for women to hold the office of deacon; in the Protestant Reformed Churches, deacons sometimes enlist the aid of godly women to accomplish aspects of the work they cannot perform, but they are not officebearers.

4 Neander, *General History*, 1:189; emphasis added.

DEVELOPMENT OF THE EPISCOPAL SYSTEM

Toward the end of the second century these practices began to change. The changes, made slowly, brought about an entirely different system of church government—the episcopal system. It is strange that these changes began so early in the history of the church, but circumstances often were to blame.

An episcopal system is one in which various levels of authority are created within the church, each level higher than the one below it. As we have seen, the New Testament words for elder are *presbyter* and *episcopos*, and both terms refer to the same office and are interchangeable.[5] Later the church made a distinction between the terms, and the whole papal system of the Roman Catholic Church developed from that mistake. The church began to teach that one of the elders was a bishop, who exercised an authority in the church that surpassed the others. This system is hierarchical, and it has reached its highest development in the Roman Catholic Church, where deacons are the lowest, then priests, bishops, archbishops, cardinals, and finally the pope sitting on the top of the pyramid. This mistake in church government was not corrected until the time of the Genevan Reformation in the sixteenth century. Reformed and biblical church polity forbids one officebearer to assume a higher position than another.[6]

Several factors contributed to the development of this unbiblical system of episcopal church government. One reason was severe persecution by the Roman Empire, which left many special offices in the church vacant. Officebearers were frequently killed or imprisoned. Some officebearers, especially ministers, who were the chief target of persecutors, fled to places of safety. On occasion some officebearers denied their Lord. This left vacancies, which were filled by others so that the church might continue to function. Offices and the specific duties of each individual office became confused.

A second factor that steered the church in the direction of hierarchy was a radical distinction that gradually appeared between *clergy* (those who hold the special offices of minister, elder, or deacon in the church) and *laity* (those who hold the office of all believers but do not hold the special offices in the church). The laity, sometimes

---

5   Neander, *General History*, 1:192.

6   "No church shall in any way lord it over other churches, no minister over other ministers, no elder or deacon over other elders or deacons" (Church Order 84, in *Confessions and Church Order*, 403). Although the article does not explicitly speak of one officebearer in one office lording it over another officebearer in another office (as a minister over an elder), the article has consistently been interpreted to mean the parity of the offices. Parity (equality) of offices is fundamental to biblical church polity.

under the pressure of persecution, were pushed aside and their office ignored. The ministers and elders had to take care of pressing matters in the church when persecution made it impossible for a congregation to operate normally. This paved the way for the development of a priesthood of the clergy, and the priesthood of all believers became less and less a part of church government.[7]

It must, however, be remembered that the laity, the regular members of the church, the people in the pew, hold the office of believer; and in holding that office, they have a God-given right to participate in the work of the church. They have the right to consent to the installation of clergy, both elders and deacons. Scripture gives them the right to participate in the rule of the church and in the work of the ministry.

A third reason for the early rise of the episcopacy was the gradual loss of the special offices of elder and deacon. In a ruling body of presbyters, one man, usually with the greatest gifts, assumed the chairmanship and the leadership of the body. At first his leadership was purely ethical; that is, he had the greatest gifts for teaching and leading meetings. His position was like a minister today in consistory meetings. He was first among equals (*primus inter pares*). But in the early church the superiority of his gifts and the pressures of persecution soon moved him from a *primus inter pares* to one with greater authority than the elders. The office of elder slowly faded into the background.

This gradual loss of the office of elder was hastened by another development. The idea of the Lord's supper as a sacrifice suggested also the need of a priest to perform the sacrifice. In this way ministers became priests instead of ministers of the gospel. These priests assumed increasing responsibility and gradually took over the work of elders, so that this important office in the church disappeared.

The same thing happened to the office of deacon. While deacons, in the beginning, manifested their own unique authority, this too gradually changed. Decisions had to be made to help those who had lost husbands and fathers. Because these problems often required immediate decisions, and the deacons were often killed or in prison, these decisions were made by a bishop.

SUPPORT FROM THE APOSTOLIC FATHERS

One can find early support for giving the office of bishop authority over the other offices. The apostolic fathers were a handful of men who were greatly respected in the

---

7 The office of all believers, a principle Martin Luther restored to the church, was sometimes called the priesthood of all believers.

post-apostolic church due to their close ties with the apostles. They included Clement of Rome, Ignatius of Antioch, Hermas of Rome, Barnabas of Alexandria, Papias of Hierapolis, and Polycarp of Smyrna. Some of these men gave bishops increasing authority in the churches. For instance, Clement of Rome taught *apostolic succession*, the idea that bishops are successors of the apostles, while Ignatius of Antioch was the first to distinguish between bishops and elders.

THE APOSTOLIC FATHERS AND EARLY WRITINGS [8]				
Name	Dates	Places of Ministry	Writings	Notable Facts
Clement of Rome	c. 30–100	Rome	1 Clement	Considered the fourth pope by Roman Catholic Church. Is perhaps mentioned in Philippians 4:3. Was martyred under Domitian. His letter stresses apostolic succession.
Ignatius	d. 107	Antioch in Syria	To the Ephesians To the Magnesians To the Trallians To the Romans To the Philadelphians To the Smyrnaeans To Polycarp	His letters were written en route to martyrdom in Rome—a fate he joyfully espoused. Was the first to distinguish between bishops and elders. Opposed gnostic heresies. Was martyred under Trajan.
Hermas	Late 1st–early 2nd century	Rome	The Shepherd	Was a contemporary of Clement. Wrote of visions and parables. Was perhaps a former slave. Was probably Jewish.
Barnabas of Alexandria	Late 1st–early 2nd century	Alexandria	Epistle of Barnabas	Was probably an Alexandrian Jew. Was familiar with allegorical methods of Philo.
Papias	c. 60–130	Hierapolis	Exposition of the Oracles of Our Lord	Was an acquaintance of the apostle John. Held a premillennial view of eschatology. Claimed Mark's gospel was based on Peter's words. Said that Matthew's gospel was originally written in Aramaic.

---

8 Chart taken from Walton, *Chronological and Background Charts*, chart 13.

THE APOSTOLIC FATHERS AND EARLY WRITINGS				
Name	**Dates**	**Places of Ministry**	**Writings**	**Notable Facts**
Polycarp	c. 69–155	Smyrna	*Epistle to the Philippians*	Was an acquaintance of the apostle John. Compiled and preserved the epistles of Ignatius. Is said to have confronted Marcion as "the first-born of Satan." Was martyred under Antoninus Pius
Unknown author	Early 2nd century	Syria	*Didache*	Early manual of church practice. Contrasts way of life and way of death. Gives instruction for fasting, baptism, Lord's supper. Tells how to recognize false prophets. Considered by some for inclusion in New Testament canon.

Ignatius of Antioch lived from the latter part of the first century to the early part of the second century. A former acquaintance of the apostle John, he later became the bishop of the church in Antioch of Syria. He was tried and sentenced to die in the Coliseum in Rome at the time of the Emperor Trajan around 107. On his way to Rome he wrote seven letters to various churches, which still survive. In these letters he taught that a godly bishop must hold his office as a visible symbol of the unity of the church under Christ. Such a bishop occupied a prestigious position of authority that excelled the positions of other officebearers. Ignatius's fearless martyrdom in Rome gave his views on church government added weight.

These changes from biblical church government to episcopal church government did not happen overnight. Into the third and even fourth centuries the elders and deacons fought to retain their offices. Presbyters insisted that the bishop (or minister) could do nothing without their consent and approval. The changes also appeared in some parts of the empire more quickly than in other parts. Even in the days of Augustine of Hippo (354–430), the presbyters were still maintaining their authority in

Ignatius of Antioch

parts of the Western church. However, these unbiblical changes gradually became universal.

MULTIPLICATION OF OFFICES

Another factor in the rise of the episcopal system was the multiplication of church offices. Many minor offices were invented to facilitate the work of the church.[9] There were sub-deacons, readers and lectors (who read the scriptures in church and were keepers of manuscripts), acolytes (who assisted the bishop), exorcists (who attempted to cast out devils in parts of the church where demon possession was thought to be common), janitors (who cleaned the churches), instructors (who had special teaching responsibilities), and others. Many of these offices were added in the third century. Although these church helpers were not always considered officebearers, gradually the idea grew that they too had official standing in the church. Over them all ruled the bishop, who coordinated their work, gave them their orders, and was responsible for their faithfulness. This strengthened the power of bishops.

One writer illustrates how these offices multiplied over the next few centuries: "In the year 612, on the staff of the Church of the Holy Wisdom, there were 80 priests, 150 deacons, 40 deaconesses, 70 subdeacons, 160 readers, 25 cantors, and 100 doorkeepers."[10]

EXPANSION OF THE HIERARCHY

In addition to the multiplication of offices within the churches, the episcopal system of church government grew in the number of hierarchical levels. Only the seeds were sown in the first two centuries of the church, but with the sowing of those seeds, a point was reached from which there was no turning back without complete reformation of the entire church.

---

9 I remember a time I was worshiping in a small congregation in Rapid City, South Dakota. The church had "installation of officebearers" in the evening worship service. Those chosen or appointed to offices were piano players, janitors, Sunday school teachers, a librarian, one whose responsibility it was to open windows when the weather turned hot, and other offices. At last every member of the congregation came to the front to be installed. My wife and I were the only ones left in the pews. The minister, with a sort of self-conscious grin, said to my wife and me, "In a small church we all have to do our part." He then proceeded to "install" them all.

10 Timothy Ware, *The Orthodox Church* (Hammondsworth, Middlesex: Penguin Books LTD, 1963), 270.

The church began to distinguish between *city bishops* and *country bishops*. Toward the end of this period, city bishops assumed control over country bishops. Even during the time of the apostles, the practice in the mission work of the church was to establish centers of mission work in major cities. From these centers evangelists would go out into the surrounding countryside to preach and establish new churches. This work was controlled by the elders of the city church. When bishops were introduced into the church structure, these city bishops considered themselves to possess higher authority than the ministers in the country churches. These new ministers who were ordained by a city bishop rather naturally fell under the city bishop's authority. It was something similar to a calling church in our day assuming authority over a mission field and then over a congregation established in that field. City bishops were sometimes only interested in adding to their power.

In addition, the general opinion in the churches was that some city churches were more important than other city churches. The larger cities were believed to be more important than the smaller cities (e.g., Ephesus became more important than Smyrna and Laodicea). The missionary centers were more important than the cities that had not actively functioned as centers of mission work (e.g., Rome was more important than Three Taverns [Acts 28:15]). The cities where the apostles had preached were more important than the cities that had never heard a sermon from the lips of an apostle. This latter was the case because many were of the opinion that all the teachings of the apostles, even those that had not been incorporated into the scriptures, were authoritative. The apostolic cities became the guardians of an authoritative tradition along with the scriptures.[11]

Even before the end of the Post-Apostolic Period, the bishops of Rome attempted to assume control over the other churches. In the late second century, bishop Victor I of Rome attempted to impose his views on all the churches in Asia Minor in the controversy over the date of Easter. In the mid–third century, bishop Stephen I of Rome excommunicated single-handedly and arrogantly all the churches of North Africa over the matter of whether the church should recognize the validity of baptisms by heretical ministers.

The bishops of Rome attempted to justify their authority over the churches with preposterous claims and even persuaded a faction of the church to agree with them. They pointed to the antiquity of the church of Rome and the position of Rome as

---

11 Some considered Ephesus and Corinth to stand in the place of Jerusalem, which had been destroyed in AD 70; Constantinople did not assume importance until Constantine moved the capital of the empire to that city in 330.

the capital of the Roman Empire. They mentioned the role of the church in Rome in the formation of the Apostles' Creed. They highlighted Rome's splendid record in martyrdom. They even claimed that Peter had primacy over the other apostles and was the first bishop of Rome. While the majority in the church in the Post-Apostolic Period resisted these presumptuous claims, such beliefs would be accepted by a majority of the Western church in time.

The result of these unbiblical developments would be that the early church gradually lost the apostolic form of church government and sowed the seeds of the papacy, which was to rule the church world until the reformers brought her back to the scriptures and the biblical form of church government.

DEVELOPMENT OF THE EPISCOPACY IN THE FIRST FIVE CENTURIES[12]		
Period	Source(s)	Description
1st century	New Testament	Elder-bishops and deacons in each church were under the supervision of the apostles.
Early 2nd century	Ignatius	Elders and bishops differentiated. Each congregation governed by a bishop, elders, and deacons.
Late 2nd century	Irenaeus Tertullian	Diocesan bishops (i.e., a bishop now oversaw a group of congregations in a geographical area); they were thought to be successors of the apostles.
Mid 3rd century	Cyprian	Priesthood and sacrifice; elders (presbyters) come to be seen as sacrificing priests. Primacy of bishop of Rome asserted.
Early 4th century	Council of Nicaea	Metropolitan bishops (archbishops) by virtue of their location in population centers gain ascendancy over country bishops.
Late 4th century	Council of Constantinople	Special honor given to bishops of Rome, Alexandria, Antioch, Constantinople, and Jerusalem—called patriarchs. Patriarch of Constantinople given primacy next to bishop of Rome.
Mid 5th century	Leo I Council of Chalcedon	The supremacy of Rome; Leo I claimed authority over the whole church on the basis of succession from Peter.

12 Chart taken from Walton, *Chronological and Background Charts*, chart 22.

THE RISE OF SYNODS

However, developments in church organization at this time were not all bad. The church, during these early years, came to see the great importance of meeting at synods in order to express the unity of the body of Christ.

Prior to the third century, few synods of any kind met besides the apostolic Jerusalem Council described in Acts 15. However, because of the pressing need for unity and conformity in all matters of faith, bishops began to come together to consult each other on problems of mutual concern. These various synods represented churches in both smaller and larger areas.

The rise of synods was an important development in the history of the church. Synods were necessary meetings for churches to decide on matters of the truth of scripture and ecclesiastical practices. While none of the synods held before the Council of Nicaea (325) were ecumenical (involving representatives from the entire church), many decisions were adopted by local synods in various parts of the empire.

The rise of synods in the early church is important to note. The requests and meetings of various synods indicate that the early church recognized the importance of seeking the unity of the church, as is required by scripture (Eph. 4:1–9). Independentism, so common among churches today, is condemned by scripture and the early history of the church. Synods are instruments of preserving that unity, for matters of disagreement between local congregations can be resolved at meetings formed after the pattern of Acts 15, which establish biblical truths to which all the churches adhere.

The opposite extreme is, of course, a false ecumenism that supposedly unites churches into one organization by ignoring biblical truths and seeking the lowest common denominator in scripture's teachings on doctrine, worship, and church government.

Every believer and every church must do everything possible to maintain the unity of the body of Christ.

CHAPTER 9:
THE WORSHIP OF THE EARLY CHURCH

God is a Spirit: and they that worship him
must worship him in spirit and in truth.

—JOHN 4:24

SIMPLICITY OF WORSHIP

Every child of God should be interested in how the early church worshiped. After all, the worship of God on the Lord's day is the center of the Christian's life.

In the Apostolic Period and during the first century after the death of the apostles, worship was simple, following the pattern of worship taught by the apostles in scripture. Early worship consisted of scripture reading, preaching, the Lord's supper, prayers, collections for the poor, and singing—all done "in spirit and in truth" (John 4:24). However, toward the end of the Post-Apostolic Period, the worship of the church became increasingly complicated and elaborate. This was probably because people love external and visible decorations and rituals. The material love of externals is due to the difficulty of worshiping God from the heart. But the church of Jesus Christ must seek to worship God in simplicity, "in spirit and in truth."

From the very beginning the church of the Post-Apostolic Period worshiped on the first day of the week, a practice that was customary already during the time of the apostles (Acts 20:7; 1 Cor. 16:2). It seems that Pentecost itself was on the first day of the week[1] and that the church in the first century after Pentecost understood that

---

1   See Herman Hoeksema, "New Testament History Syllabus" (syllabus, Theological School of the Protestant Reformed Churches, 1978), 61–62.

Christian worship in the catacombs

the resurrection of Christ on the first day of the week was the fulfillment of the Old Testament sabbath.

The places of worship were simple. The church met in private homes (Philemon 2) and in small, unadorned meeting places. Sometimes they gathered in caves, in open fields, in cemeteries, at the graves of martyrs, and occasionally in the catacombs. In the second century, when persecution eased and the church was able to worship in peace, more elaborate and costly buildings were erected. But when persecution once more became imperial policy, these buildings were seized by the authorities. This confiscation of property happened especially during the final Roman persecution, the "Great Persecution" of the emperors Diocletian and Galerius (303–11). When the Christian emperor Constantine brought an end to persecution with the Edict of Milan in 313, one of his first decrees was that all seized church property must be restored to the church.

The worship services were also simple and included those elements required by scripture. In the preaching of God's word, the church clung to the simple truth of salvation for sinners in the suffering and death of their Lord Jesus Christ on the cross. This truth is the heart of the gospel, and it was central to the life and worship of the early church. The sacraments were administered in biblical simplicity too. Baptism was practiced, and the Lord's supper was administered, sometimes in connection with love feasts, a practice that had begun in apostolic times (1 Cor. 11:20–22). These love feasts were gatherings of the members of the congregation to dine together for purposes of fellowship. Some brought food for themselves and for the poor.

Although images in worship were condemned, the early church made wide use of symbols, especially the symbols of the cross (a symbol of salvation through Christ's death), the fish (because the Greek word for *fish* is composed of the first letters of each word in the phrase "Jesus Christ, God's Son, Savior"), and the dove (a symbol of the Holy Spirit at the baptism of Christ [Matt. 3:16]).

EARLY SYMBOLS OF CHRISTIANITY[2]	
Name and Symbol	Significance
Alpha-Omega	Eternality of Christ (see Revelation 1:8)
Anchor	Hope (see Hebrews 6:19)
Bread and Wine	Eucharist—Death of Christ
Chi-Rho	First two letters of "Christ" in Greek superimposed
Cross	Death of Christ
Dove	Holy Spirit as manifested at the baptism of Christ
Fire	Holy Spirit on the day of Pentecost
Fish	Initial letters of "Jesus Christ, God's Son, Savior" in Greek, spelling ICHTHUS, the Greek word for "fish"; feeding of 5,000, "fishers of men"
IC XC NIKA	Symbol of Christ the Conqueror, consisting of the first and last letters of the Greek words for "Jesus" and "Christ" and the Latin for "Victory" around the cross
IHS (sometimes IHC)	First three letters of "Jesus" in Greek
INRI	Initial letters of inscription on Christ's cross in Latin—*Iesus Nazarenus Rex Iudaeo-rum* (Jesus of Nazareth, King of the Jews; see John 19:19)
Lamb	Christ's self-sacrifice
Palm Branch	Christ's triumphal entry; also associated with martyrdom
Phoenix	A legendary bird that burns itself on a funeral pyre then comes back to life; it was used as early as the writings of Clement of Rome as a symbol of the Resurrection
Shepherd	Christ's care for his people
Ship	Church (Noah's ark; cf. baptism, 1 Peter 3:20–21)
Vine	Christ's union with his people; wine of Eucharist

---

2   Chart taken from Walton, *Chronological and Background Charts*, chart 11.

THE SACRAMENTS

While the Roman Catholic Church corrupted the number of sacraments during the apostasy of the Middle Ages, the early church recognized only two sacraments: baptism and the Lord's supper.

Because many adult converts were brought into the church during this period, adult baptism was very common, following the example of Philip the Evangelist and his baptism of the Ethiopian eunuch (Acts 8:26–40). The early church instructed these new adult converts, called *catechumens*, and prepared them for baptism, when they would be permitted to attend the entire worship service and become full members of the church. Infants were also baptized.[3] The early church fathers Irenaeus of Lyons (c. 130–202), Origen of Alexandria (185–254), and Cyprian of Carthage (c. 200–258) all mention that infant baptism was commonly practiced throughout the church.

An early depiction of baptism

While baptism was, in the first part of the period, a simple ceremony administered in the name of the Trinity, adult baptism sometimes became more complicated. The newly instructed convert was required to renounce Satan, give himself to Christ, and make confession of faith in the words of the Apostles' Creed. Immersion, partial immersion, and sprinkling with water were all used in the early church.

However, as the period continued, certain parts of the church made additions to the sacrament of baptism. Gradually the sacrament more and more became an outward ritual that included the laying on of hands as a sign of the giving of the Holy Spirit and an anointing with a mixture of milk and honey to point to entry into the spiritual land "flowing with milk and honey." In 256, the provincial Synod of Carthage introduced exorcism, the casting out of devils, as a part of the ceremony, and the church fathers Tertullian (c. 160–225) and Cyprian wanted anointing with oil as a symbol of consecration to the spiritual priesthood of believers.

Baptism was considered to be a sign and seal of the washing away of sins—as indeed it is. But already in this early period, some ascribed power to the water of baptism used in the sacrament. This was the beginning of the Roman Catholic doctrine that describes the operation of the sacrament as *ex opere operato* ("by the work

---

3   See Joachim Jeremias, *Infant Baptism in the First Four Centuries*, trans. David Cairns (London: SCM Press LTD., 1960). See especially chapter 32, pp. 43–58.

worked"). This doctrine taught that the water of baptism itself could wash away sins, for it was a special water, consecrated by the church and given that power by God through the church. It became accepted doctrine when the church became the Roman Catholic Church and is still taught today as the doctrine of baptismal regeneration.

Some held that baptism washes away all sins committed prior to baptism, an erroneous view that led some members to postpone baptism until just before they died. For example, the emperor Constantine was not baptized until shortly before his death, for it was thought preferable to have as many sins as possible washed away before one appeared before the judgment seat of Christ.

An early depiction of the Lord's supper

The second sacrament instituted and commanded by Christ to be observed by the church was the Lord's supper. The celebration of the Lord's supper was a very important part of the worship service. Because the Lord had commanded the church to celebrate this sacrament in remembrance of him, it was administered every Lord's day and frequently at every service, but without the lengthy liturgical form that we use today.

In this period of the church's life, none of the trappings that were later added to the administration of the Lord's supper corrupted the sacrament. The sacrament was considered a sign and seal of Christ's suffering and death on the cross and of our blessedness through his death. It was celebrated in a simple way, following the words of Christ at the Last Supper, and often was celebrated at the end of the service. Congregants shared a common loaf and a common cup.

The early church often referred to the Lord's supper as the *Eucharist*, which simply means "thanksgiving." Because the bread was broken and the wine poured out, the sacrament was considered by some to be a sacrifice, but not a repetition of the one sacrifice of Christ as the Romish church claims for the mass; it was a sacrifice of thanksgiving to God for salvation in Christ.

CHRISTIAN DISCIPLINE

Although the church was not consciously practicing the three marks of the true church, added to the preaching and the administration of the sacraments was the exercise of Christian discipline. Discipline was faithfully practiced, and those guilty of heresy, schism, and other gross crimes were excommunicated.

The church was aware of the need to discipline members for impenitence only. Those who refused to repent of gross sins were excommunicated. It was understood that an excommunicated sinner could be restored to the church only after repentance and confession, but the church struggled with the question of determining whether a confession was genuine or only external.

Strange distinctions were made and various names given to penitents: *weepers*, who prostrated themselves at the door of the church seeking reentrance; *hearers*, who were permitted to listen to the sermon but were not permitted to join in the rest of the service until there was clear evidence of their genuine sorrow for sin; *kneelers*, who attended public prayers while kneeling; and *standers*, who were permitted to be present at the entire worship service, excluding the Lord's supper.

Scripture makes clear that the church of Christ must receive the confession of sin that a sinner makes (Matt. 18:15–35). No one can judge the heart except God. The elders must take a sinner at his word and leave the matter with God—unless the sinner gives clear evidence that his confession is not sincere. But it must be remembered that true confession implies repentance, and repentance implies forsaking sin.

Unlike much of the church today, the early church took sin very seriously. One sin, the sin of apostasy, stood out above all others, especially when, under the pressure of persecution and torture, members of the church would renounce their faith. Much controversy arose in the church regarding whether those unfaithful people could be readmitted to the church when persecution ceased and they wanted to return to the fellowship of the saints. These people, called the *lapsed*, had escaped persecution by denying their faith to escape torture and death, while many others had suffered painful cruelties as the price of faithfulness.

Some in the church considered the lapsed to have taken the easy way, while the faithful endured what Jesus called "the burden and heat of the day" (Matt. 20:12). Others wondered whether denying the faith was such a great sin that it could never be forgiven. After all, had not Jesus said that those who denied him before men, he would deny before his Father in heaven (10:33)? Still others took the position that the only sin that cannot be forgiven is the sin of refusal to repent of sin—a position the church holds today. The church may discipline only for the sin of impenitence.

Several schisms that threatened the unity of the church resulted from these controversies, including the Novatian Schism after the persecution of Emperor Decius in the third century (see the sidebar below) and the Donatist Schism after the persecution of Emperor Diocletian in the fourth century (see chapter 16).

THE DECIAN PERSECUTION AND THE NOVATIAN SCHISM

In 250, the Roman emperor Decius initiated the first empire-wide persecution of Christians. Although the persecution was short-lived, Decius required an annual sacrifice to the emperor. Every Roman citizen was commanded to burn a pinch of incense in a temple before the image of the emperor while reciting the words "Caesar is lord." Those who complied were given a certificate called a *libellus*. Those who refused were put to death. For the Christians, it was an unavoidable test of loyalty to the Lord Jesus Christ.

The persecution produced countless martyrs and a host of apostates, those who had denied their faith to save their lives. When the persecution ended with the death of Decius in 251, churches throughout the empire were faced with an apostasy crisis. What should be done with lapsed sinners who had denied their faith? Could the church forgive apostasy? The question created a crisis throughout the ancient church world. Some argued that those who had lapsed should be banned permanently from church worship and membership. Others argued that the lapsed could be received again into the fellowship of the church.

The debate raged

A libellus from AD 250

most intensely in the church of Rome, where the new bishop Cornelius (d. 253) was opposed by the presbyter Novatian (d. 258). Cornelius argued for forgiveness and leniency after *penance*, a period of sorrow for sin. Novatian argued adamantly to keep the church pure by keeping those who had apostatized out of the church. When it became clear that the majority in the church in Rome sided with Cornelius, Novatian had himself elected as another bishop of Rome, thus creating a bitter schism in the church.

In Carthage, the great church father Cyprian (c. 200–258) sided with Cornelius and opposed Novatian. In his book *On the Lapsed*, he took a moderate position on readmission to the church. Avoiding the one extreme that there be no readmission and the other extreme that there be immediate readmission, Cyprian argued that apostates could be readmitted to the church by the bishops only after expressing sorrow for their sins through penance. In his book *On the Unity of the Church*, Cyprian emphasized the necessity of church membership for every believer. He wrote, "He can no longer have God for his Father who has not the church for his mother," and "There is no salvation outside of the church." Cyprian's views won the day. He died a faithful martyr during the next wave of persecution in 258.

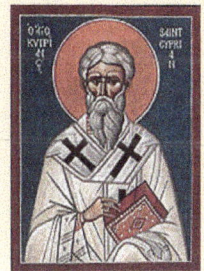

Cyprian of Carthage

CHRISTIAN HOLIDAYS

The number of weekday services gradually multiplied during the Post-Apostolic Period. Special days were set aside to observe special events in the life of Christ. Some churches set aside Wednesdays and Fridays as days of fasting and humiliation and frequently held worship services in the evenings. Before the celebration of Easter, some churches required a forty-day period of fasting, called Lent. The deaths of martyrs were also observed on the anniversaries of those deaths, and special services were held to commemorate their faithfulness. Sometimes these services were held in the cemeteries, where the mutilated bodies of the martyrs were buried.[4]

Gradually, over the course of many centuries, Christian holidays multiplied to such an extent that the Christian calendar had almost no days left for additional special days. All became a part of the growing tendency to make religion external. The words of our Lord were forgotten: "God is a Spirit: and they that worship him must worship him in spirit and in truth" (John 4:24).

The way was being paved for the erection of the imposing Roman Catholic structure of church liturgy, which structure is contrary to what the apostles had taught. All the seeds of this Romish system were sown by the end of the ancient period. It is intriguing to ask: why did our sovereign Christ permit the church to stray so soon from biblical church polity and worship, an erroneous system that lasted a thousand years—half the history of the New Testament church? While I do not have the full answer to this question, it may very well be that Christ was teaching the true church what it means to live under a false church that persecutes the faithful. Biblical church polity and worship were not restored until the Protestant Reformation of the sixteenth century, when John Calvin worked on these principles during his exile from Geneva in Strasbourg.

WORSHIP AND LIFE

Although the life of Christians in the first three centuries was not technically worship, it has much to do with worship. When the worship of the church becomes mere lip service, the life of the people of God becomes worldly. When worship is sincere and from the heart, the walk of believers in the world is holy. In the church of the first three centuries, worship was sincere and enthusiastic, and the Christians lived

---

4   This practice is still followed by some Presbyterians, especially in Scotland, who hold special services in cemeteries or in places where Scotland's martyrs suffered.

antithetically in all of their lives. In the worship of the churches believers confessed their faith by attending to preaching, singing, and praying; and in their lives these believers confessed their faith by a godly walk.

The Roman Empire was morally bankrupt. A rot had set in at the heart of the empire that doomed it to destruction. All the gods of the Greeks and Romans were worshiped. That worship included debauched and immoral practices that are beyond description. The rich lived luxuriously in gluttony and drunkenness. Government handouts and public doles were so common that people considered themselves deprived of their rights if they were not given their "bread and circuses." Pagan parents abandoned their unwanted children. Spouses lived in immorality and divorce was frequent. Cruelty to slaves was for many a way of life. And entertainment consisted in violence, bloodshed, and murder in gladiatorial contests in the arenas.

God established his church in this pagan and corrupt world and called his people to live lives in conformity with his own holiness. His words to his church were, "But as he which hath called you is holy, so be ye holy in all manner of conversation" (1 Pet. 1:15). For the most part, the people of God lived antithetical lives. They condemned the wickedness about them and lived both in their homes and families and in the church as a different people whose lives were shaped by the word of God. They condemned fiercely all idolatry and confessed that God is God alone. They shuddered at the immorality of their times and walked in faithfulness to God's commands. They not only cherished their own children but picked up abandoned children, adopted them, and taught them the ways of God. They lived simple and frugal lives, found their joy in the service of God, and condemned the cruel and murderous shows in the arenas and coliseums. They were kind to their slaves (if they had them), took them to church, taught them God's word, and in many instances gave them their freedom. They cared for the poor, visited those in prison (some-

An early depiction of an Agape Feast

times at great risk of their own lives), supported the widows, adopted the orphans, and witnessed to their faith by their lives as well as by their words.

The church in the first centuries of its existence followed closely in worship and in life the simple pattern laid down by the apostles and by Christ himself. Sadly, the medieval church gradually changed and eventually mutilated this pattern. It is still being corrupted today by all forms of contemporary worship. Because the life of God's people and the worship of God are so crucial to the church's existence in the world, it is important that the church remain faithful to scripture and to her calling as the church of Christ also in worship.

CHAPTER 10: **THE MONARCHIAN HERESIES**

And without controversy great is the mystery of godliness:
God was manifest in the flesh, justified in the Spirit, seen of angels,
preached unto the Gentiles, believed on in the world, received up into glory.

—1 TIMOTHY 3:16

IMPORTANT QUESTIONS

At the end of the second century the church began to be troubled by differences over the question of the unity of God and the divinity of Christ. These were important questions, for they involved the basic truths of the Christian religion. Yet they were also very difficult questions to answer, and the debate over these questions lasted more than two and a half centuries (c. 180–451).

These questions have been long settled, and we take the answers to them for granted. However, in the days of the early church they were puzzling. The church had to study hard to understand scripture's teachings.

The church lived in a pagan world in which dozens of gods were worshiped. The Christians knew that polytheism was wrong and that the scriptures taught only one true God. The idols of the heathen were the work of men's hands; the God of scripture alone was God. The church readily confessed this truth.

But the problem arose in connection with the doctrine of our Lord Jesus Christ. The church confessed that Jesus was divine. Yet scripture spoke of him as distinct from God. The heathen were quick to pick up this point, and they frequently charged the Christians with teaching a plurality of gods: God the Father and Jesus Christ, who is also divine. How could this problem be explained?

The ancient apologists had wrestled with this question. Church historian Philip Hughes writes,

So it was with the mystery we know as that of the Trinity. God was one. Jesus Christ was God because the Logos [the Word] incarnate. And yet Jesus Christ was not God the Father…The Apologists boldly showed the way to eighteen centuries of Christian thinkers. Like pioneers of every type they had to devise instruments and machinery as they went along. The road was unplotted, the obstacles unknown and, when known, for long not fully understood, the rough tools sometimes a hindrance as well as a help. They use for example the concepts and language of the philosophical schools to which they at one time adhered, and thence ensues a host of new difficulties of such high speculation, thanks to a tested technical language which they lacked. Of that language they were the founders. In their stumblings and groping, it was born. Inevitably there is at times in their speculation an uneasiness, a confusion and an obscurity which leave room for contrary interpretations of their meaning.[1]

EASTERN AND WESTERN CHURCHES

A significant factor in the debate and controversies over these questions was the wide difference bet ween the Greek-speaking Eastern church (Egypt, Palestine, Syria, Asia Minor, and Greece) and the Latin-speaking Western church (Italy, Gaul, Spain, and North Africa). These two regions of the Roman Empire surrounding the Mediterranean Sea had been settled by different branches of the descendants of Japheth and were characterized by different languages and different ways of thinking.

The Greek-speaking Eastern church, occupying lands from which in past centuries had emerged elaborate systems of philosophy, was far more speculative than the Western church. One need only study Platonic philosophy (the thinking of Plato) and Aristotelian philosophy (the thinking of Aristotle) to realize how abstract the Greek mind could be.

The Latin-speaking Western church, in contrast, was dominated by the Roman way of thinking. The Romans were not speculative but very practical and pragmatic, believing that something is good if it works. From the Roman mind came a system of law and order. In the Roman part of the empire were developed the fundamental laws that are still the basis for all law in Western civilization.

---

1 Hughes, *A History of the Church*, 1:104.

The Church in the Roman Empire

West

East

Chart 54

Taken from *Charts of Ancient and Medieval Church History* by John D. Hannah. Copyright @ 2001 by John David Hannah. Used by permission of Zondervan, www.zondervan.com.

Due to these differences, misunderstandings often arose, and two vocabularies (one in the Greek language, the other in Latin) had to be developed for the Eastern and Western churches to answer these perplexing questions. It is interesting that almost all the controversies regarding the Godhead and the divinity of Christ took place in the Eastern church, while the Western church was never deeply troubled by these controversies and never was torn apart by heretical solutions to them.

Yet despite these differences, the early church, both Eastern and Western, was one; and unity was necessary to understand the doctrine of God, which was, after all, the most fundamental truth of the Christian faith.

DYNAMIC MONARCHIANISM (ADOPTIONISM)

The first efforts to solve the problem were made by men who were trying to understand the scriptural data and formulate it in doctrinal teachings. Monarchianism was the earliest proposed solution. The term *monarchianism* comes from two Greek words that mean "a single ruler," from which we get our word "monarch." Fearing that an explanation of Jesus Christ as God would compromise the essential oneness of God the Father, monarchianism stressed the unity and authority of God at the expense of teaching the diversity of persons within the Godhead.

Two kinds of monarchianism were present in the early church: dynamic monarchianism (sometimes called adoptionism) and modalistic monarchianism (sometimes called modalism or Sabellianism). While these agreed on the question of the oneness of God, they disagreed on the question of the divinity of Christ. We will take a brief look at both.

The founder of dynamic monarchianism was Paul of Samosata (c. 200–275), a bishop of the important church in Antioch of Syria, which church had sent out Paul and Barnabas. Paul of Samosata reportedly loved pomp, show, wealth, applause, and power. He was charged with acquiring wealth in reprehensible ways and permitting prostitutes in his entourage. The fact that such a man was permitted to be bishop is evidence of how low the church had already sunk, in some places, by the third century.

Paul must have thought himself to be a gifted theologian as well, for he proposed to settle the problem of God's nature and being by making a distinction between the eternal Logos (Word) and Jesus. Jesus was a mere man in all respects, he said, but at his baptism he was filled with the Logos. The Logos was divine, although not as divine as God; it was a sort of emanation from the being of God, much like a stream emanates from a fountain. The Logos was an impersonal attribute or power, like human reason. This entrance of the Logos into the man Jesus made him divine, but he possessed a lesser divinity than God himself. To make matters worse, Paul also denied that the Holy Spirit was a person and spoke of him only as a divine power.

Because Paul of Samosata taught that the man Jesus was given divine power at his baptism, this heresy is called *dynamic* monarchianism. (The word *dynamic* comes from the Greek word *dunamis*, meaning "power.") Because he taught that God adopted Jesus as his Son after Jesus's death, this heresy is also called *adoptionism*.

Because Paul denied both the full deity of Jesus Christ and the person of the Holy Spirit, the church realized that it needed to respond swiftly. Paul of Samosata's heretical views were condemned by three synods in Antioch from 264 to 268, and he was deposed from his office.

Adoptionism and Modalism Compared

ADOPTIONISM (Dynamic Modalism)	MODALISM (Modalistic Monarchianism, Sabellianism, Patripassionism)
Stress Oneness of God	Stress Oneness of God
Deny Deity of Christ	Affirm Deity of Christ
Affirm Humanity of Christ	Deny Humanity of Christ
Holy Spirit = a power	Holy Spirit = a mode of God's existence

Chart 60

Adoptionism and Modalism Compared. Taken from *Charts of Ancient and Medieval Church History* by John D. Hannah. Copyright @ 2001 by John David Hannah. Used by permission of Zondervan, www.zondervan.com.

MODALISTIC MONARCHIANISM (MODALISM)

Modalistic monarchianism was taught first in the late second century by Noetus, the bishop of Smyrna. A pupil of Noetus named Praxeas then brought his teachings to Rome, where Sabellius, a third-century priest and would-be theologian, also taught the heresy and became its chief defender. For this reason, modalistic monarchianism is often called Sabellianism.

Sabellius taught that God is one divine being and person and that the one person of God manifests himself in three different ways or "modes" (hence the name *modalistic monarchianism* or *modalism*) at various times and for various reasons. He taught that God manifested himself as Father and Creator, as Son and Redeemer, and as Holy Spirit and Sanctifier. He claimed that any other view was tritheism (the

Sabellius (Third Century)

Sabellius was a North African presbyter and theologian who moved to Rome for a time and later to Alexandria. Although little is known about Sabellius's life, he is widely recognized as the leading proponent of an early heresy called modalistic monarchianism (also called Sabellianism, modalism, or patripassianism). While Sabellius correctly taught that there is one God, he failed to affirm that God is three in person. Instead, he declared that God reveals himself in three temporary ways, or modes. For this, he was excommunicated by the churches in Rome and Alexandria. To learn more, read "Sabellius: First Unitarian," chapter 4 of Herman Hanko's *Contending for the Faith*.

worship of three gods) and a return to pagan polytheism.

Tertullian of Carthage, one of the great church fathers, opposed Sabellius, charging him with the heresy of deposing the Holy Spirit and crucifying the Father. Because Sabellius taught that the Father suffered and died, his followers were sometimes called "patripassianists," a word from the Latin *patri* ("father") and *passio* ("suffering"). Despite the fact that Sabellius was opposed by Tertullian and excommunicated twice, first by bishop Callistus of Rome in 220 and then by bishop Dionysius of Alexandria in 260, he retained a great deal of influence.

WRONG EXPLANATIONS OF THE RELATION OF THE SON TO THE FATHER

What was the relation of the Son to the Father?...

The church's theologians proposed various solutions. One solution was that Christ was not the natural Son of God, but the *adopted* Son. The status of sonship was conferred on Christ either at his baptism or at his resurrection. But this was unsatisfactory, for it denied that Christ was really God.

Another solution was that Christ was *derived from* the Father. In this view, the Father was greater than the Son, although great honor was ascribed to the Son. Maybe

he was a very high angel, maybe a spirit, maybe the Logos of which John speaks in the first chapter of his gospel narrative, or maybe just a son. But for all the greatness he possessed, he was still inferior to the Father. Maybe he was in some sense "divine," but his divinity was not the same as that of the Father.

Then a third solution was suggested. This one was really the gravest threat of all to the church in the third century. The theory suggested that Christ was *the same person as* the Father. There was really no difference between the Son and the Father. Just the names given to God were different. Sometimes God was referred to as Father, sometimes as Son, and other times as Holy Spirit. The three names were only three different names for one God, three different ways to refer to him, three different ways of thinking about the one and the same God.

—Herman Hanko, *Contending for the Faith*, 30.

THE ANSWER OF THE CHURCH

We must remember that the early church did not yet fully understand the teachings of scripture on the questions of the Trinity and the divinity of Christ. Nor did the church possess a vocabulary to express many biblical truths. The Bible does not provide a ready-made doctrinal vocabulary, and the church had to find terms not found in scripture to express the Bible's teaching. Not only did these terms have to be developed, but the church as a whole had to agree on what these terms meant as applied to the problems it confronted.

The result was that in the synods where these heresies were considered and rejected, no positive statement of the truth was made. It was as if the church at her synods said, "We do not yet understand completely these doctrines, but we do know with certainty that the solutions we now consider are not scripture's teaching."

Tertullian, from the Latin Western church, did more than any other to establish orthodoxy in the Western half of the church. He wrote a concise and brilliant book against the monarchians called *Against Praxeas*. To Tertullian we owe the

Tertullian of Carthage
(c. 160–225)

The son of a Roman army officer in Carthage, Tertullian was a gifted Latin lawyer who was converted from paganism as an adult. He became a fierce apologist, defending the faith against paganism and a host of heresies, including gnosticism, Marcionism, and Sabellianism. Tertullian was the first great church father to write in Latin, and his writings on the Trinity are the earliest expression of the truth that God is one in essence and three in person. Sadly, he joined the heretical Montanists during the last years of his life. To learn more, read "Tertullian: Theologian of the Trinity," chapter 3 of Herman Hanko's *Portraits of Faithful Saints*.

words *Trinity*, *essence*, and *person*, although even these terms, not found in the Bible as applied to God, had yet to be carefully defined.

Although Tertullian settled these trinitarian and Christological issues in the Latin Western church already by the third century, the Greek Eastern church would continue to wrestle with them for centuries. So began the great controversies that would not be fully resolved until the Council of Chalcedon (451) and would require no less than four major church councils to solve the problems and establish the truth concerning God and Christ.

Yet these truths had to be established, for the doctrine of the Trinity is the truth of God himself and thus the sum of all the truth of scripture. And the truth concerning Christ is the truth of the eternal Son of God in our flesh, upon which truth Christ himself said, "Upon this rock I will build my church" (Matt. 16:18).

Part Three

The Nicene
and Post-Nicene Period

(AD 313–590)

INTRODUCTION TO THE NICENE
AND POST-NICENE PERIOD

In 313, a Christian emperor named Constantine and a pagan emperor named Licinius met near Milan in northern Italy and issued a momentous decree, one that would profoundly impact the history of the church. The document that they produced is called the Edict of Milan, and it established a new religious policy for the Roman Empire, one of freedom and toleration for everyone, including Christians. The document stated that "Christians and all others should have freedom to follow the kind of religion they favoured."[1]

Ten years earlier, a Christian emperor and a policy of religious freedom would have been unimaginable. In 303, the pagan emperor Diocletian initiated the worst persecution of Christians in ancient history, the climax of a 250-year effort on behalf of the Roman Empire to exterminate the church of Jesus Christ. For nearly a decade, the cruel Diocletian and his sinister successor Galerius presided over a shocking, empire-wide campaign of brutality, bloodletting, and Bible burning. Christians called it the "Great Persecution."

So how did it happen that in just ten years the Roman Empire shifted from a policy forbidding Christianity to a policy promoting it? How was it that almost overnight it became fashionable for Romans to identify as Christians, and that in just a generation the church became a privileged majority after centuries as a persecuted minority? The answer lies in the inscrutable wisdom of God, who brought about the unpredictable rise of Constantine the Great, the first Roman emperor to call himself a Christian.

After claiming to have seen a vision from Christ before a decisive military victory

---

1   Henry Bettenson and Chris Maunder, eds., *Documents of the Christian Church*, 3rd ed. (Oxford: Oxford University Press, 1999), 17.

in 312, Constantine proclaimed himself a Christian emperor and promoted the church throughout his reign. He legalized Christianity, built grand churches throughout the empire, created the Christian capital of Constantinople, and assembled the illustrious Council of Nicaea. Constantine's reign marks a major turning point in church history.

While the Nicene and Post-Nicene Period (313–590) begins with the legalization of Christianity under Constantine the Great (313) and ends with the rise of the medieval papacy under Gregory the Great (590), the period is named after its most important event—the Council of Nicaea (325). This first ecumenical church council was a triumph of orthodoxy over the heresy of Arianism. It defined the doctrine of the Trinity and produced the Nicene Creed.

Perhaps no period of church history had such contradictory characteristics. On the one hand, many developments were negative: Christianity became the state religion; the church was increasingly plagued by worldliness and superstition; rivalries, heresies, and schisms threatened church unity; worship services became innovative and elaborate; asceticism and monasticism became widely popular; and the growing hierarchy of the church paved the way for the Roman papacy of the Middle Ages.

On the other hand, many developments were positive: the church was able to worship and flourish free from persecution; the church fathers settled the trinitarian and Christological controversies at the great councils and wrote the ancient creeds; the theologian Augustine of Hippo wrote timeless Christian literary classics and masterfully championed the truth of sovereign grace; and the missionary monks preached the gospel of Jesus Christ to the myriad barbarian tribes outside the empire's borders.

A fascinating and complex period of the church, the Nicene and Post-Nicene Period is important for all these reasons; but it also serves as a reminder that the church of Jesus Christ is called to live antithetically in the midst of a wicked world and that only when Christ comes again on clouds of glory will the kingdoms of men become the kingdom of our God.

Timeline of the Nicene and Post-Nicene Period

313	Emperor Constantine issues the Edict of Milan, legalizing Christianity and tolerating all religions.
314	The Synod of Arles considers the Donatist Schism; the Synod of Ancyra writes canon law.
320	Constantine builds the old St. Peter's Basilica in Rome; Pachomius founds the first monastery.
324	Eusebius of Caesarea completes his *Ecclesiastical History*, the very first book of church history.
325	The ecumenical Council of Nicaea defines the Trinity, condemns Arianism, and drafts the Nicene Creed.
330	Constantine moves the capital of the Roman Empire to Byzantium and renames it Constantinople.
335	Arianism begins a resurgence; the Council of Tyre condemns Athanasius, the defender of Nicaea.
337	Constantine, the first Christian emperor, abolishes crucifixion and is baptized shortly before his death.
356	The hermit Anthony of Egypt dies at 105 years old; Athanasius writes *Life of Anthony* the next year.
362	Emperor Julian "the Apostate" tries to revive paganism, but his attempt is unpopular and he dies in 363.
367	Athanasius writes an Easter letter that includes the first complete list of books in the Bible.
380	Emperor Theodosius I issues the Edict of Thessalonica, making Christianity the official state religion.
381	The ecumenical Council of Constantinople condemns Arianism, Apollinarianism, and Macedonianism.
386	Augustine of Hippo is converted to Christianity in a garden in Milan when he reads Romans 13:13–14.
390	Ambrose of Milan disciplines Theodosius for a massacre at Thessalonica and brings him to repentance.
395	Augustine becomes the bishop of Hippo; the Roman Empire is permanently divided into East and West.
397	The Council of Carthage defines the New Testament canon; Augustine of Hippo writes *Confessions*.
398	John Chrysostom, the "golden-mouthed" preacher, becomes the patriarch of Constantinople.
405	Jerome completes his translation of the Latin Vulgate, the Bible used throughout the Middle Ages.
410	The city of Rome is sacked by Alaric I, the king of the Visigoths; the Roman army abandons Britain.
411	The Synod of Carthage, at which Augustine plays a major role, condemns the schismatic Donatists.
430	Augustine of Hippo dies while the barbarian Vandals besiege Hippo and ravage North Africa.

431	The ecumenical Council of Ephesus condemns the heresies of Nestorianism and Pelagianism.
432	Patrick begins his mission in Ireland after having been kidnapped from Britain and enslaved by the Irish.
440	Leo I ("the Great") is consecrated bishop of Rome and defends the doctrine of papal supremacy.
445	The edict of the emperor Valentinian III strengthens the primacy of Rome by making it law.
451	The ecumenical Council of Chalcedon condemns Eutychianism and writes the Creed of Chalcedon.
452	Leo the Great persuades Attila the Hun not to invade Rome; Leo is widely celebrated as a hero.
455	Leo the Great persuades Gaiseric the Vandal not to burn the city of Rome and slaughter the people.
476	The Western Roman Empire falls to the barbarians when Emperor Romulus Augustulus is deposed.
496	Clovis, the king of the Franks, and his three thousand troops are baptized by Remigius, the bishop of Reims.
525	Dionysius Exiguus creates a Christian calendar, using "AD" and fixing Christ's birth at December 25.
529	Justinian I publishes his legal *Code*; Benedict founds Monte Cassino; the Synod of Orange meets.
540	Benedict writes his famous *Rule*, which profoundly impacts the history of Western monasticism.
553	The ecumenical Council of Constantinople condemns monophysitism (Eutychianism) a second time.
563	Columba establishes a monastery and missionary headquarters on the island of Iona in Scotland.
589	The Council of Toledo adds the controversial *filioque* ("and the Son") clause to the Nicene Creed.
590	Gregory I ("the Great") is elected the pope of Rome; Columbanus sets up Celtic monasteries in Gaul.

Map of the Nicene and Post-Nicene Period

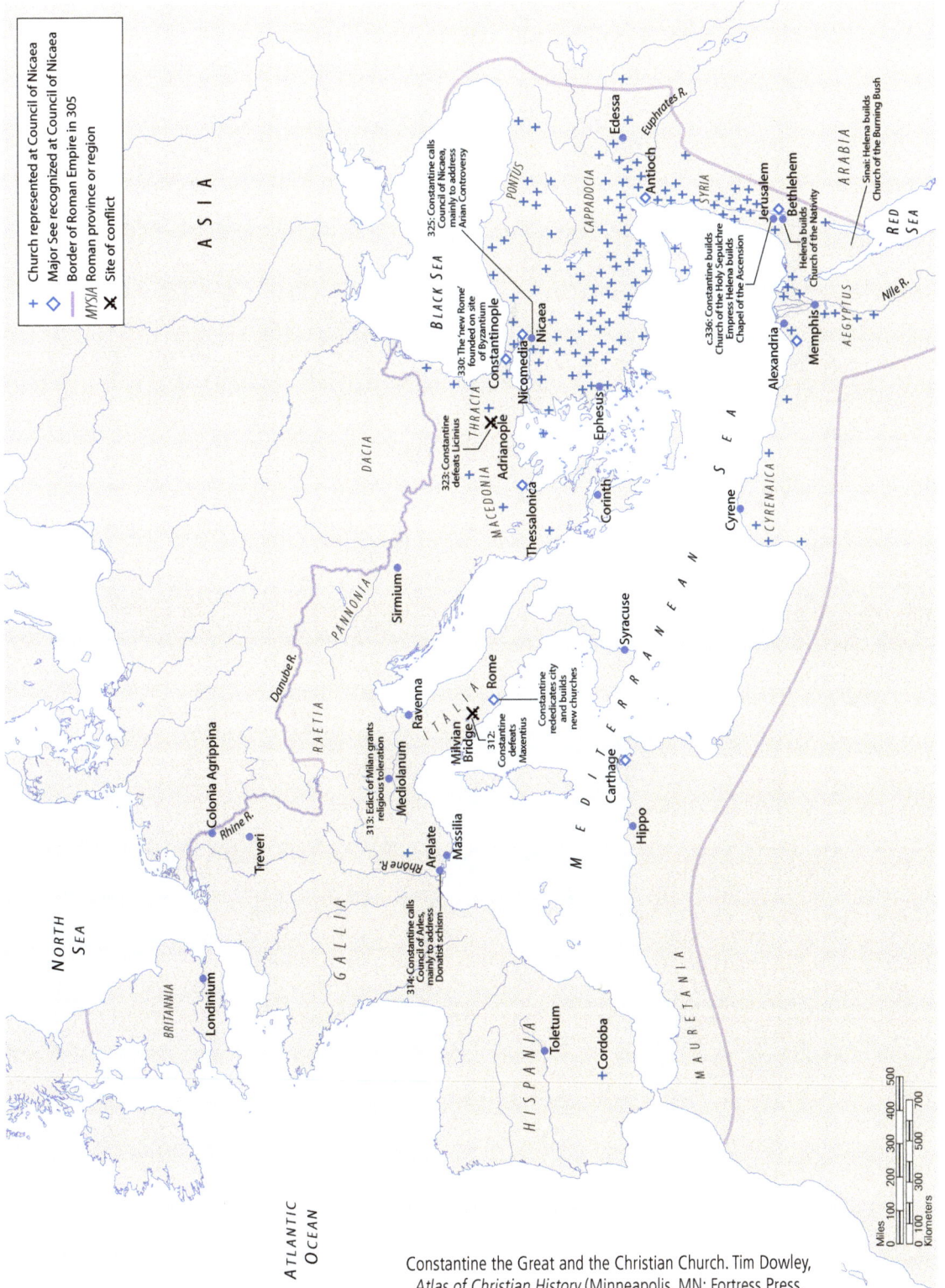

Church represented at Council of Nicaea
Major See recognized at Council of Nicaea
Border of Roman Empire in 305
MYSIA Roman province or region
Site of conflict

ASIA

Edessa
Euphrates R.
Antioch
SYRIA
CAPPADOCIA
PONTUS
ARABIA
Jerusalem
Bethlehem
Sinai: Helena builds Church of the Burning Bush
RED SEA
Nile R.
AEGYPTUS
Memphis
Alexandria
Helena builds Church of the Nativity
c.336: Constantine builds Church of the Holy Sepulchre; Empress Helena builds Chapel of the Ascension

325: Constantine calls Council of Nicaea, mainly to address Arian Controversy

330: The 'new Rome' founded on site of Byzantium
Constantinople
Nicaea
Nicomedia
BLACK SEA

Ephesus
THRACIA
323: Constantine defeats Licinius
Adrianople
MACEDONIA
Corinth
Thessalonica
DACIA
CYRENAICA
Cyrene
SEA

PANNONIA
Sirmium
Syracuse
Danube R.
RAETIA
Ravenna
ITALIA
Rome
Milvian Bridge
312: Constantine defeats Maxentius
Constantine rededicates city and builds new churches
Carthage
Hippo
MEDITERRANEAN SEA

Colonia Agrippina
Rhine R.
Treveri
313: Edict of Milan grants religious toleration
Mediolanum
Arelate
Massilia
Rhône R.
GALLIA
314: Constantine calls Council of Arles, mainly to address Donatist schism

NORTH SEA
BRITANNIA
Londinium

HISPANIA
Toletum
Cordoba
MAURETANIA

ATLANTIC OCEAN

Miles
0 100 200 300 400 500
Kilometers
0 100 300 500 700

Constantine the Great and the Christian Church. Tim Dowley, *Atlas of Christian History* (Minneapolis, MN: Fortress Press, 2016), 18–19. Used with permission from 1517 Media.

CHAPTER 11: **THE CHRISTIAN ROMAN EMPIRE**

Submit yourselves to every ordinance of man for the Lord's sake: whether it be
to the king, as supreme; or unto governors, as unto them that are sent by him
for the punishment of evildoers, and for the praise of them that do well.

—1 PETER 2:13–14

Because the history of the church during the Nicene and Post-Nicene Period is closely connected with the history of the Roman Empire, a discussion of this period should begin with a brief survey of the most important emperors who ruled during these years. This chapter will examine the religious policies of five Roman emperors who shaped church history throughout the period.

The chapter highlights the stunning transformation of the pagan Roman Empire into a nominally Christian Roman Empire through the reigns of Diocletian (r. 284–305), who started the "Great Persecution"; Constantine I (r. 306–337), who legalized and promoted Christianity; Julian the Apostate (r. 361–63), who failed in his efforts to revive paganism; Theodosius I (r. 379–95), who established Christianity as the state religion; and Justinian I (r. 527–65), who thoroughly united the Christian church and the Roman state.

EMPEROR DIOCLETIAN

Of these emperors, Constantine the Great ranks as the most important. But Constantine's rise to power must be considered against the background of the rule of Diocletian (r. 284–305). Diocletian led the Roman cavalry on the frontiers of the empire, as Roman legions attempted to keep the barbarians at bay. He rose through the ranks and became emperor, ruling for twenty years. In many respects Diocletian was an able emperor who, by his reorganization of the empire, gave Rome stability and greater strength. His main work of reorganization was the division of the empire into a tetrarchy (a rule of four) with four separate realms, two in the East and two in the West. Diocletian made Maximian the Augustus (emperor) in the West, while he remained the Augustus in the East. To complete the tetrarchy, Diocletian appointed two Caesar-successors to rule under the Augusti. Galerius was appointed Caesar under Diocletian in the East, and Constantius Chlorus (the father of Constantine) was appointed Caesar under Maximian in the West.

Emperor Diocletian

Despite his effective reorganization of the empire, Diocletian was the cruelest persecutor of all the Roman emperors. In 303, he started the empire-wide "Great Persecution," ordering all Christian churches to be destroyed, all Christian literature—including the Bible—to be burned, and all Christians who refused to declare the emperor to be a god to be imprisoned and killed.

When Diocletian, weary of ruling, retired to cultivate cabbages on the shores of the Black Sea, he appointed his Caesar Galerius (r. 305–11) to succeed him. Galerius continued the policy of persecution with even greater ferocity. However, while dying from a grave illness, Galerius changed his mind and issued an official edict of toleration in 311. Lactantius (c. 240–320), the church father and apologist, quoted Galerius as saying, "In return for this indulgence of ours it will be the duty of Christians to pray to God for our recovery, for the public weal and for their own; that the state may be preserved from danger on every side, and that they themselves may dwell safely in their homes."[1] Galerius died shortly thereafter, and Licinius (r. 308–24) replaced him as the Eastern emperor.

EMPEROR CONSTANTINE

Constantine I (r. 306–37) was born around 272 in Illyricum to Constantius Chlorus and his wife Helena. During the years of Diocletian's tetrarchy, Constantius Chlorus, first a Caesar and then an Augustus, ruled Gaul, Spain, and Britain. He was tolerant of Christians in his realm, even during the bloody days of the emperor Diocletian's persecution.

---

1 Bettenson and Maunder, *Documents of the Christian Church*, 17.

When Constantius Chlorus died in 306, his troops hailed his son Constantine as the new emperor. In 312 Constantine marched on Maxentius, a usurper who claimed to be the emperor in the West after the death of Diocletian. In a historic victory, Constantine defeated Maxentius at the Battle of the Milvian Bridge, near a bridge over the Tiber River and the quickest road to Rome.

Before the battle, Constantine claimed to see a vision of a cross in the sky with the Latin words *In hoc signo vinces* ("by this sign, conquer"). The vision, whether real or not, was a turning point in the history of the church. Suddenly proclaiming himself a Christian, Constantine required that his soldiers paint the cross on their shields as they marched into battle. When his outnumbered troops won the battle, Constantine claimed victory by the sign of the cross of Christ. The body of Maxentius was dragged out of the

Constantine's vision

Tiber River into which it had been tossed. It was decapitated, and the headless body was sent to Carthage to prove that Maxentius had been killed.

The Battle of the Milvian Bridge belongs to those crucial battles in which God altered the entire course of history. It stands along with the Battle of Carchemish and the Battle of Tours as decisive for succeeding events.[2] The unexpected victory at the Milvian Bridge opened the way to Rome and Constantine's accession to the throne of the empire as the first Christian emperor.

The Battle of the Milvian Bridge

---

2 The Battle of Carchemish was between the forces of Egypt under king Pharaoh Necho and the Babylonian armies. It was on the way to Carchemish that Josiah, good king of Judah, challenged Pharaoh Necho and was killed (2 Kings 23:29–30). The victory of the Babylonians opened the door to Babylon becoming the world power, which world power brought Judah into captivity. The Battle of Tours in 732 was fought by Charles Martel against the Muslims. The Muslims were defeated, and Europe was saved from Islam.

In 313, Constantine, who now ruled the entire Western half of the empire, met Licinius, successor to Galerius and emperor over the Eastern half of the empire, and worked out with him the famous Edict of Milan, which granted freedom of religion to Christians and opened the door for the support of the church by the state.

Almost immediately Constantine used his favorable attitude toward Christianity to benefit the church. In 319, Constantine forbade all heathen sacrifices and excluded the Christian clergy from taxes. In 321, he gave permission to the church to receive legacies.[3]

Constantine also unseated and executed the Eastern emperor Licinius and established himself as head of the entire Roman Empire in 324. In 330, he moved the capital of the empire from Rome to Byzantium on the farthest edge of Greece. The city was located on the Bosporus, that crucially important body of water that connects the Black Sea with the Mediterranean. The city stands astride the important trade routes of East and West and was the boundary between Europe and Asia. Although Constantine called it "New Rome," it soon became known as Constantinople in honor of his greatness. The city was destined to play a major role in the history of the world and of the church.

Map of Constantinople

This change of capital had an important effect upon the church. It brought the seat of the empire to a strongly Christian center, and it left the bishop of Rome in a position of tremendous power in that city. Rome was no longer the capital of the empire, nor even of the West, leaving a political vacuum that the pope could fill. And while the pope's rule was, at the beginning, only ecclesiastical, he soon extended his

---

3 Legacies are gifts from individuals to the church that, because they were given to the church, were tax-free.

rule to the secular government of the city and, when possible, to the Western part of the empire.

A much-debated question is this: was Constantine a genuine Christian?[4] Of course, only God knows who are his elect and when he has regenerated them. However, arguments can be raised in support of both sides of the debate. His life was filled with contradictions.

On the one hand, Constantine claimed to be converted, and he declared as imperial policy that Christianity was to be tolerated throughout the empire. He urged people to join the church and attended church himself. He forbade pagan practices that he considered detrimental to the welfare of the church, such as pagan sacrifices (although the edict was widely ignored), and he passed a law against work on Sunday. He preached in the court in Constantinople and even referred to himself as the "bishop of bishops," that is, the ecclesiastical head of the church. He called the Council of Nicaea in 325 to settle the question of the Arian heresy and accepted the final decision of Nicaea, which condemned Arianism.[5]

On the other hand, Constantine postponed his baptism until shortly before he died at the age of sixty-five. Although he was not a theologian and perhaps did not understand the doctrinal issues involved, the baptism of infants and new converts was the common practice in the church. Furthermore, Constantine killed Licinius after the Battle of Adrianople (324), even though he had promised him mercy; he killed his own son Crispus because he considered him a threat to the throne; and many historians claim that he murdered his wife Fausta, whom he suspected of treachery.

It is possible that Constantine saw the moral decay of the empire and its gradual disintegration and decided that the empire could only be preserved through breathing new life into it by the power of Christianity. His conversion then would be as much political and a matter of statesmanship as a religious change of life. He was a man who stood with one foot in the old age and one foot in the new; his attempts to bridge the gap by becoming a Christian were on the whole successful. Although I doubt the genuine character of Constantine's religion, I leave the matter with God.

---

4   For a well-reasoned defense of the Christianity of Constantine, see Peter J. Leithart, *Defending Constantine: The Twilight of an Empire and the Dawn of Christendom* (Downers Grove, IL: InterVarsity Press, 2010).

5   The great controversy of the period we are now discussing over the divinity of our Lord.

EMPEROR JULIAN

The toleration of Christianity, begun by Constantine, did not result in a completely Christian Roman Empire. The emperors who followed Constantine were usually favorable toward Christianity, but the degree of their support differed with each emperor.

When Constantine died, the empire was divided between his three sons: Constantine II, Constans, and Constantius II. The three sons were rivals for the throne until Constantius II (r. 337–61) became sole emperor.

The death of Julian the Apostate

Constantius followed the religious policies of his father and forced the heathen to forsake their pagan practices. This brought about a surge of growth in the church.

When Constantius died, his successor Julian (r. 361–63) made a brief attempt to restore paganism; but he reigned for only three years and his experiment failed. Julian tried to reduce Christianity to a sect so that paganism could once again become the empire's official religion. He reinstated the worship of the gods and rebuilt their temples. He rewarded those who apostatized from the Christian faith and oppressed the Christians with heavy taxes and confiscation of property and schools. The schools were changed into pagan institutions of learning. He tried to set one part of the Christian church against another part and made plans to encourage Judaism by rebuilding the old temple.

Julian failed in his efforts. His persecution of Christians was widely unpopular. Fatally wounded by a spear in battle with the Persians on the eastern border of the empire, he reportedly said, "Thou hast conquered, Galilean." Because he was born of Christian parents, he has become known in history as Julian "the Apostate."

EMPEROR THEODOSIUS

After the death of Julian, the Roman state gradually gained more power and influence in the affairs of the church. Because the barbarian Goths were pressing in on the empire in the West, and because Emperor Theodosius I (r. 379–95) was the last emperor of a united Roman Empire, his rule is important.

Theodosius strongly favored Christianity and opposed paganism. He showed his power by declaring Christianity the official religion of the empire in 380. Theodosius declared, "It is Our Will that all the peoples we rule shall practise that religion which the divine Peter the Apostle transmitted to the Romans. We shall believe in the single Deity of the Father, the Son, and the Holy Spirit, under the concept of equal majesty and of the Holy Trinity."[6] Theodosius's edict meant that other religions were no longer permitted, including paganism. He was strongly intolerant of paganism and began the punishment of heretics as official policy. During his reign, overly zealous monks and clergy began to destroy pagan idols and temples.

In addition, Theodosius was an orthodox emperor who opposed the heresy of Arianism and promoted the Nicene Creed. He called the church together at the Council of Constantinople in 381 to defeat Arianism a second time.

But the church also exercised some authority over this powerful emperor. In an unjustifiable fit of temper, Theodosius ordered the Thessalonians slaughtered for rebelling against their local ruler. Although Theodosius almost immediately recalled the order to kill them, the slaughter began before his second order arrived. Thousands were brutally murdered. Ambrose of Milan (c. 339–97), the bishop who had ecclesiastical authority over Theodosius, informed him that he could not partake of the Lord's supper unless he repented and confessed his sin. Theodosius, who held an exalted notion of his own eminence, at first refused. But when Ambrose was adamant, Theodosius, in fear of being excluded from

John Chrysostom (c. 349–407)

Serving the church as a popular and eloquent bishop and patriarch, first in Antioch and then in the imperial capital of Constantinople, John Chrysostom is remembered as the greatest preacher of the ancient church. His nickname, *Chrysostom*, means "golden-mouthed." Although active when Roman emperors such as Theodosius were exercising increasing power over the church, John fearlessly challenged leaders of both church and state who abused their authority. Banished by the Empress Eudoxia, he died a martyr's death at the hands of the Roman state. To learn more, read "John Chrysostom: Golden-Tongued Preacher," chapter 6 of Herman Hanko's *Portraits of Faithful Saints*.

Ambrose disciplines Theodosius

---

6   Bruce L. Shelley, *Church History in Plain Language*, 3rd ed. (Nashville, TN: Thomas Nelson, 2008), 96.

the church, confessed his sin. A lowly bishop had brought an emperor of the world to his knees!

EMPEROR JUSTINIAN

The Roman emperors were responsible for a gradual growth in the influence that the state had over the church. This was demonstrated many years later in the rule of Justinian I (r. 527–65). Ruling the Eastern Roman Empire after the fall of the Western Roman Empire to the barbarians, Justinian reconquered much of the West and revitalized the East from his capital of Constantinople. His empire was a continuation of the Eastern Roman Empire but was called the Byzantine Empire (centered as it was in Constantinople, the old city of Byzantium), and it lasted for almost a millennium. Justinian was the first and the greatest Byzantine emperor.

Emperor Justinian

Justinian used his vast power and influence to strengthen and promote the church. He built magnificent churches, such as the Hagia Sophia (Church of Holy Wisdom) in Constantinople. He summoned church councils, such as the Second Council of Constantinople in 553. And he frequently determined for the whole church which teachings constituted heresy and which teachings were orthodox.

The Hagia Sophia in Constantinople

Justinian also made a major contribution to both church and state with his formation of a body of canon law called the Justinian Code. This code of canon law mixed Roman jurisprudence with ecclesiastical decisions of permanent value. It was a body of legislation that became the fundamental church order and the basic law of the nations. It has been described as "the universal law of the Roman empire, the sole text-book in the academies at Rome, Constantinople, and Berytus, and the basis of the legal relations of the greater part of Christian Europe to this day."[7]

ADVANTAGES OF A CHRISTIAN STATE

From an earthly point of view, a Christian state had advantages. Christian emperors exerted considerable influence in church affairs by calling for major church councils in order to settle doctrinal controversies, by sending their representatives to these ecclesiastical assemblies, and by writing letters to bishops expressing "the will of the emperor" condemning heresy. The force of these letters was: "Do as I say, or else."

Ecclesiastical groups within the church who held positions contrary to the church sometimes sought assistance and support from the government in their causes. The result was that the emperor had an increasingly important say in ecclesiastical controversies.

The state also supported the church financially. The wealth of closed pagan temples was given to the church; property confiscated from heretics was put into the hands of the church; travel expenses to and from council meetings were underwritten by the state; and assistance was given for the support of the poor.

Labarum.
The Chi-Rho
military standard

In addition, the state gave legal sanction to Sabbath observance and to worship on other Christian holidays. It also gave to the church the right of legal incorporation and exemption from military service and from taxes for the clergy.

Finally, Christianity was now free from persecution and could concentrate its efforts on its calling as the church of Christ in the world. This was especially true in the area of missions. The church was also now in a position to exercise a wholesome influence on family life and public morals. But the greatest benefit—if we may call it that—was the rapid growth of the church.

DISADVANTAGES OF A CHRISTIAN STATE

However, the disadvantages seemed to outweigh the many advantages. From a spiritual point of view, the cessation of persecution did the church no good. Under

---

7 John McClintock & James Strong, *Cyclopedia of Biblical, Theological, and Ecclesiastical Literature* (Grand Rapids, MI: Baker Book House, 1969), 4:1111.

the hammer blows of persecution, the church learns that her only real defense in the world is Christ, and that the treasures of heaven are far more important than earthly possessions. In times of prosperity and freedom from persecution, the dangers of materialism and worldly prosperity are very real. So it was in the church during the fourth, fifth, and sixth centuries: the spirituality of the church was diminished.

Under the benevolent and watchful eye of the emperors the church grew rapidly, for to belong to the Christian church became fashionable. Many who joined the church lacked the grace of God, and they brought into her fold the vices of the heathen and created an atmosphere of moral laxity, secularization, and a subsequent weakening of the third mark of the true church—discipline.

Along with the rapid growth in membership came also a growing wealth. The church became so extremely rich that some historians claim that the church owned one-tenth of all landed property in the empire. Wealth enabled the church to erect costly and ornate places of worship. Outward form took the place of worship that was in spirit and in truth (John 4:24). The clergy were the primary recipients of the wealth. As a result, the clergy did not need the contributions of the laity to sustain them, and a hierarchy arose independent of the laity, which contributed to the rapid growth and power of the episcopacy. The members of the church no longer felt the need to support the poor and the causes of God's kingdom, and an essential part of worship was all but lost. In the meantime, the wealth of the clergy produced clerics who loved pomp and external show, who were models of laziness and lovers of luxury, but poor in spiritual life. Today's modern church-growth specialists will not learn from history's sharp lessons.

These sins did not characterize all the congregations and all the clergy, but the spiritual energy of many was sapped by such carnality.

With the support of the secular powers, the church lost some of its independence, because the state exerted influence in ecclesiastical affairs. The old adage is true: the one who supplies the money has the right to dictate how the money is used.

But the relation between church and state and of clerics and government officials was a two-way street: government officials often influenced clerics, but powerful clerics took an active part in the secular and political problems of the day and heavily influenced the direction the empire took. As the empire weakened in the West through the pressures of barbarians on the frontier, the power of the church grew until the church claimed for itself genuine secular as well as ecclesiastical power. Unfortunately, the church gradually lost her first love—Christ—and became married to the state; and that marriage would in time produce a monster: the tragic reality of the medieval papacy.

CHAPTER 12: **THE TRINITARIAN CONTROVERSIES**

Hear, O Israel: the LORD our God is one LORD.

—DEUTERONOMY 6:4

And without controversy great is the mystery of godliness:
God was manifest in the flesh.

—1 TIMOTHY 3:16

THE COMPLICATED BACKGROUND

The Council of Nicaea ranks among the most important events in the history of the church. In 325, God used Emperor Constantine to assemble a large body of churchmen from throughout the Roman Empire to wrestle with a heresy called Arianism and to establish the foundational doctrine of the Trinity. The Council of Nicaea also formulated the Nicene Creed, which established that Jesus Christ is both fully God and fully man.

This council has a complicated background. Before Constantine became emperor and gave the church rest from persecution, the church had faced several errors regarding the doctrine of God and Christ. These doctrines had not yet been significantly developed. The church had not yet reached the point at which it was able to say what scripture teaches regarding these fundamental doctrines. The history of the defense of the doctrines of the Trinity, of our Lord's divinity, and of the union of the two natures of Christ in one person is complicated.

First, this history is complicated because the doctrinal issue itself is complex: How can there be one God and yet three to be worshiped? And how can our Lord Jesus Christ be both God and man at the same time?

Second, this history is complicated because the church had no fixed terminology to express the doctrines of scripture. The Bible does not supply the church with a

145

vocabulary to use in defining and explaining the Trinity and the divinity and humanity of our Lord. Such terms as *Trinity*, *person*, *nature*, *essence*, and *being* had not been discovered, and even when they were used in one part of the church, they would often mean something entirely different somewhere else. The church had to invent a vocabulary but also had to agree on the meaning of key terms.

A third complicating factor in this history was that heretics, attempting to solve the matter of Christ's divinity, were everywhere spouting their views and gaining followings. The church was beset by the lingering influence of the early monarchian heresies of adoptionism and modalism. Although these heresies had been condemned by the early church, many still clung to and taught these erroneous views. Furthermore, false teachings about God and Christ held by a brilliant scholar named Origen of Alexandria were still popular in the early fourth century.

ORIGEN OF ALEXANDRIA (C. 185–254)

One of the most influential heretics was Origen (c. 185–254). He was a strange man. When he was still a boy, his mother had to hide his clothes, because when his father was taken away to be killed for his faith, Origen wanted to be a part of his martyrdom and could be kept in the house only because he was too modest to appear naked in the streets. When he became a young adult, he mutilated himself, thinking that in this way he would be obedient to Christ and would become a eunuch for the kingdom's sake.

Origen was extremely brilliant and far ahead of his times in his theology. Though brilliant, he was also erratic, and many of the heresies that appeared in later years in the church can be traced back to him.

Origen had a direct role to play in the controversy that surrounded the heretic Arius. Origen was a man to whom both the orthodox and the heretics appealed—each with some justification. The orthodox appealed to him because he taught the absolute divinity of Jesus Christ and insisted that Christ was very God. The heretics, including Arius, appealed to him because he said that Christ's generation by the Father, though eternal, was an act of God's will. This was a serious error, because obviously this made Christ less than the Father. If Christ was begotten by an act of the Father's will, then Christ's will, according to his divine nature, could not be the same will as the Father's. Thus God and Christ would not be the same in essence, a view that is a denial of the unity of God.

—Herman Hanko, *Contending for the Faith*, 34–35.

A final complicating factor in this history was the rivalry between the two ancient seminaries of Alexandria in Egypt and Antioch in Syria. These two influential theological schools used different methods of biblical interpretation and emphasized the doctrine of Christ differently. This rivalry between the two seminaries played an important role in the Arian controversy and would affect the church in her struggles for another two hundred years.

Against this background of such confusion, the Arian controversy began. In the center of it was the man for whom this heresy is named: Arius.

THE ARIAN CONTROVERSY

Little is known of Arius (c. 250–336), because references to him were burned by order of Emperor Constantine after his condemnation at the Council of Nicaea in 325. Any remaining references that could be found were later destroyed by orthodox theologians.

Arius of Alexandria

Arius was born around the time of the empire-wide Decian persecution in 250, perhaps in Libya in North Africa. He later studied in the seminary of Antioch, where he was heavily influenced by monarchian ideas. Arius was a pupil of Lucian of Antioch (c. 240–312), who had been a pupil of the monarchian Paul of Samosata (c. 200–275).

From Antioch, the young Arius moved to Alexandria, taking his views with him. In Alexandria, Arius served first as a deacon, then a presbyter. But he was excommunicated by the bishop, Peter of Alexandria, for supporting the schismatic views of Meletius of Lycopolis, who had taught that Christians who denied Christ under torture should not be readmitted to the church, even when they confessed their sin. Arius was later readmitted and became a well-known presbyter in an important church.

Arius was known for his asceticism and his courtly manners. He was tall and thin and had the general appearance of a scholar. He was a man of ability, learning, and piety. He made a favorable impression on the people whom he met. But beneath his external demeanor was a burning pride.

The controversy began after Arius's move to Alexandria. He soon made his office as presbyter in the church of Alexandria a powerful launching pad for his views. As presbyter, he began to teach some strange views, the most important of which was that the Logos (the Word, the Son of God, Jesus Christ) was created. The Logos was the firstborn, he said, the means by which the rest of the creation was formed, the greatest under God and as much like God as it is possible to be, but the Logos was not eternal God. Arius insisted that "there was a time when the Son was not." He explained that the Logos entered the body of Christ when he was born of Mary, and thus Christ became as much like God as was possible. But Christ was not God.

Alexander of Alexandria (c. 250–326), the bishop who had taken Peter's place, condemned these wrong views and attempted to change Arius's mind, but without success. So Arius was condemned by a synod held in Alexandria. He fled to Palestine and then to Nicomedia, where he was supported by some Eastern bishops, especially the influential Eusebius of Nicomedia (d. 341), who supported him even after the Council of Nicaea.

But Alexander would not allow *any* part of the church to be persuaded of Arius's false doctrines. He informed all the churches of what had happened in Alexandria. The result was not that peace and unity came about in a universal condemnation of Arius, as Alexander had hoped, but that the controversy spread rapidly throughout the entire empire and threatened to divide the entire church.

It is therefore not surprising that Emperor Constantine entered the fray, for the unity of the empire, which he had labored so hard to restore, was once again threatened, this time by religious conflict. Such disunity was particularly disturbing to Constantine, because he had hoped that Christianity would breathe new life into the dying Roman Empire and thus restore unity among its many factions.

Constantine appointed Hosius of Cordova (c. 257–357), a bishop in Spain, to restore peace and unity. Hosius was orthodox in all respects even before the Arian controversy. He must have been an influential theologian and gifted administrator for Constantine to summon him from Spain to perform a vital work in the church and empire. Both Constantine and Hosius thought a solution to the problem was possible. Constantine considered the disagreement to be over "an unprofitable question." Both men failed to appreciate the seriousness of the matter and the antagonism that can arise in Christian circles over doctrinal questions. All efforts to restore unity failed.

THE COUNCIL OF NICAEA

Almost in desperation, Constantine called the Council of Nicaea, one of the great ecumenical meetings in the entire history of the church. All expenses were to be paid out of the imperial treasury, and transportation was provided by the emperor so that the bishops could come from every part of the Mediterranean world. The year was 325, more than ten years after Constantine came to power. Nicaea was a rather unpretentious town in the northwestern part of Asia Minor (now Turkey).

Present at this meeting were 318 bishops, all but seven of whom came from the Eastern church. It was a diverse group. Some had been tortured by the authorities during the Diocletian persecution. They bore in their bodies the broken limbs and scars left from the cruel tortures of their persecutors. Others were from prestigious cities where bishops had already become accustomed to some pomp and show. They came with their retinues and attempted to impress the council with their wealth and religious trappings. Emperor Constantine himself was present, though he did not preside over the deliberations. The presence of the Roman emperor was bound to have its effect on the meeting; yet Constantine did not interfere with the decisions that were made.

One delegate, the scholarly bishop Eusebius of Caesarea (c. 260–340), known today as the father of church history for his writing of the very first church history book, described the opening ceremonies this way:

> After all the bishops had entered the central building of the royal palace, on the sides of which very many seats were prepared, each took his place with becoming modesty, and silently awaited the arrival of the emperor. The court officers entered one after another, though only such as professed faith in Christ. The moment the approach of the emperor was announced by a given signal, they all rose from their seats, and the emperor appeared like a

---

Arius of Alexandria (c. 250–336)

Arius may be the most infamous heretic in church history. As a presbyter and preacher in the influential church of Alexandria, he taught that Christ is an eternally created being who is less than God. He used street tunes to popularize the idea that "there was a time when the Son was not." After his condemnation at an Egyptian synod and his excommunication from the Alexandrian church, Arius took his heretical ideas to Palestine and Asia Minor, stirring up an empire-wide controversy that led to the Council of Nicaea. Although Arianism was condemned, Arius was banished, and his writings were banned, Emperor Constantine permitted Arius to return just a few years later, resulting in a disastrous resurgence of Arianism and a renewed battle for trinitarian truth. To learn more, read "Arius and the Council of Nicaea," chapter 5 of Herman Hanko's *Contending for the Faith*.

Eusebius of Caesarea

heavenly messenger of God, covered with gold and gems, a glorious presence, very tall and slender, full of beauty, strength, and majesty. With this external adornment he united the spiritual ornament of the fear of God, modesty, and humility, which could be seen in his downcast eyes, his blushing face, the motion of his body, and his walk. When he reached the golden throne prepared for him, he stopped, and sat not down till the bishops gave him the sign. And after him they all resumed their seats.[1]

The issue before the council was the divinity of our Lord Jesus Christ. Arius was ready to admit the Lord's divinity, but he insisted that the divinity of the Lord was less than that of the Father. Eagerly taking hold of Origen's teaching that the Son of God was begotten by the Father as an act of God's will, he argued that Christ could only be divine in a created way since creation was an act of God's will.

The Council of Nicaea, AD 325

The orthodox delegates insisted that Christ is divine in the same sense as the Father is divine, that he was begotten by God as a *necessary* relation between the Father and the Son within the divine essence. The word *necessary* was determinative. He was not begotten by the will of God, but by a *necessary* act of the Father within the eternal Trinity. The battle raged around those fundamental differences.

The council was divided into three groups who differed on the question of Arius's teachings. About twenty bishops, led by Eusebius of Nicomedia, were Arians. A smaller group composed of gifted

1 Eusebius, quoted in Philip Schaff, *History of the Christian Church*, vol. 3, *Nicene and Post-Nicene Christianity: From Constantine the Great to Gregory the Great, AD 311–600*, 5th rev. ed. (New York: Charles Scribner's Sons; repr., Grand Rapids, MI: Wm. B. Eerdmans Publishing Co., 1964), 624–25.

theologians represented the orthodox position and was led by Alexander of Alexandria and his deacon Athanasius. The majority, led by Eusebius of Caesarea, were closer to the orthodox position than to that of Arius, but they were generally followers of Origen and his mistaken notion of the Father begetting the Son by an act of his will.

Arius himself proposed a statement. This formulation was shouted down by a great uproar.[2] Eusebius of Caesarea then proposed another statement. This one was vague on the exact point at issue. The orthodox were suspicious of the confession proposed by Eusebius, chiefly because the Arians themselves were willing to sign it, and it was obviously designed to please both parties. It was a compromise that did not satisfy them. Compromises do not work when the truth of God is at stake. The orthodox wanted to be sure that no doubt could be left regarding the meaning of scripture.

The orthodox began to use a term that made their position unmistakably clear: *homo-ousios*, a Greek term that means "same essence." These orthodox theologians insisted that Christ was of the same

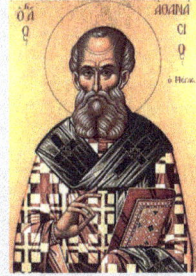

Athanasius of Alexandria
(c. 296–373)

Few figures in ancient church history play such an important role as that of Athanasius. As a deacon, he attended the Council of Nicaea and championed the doctrines of the Trinity and the full divinity of Jesus Christ. As an author, he defended sovereign grace in *On the Incarnation*, encouraged the ascetic movement in *The Life of Anthony*, and was the first to provide a complete list of New Testament books in his Easter letter of 367. As a bishop, he led his Alexandrian flock faithfully for decades and endured no less than five banishments for his uncompromising stand for the truth. The church later honored him by placing his name on the Athanasian Creed. To learn more, read "Athanasius Against the World," chapter 5 of Herman Hanko's *Portraits of Faithful Saints*.

essence as the Father. To avoid any misunderstanding, the orthodox insisted on adding the term *homo-ousios* to any statement adopted by the council, and they finally succeeded. So we have those memorable words in the Nicene Creed: "And [I believe] in one Lord Jesus Christ, the only-begotten Son of God, begotten of the Father before

---

2   Some church historians say that it was torn to pieces and trampled on the floor.

all worlds, God of God; Light of Light, true God of true God; begotten, not made, being of one essence [*homo-ousios*] with the Father."[3]

Athanasius (c. 296–373), a deacon in the church of Alexandria, put the debate in its proper context. He insisted that the debate was not merely about an abstract theological issue. Because scripture is the written record of the revelation of God who is the God of our salvation, this debate regarded our salvation in Jesus Christ.

Athanasius argued that we are saved by God alone, not by our efforts. If we are saved by God and by Christ's work, then Christ must be God. Our salvation rests upon that truth. The argument was cogent and persuasive. It was the very first defense of sovereign grace.

To make matters sure, the council drew up the Nicene Creed. All of the bishops present at the council signed this confession, except for two delegates and Arius. The words of the original Nicene Creed are as follows:

We believe in one God the Father All-sovereign, maker of all things visible and invisible;

And in one Lord Jesus Christ, the Son of God, begotten of the Father, only-begotten, that is, of the substance of the Father, God of God, Light of Light, true God of true God, begotten not made, of one substance with the Father, through whom all things were made, things in heaven and things on the earth; who for us men and for our salvation came down and was made flesh, and became man, suffered, and rose on the third day, ascended into the heavens, is coming to judge living and dead.

And in the Holy Spirit.

And those that say "There was when he was not," and "Before he was begotten he was not," and that, "He came into being from what-is-not," or those that allege, that the son of God is "Of another substance or essence" or "created," or "changeable" or "alterable," these the Catholic and Apostolic Church anathematizes.[4]

---

3   Nicene Creed, in *Confessions and Church Order*, 11.
4   Bettenson and Maunder, *Documents of the Christian Church*, 27–28.

The Council of Nicaea was a great victory for the church. It established the doctrine of scripture regarding the Trinity and the person of Christ.

THE SEMI-ARIAN CONTROVERSY

If Constantine and the delegates left Nicaea thinking that the adoption of the Nicene Creed settled the matter and would bring unity to the empire, they were sadly mistaken. Even though Arius's books were burned and his followers were banished, the controversy continued.

While strict Arianism gradually waned, a new heresy arose, a modification of full-blown Arianism and a compromise position that attracted thousands. The debate after Nicaea swirled around three terms that were used to describe the relationship between the Father and the Son. The orthodox theologians continued to use the term adopted by the Council of Nicaea: *homo-ousios* (same essence). The Arian theologians had used the term *hetero-ousios* (different essence), but their position was mostly abandoned and the word fell into disuse. However, a large group in the theological middle, called the semi-Arians, began to prefer a new term: *homoi-ousios* (similar essence). After Nicaea, the theological battle lines were drawn between the orthodox Nicene party (*homo-ousios*) and the heretical semi-Arian party (*homoi-ousios*).

Imagine that the church could be aroused to heights of outrage by the difference of one small letter *i* (in the Greek called an "iota," the smallest of all the letters in the Greek alphabet)![5] Theologians today find such controversy embarrassing and even despicable. They, for the most part, do not stumble even at avowed Arminianism, though it is a horrible corruption of the truths of sovereign grace.

If we think such small differences are unimportant, let us remember that the confession of the doctrine of Christ's divinity and our subsequent salvation rests on the presence or absence of that little *i*.

More importantly, the whole question revolves around the doctrine of God himself: Is God sovereign in all he does, including the work of salvation? Or is salvation

---

5 Bruce Shelley, in commenting on this point, uses an example to illustrate the importance of "little" points. He tells of a woman who was traveling in Europe and came across a bracelet she wanted to buy. She cabled her husband: "Have found wonderful bracelet. Price seventy-five thousand dollars. May I buy it?" He cabled back: "No, price too high." But the cable operator omitted the comma, and the message the wife received was: "No price too high." The lady bought the bracelet. Shelley, *Church History in Plain Language*, 104.

partly his work, yet he needs someone outside himself to assist him? God does all things for his own name's sake; Christ who accomplished salvation for us is not *like* God; he *is* God.

The fight went on after Nicaea for over fifty years. The fortunes of the orthodox party and the semi-Arian party waxed and waned depending on whether the current emperor favored one party or the other. In the course of all the struggles it seemed at times as if semi-Arianism would prevail.

During these years, Athanasius, the orthodox deacon who had defended the divinity of Christ at Nicaea, rose to the high office of bishop of Alexandria when Alexander died. He remained the champion of orthodoxy in the years that followed, but he paid the price with five banishments. The first one was to far-off Trier, a town in the heart of the dense forests of Germany, where his enemies thought that his voice would be stifled. But he was rescued from banishment and returned to Alexandria to renew the fight. Athanasius often faced threats against his life and slander against his good name. The semi-Arians hated him and attempted to silence him. At times they seemed successful. Some local synods even vindicated the heretic Arius. All these troubles forced from the monk Jerome (c. 345–420) the plaintive cry, "The whole world groaned to find itself Arian."

In the course of time, the heretic Arius and the faithful Athanasius both died. New theologians arose to defend Nicene orthodoxy. In the East, the Cappadocian Fathers, an orthodox trio of theologians from Asia Minor, included Basil of Caesarea (c. 329–79), Gregory of Nazianzus (c. 330–90), and Gregory of Nyssa (c. 330–94). These were men of outstanding ability. They were joined by theologians in the West, like Hilary of Poitiers (c. 315–67) and Ambrose of Milan (c. 339–97), who throughout the controversy remained in the orthodox camp. Gradually, the theological climate of the church changed and the views and creedal formulations of Nicaea were accepted.

The victory was finally sealed at the ecumenical Council of Constantinople in 381, at which Arianism and semi-Arianism were condemned and trinitarian and Christological doctrine was affirmed. The council also made some minor but necessary changes to the Nicene Creed, especially regarding the doctrine of the Holy Spirit.[6]

---

6   For these changes see Schaff, *History of the Christian Church*, 3:668–69.

THE NICENE CREED

The Nicene Creed, in its original form, was adopted by the Council of Nicaea (325), which condemned the heresy of Arianism (a denial of the deity of the Son) and proclaimed the biblical doctrine regarding the Trinity and the full divinity of Jesus Christ. The Nicene Creed's confession concerning the Holy Spirit was expanded at the Council of Constantinople (381), which also condemned the heresy of Macedonianism (a denial of the deity of the Holy Spirit). The modified Nicene Creed is therefore more accurately called the Niceno-Constantinopolitan Creed. The Western church made one final change to the creed at the Council of Toledo (589), adding to the article on the procession of the Holy Spirit the words "and the Son" (Latin: *filioque*). This beautiful, ancient trinitarian creed is mentioned and affirmed explicitly in article 9 of the Belgic Confession (1561).

I believe in one God, the Father Almighty, Maker of heaven and earth, and of all things visible and invisible.

And in one Lord Jesus Christ, the only-begotten Son of God, begotten of the Father before all worlds, God of God; Light of Light, true God of true God; begotten, not made, being of one essence with the Father; by whom all things were made; who, for us men and for our salvation, came down from heaven, and was incarnate by the Holy Ghost of the Virgin Mary, and was made man; and was crucified also under Pontius Pilate; He suffered and was buried; and the third day He rose again, according to the Scriptures; and ascended into heaven, and sitteth on the right hand of the Father; and He shall come again, with glory, to judge both the quick and the dead; whose kingdom shall have no end.

And I believe in the Holy Ghost, the Lord and Giver of life; who proceedeth from the Father and the Son; who with the Father and the Son together is worshiped and glorified; who spake by the prophets.

And I believe one holy catholic and apostolic church. I acknowledge one baptism for the remission of sins; and I look for the resurrection of the dead, and the life of the world to come. Amen.[7]

---

7   Nicene Creed, in *Confessions and Church Order*, 11.

THE IMPORTANCE OF THE CONTROVERSY

When Peter made his confession that Jesus was "the Christ, the Son of the living God," Jesus defined that confession as the rock on which he would build his church (Matt. 16:13–19). The apostle John affirmed that great truth when he told us the reason for his gospel narrative: "But these are written, that ye might believe that Jesus is the Christ, the Son of God; and that believing ye might have life through his name" (John 20:31). Again, in his first epistle, John made the statement that when the Lord Jesus Christ came into the world, he came as divine, and a confession of his divinity is the difference between the true church and antichrist (1 John 4:1–3).

In other words, the church could not develop truth further until she held to the doctrine of the divinity of the Son of God in our flesh. Indeed, the church would lose her identity if she denied that great and fundamental doctrine. It was absolutely necessary for the future existence of the church that the doctrine of Christ's divinity be creedally established as the rock on which Christ would build his church.

Under the sovereign control of an all-wise God, Arius arose and taught differently. In God's hand, Arius was a goad to compel the church to define this biblical doctrine so that it could be established for all time. That establishment of the truth had to take place in the early history of the church.

These controversies were both Christological and trinitarian. While the debates swirled around the question of the divinity of Christ, the truth of the Trinity was inextricably woven into the doctrine of Christ. After all, the question had to be answered: how can Christ be fully divine as the Son of God, if the Father is God and yet there is only one God? That problem was implicitly settled at the Council of Nicaea in 325 and was finalized by the Council of Constantinople in 381. Both doctrines received their final form in the Athanasian Creed.

The confessions of the Reformed churches around the world explicitly appeal to both the Nicene Creed and the Athanasian Creed in support of the fact that Reformed churches stand on the basis of the ancient creeds.[8] In article 9, on the Trinity, the Belgic Confession states that "we

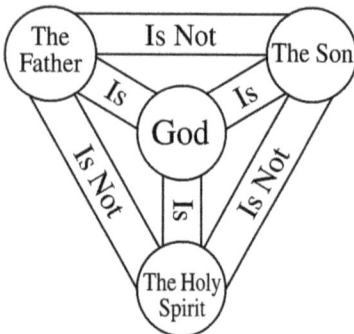

An early diagram of the Trinity

The Father — Is Not — The Son; Is — God — Is; Is Not — Is — Is Not; The Holy Spirit

---

8 Belgic Confession 8–11, in *Confessions and Church Order*, 28–33.

do willingly receive the three creeds, namely, that of the Apostles, of Nicaea, and of Athanasius."[9]

While the main issues in the controversy swirled around the question of the divinity of Christ, behind them was the question of God's nature. Christ is, with the Father, true God of true God. How could the church insist that Christ the Son and the Father are God at the same time and yet avoid polytheism? The doctrine of the Holy Spirit was a part of the discussion as well. Scripture also ascribes to the Holy Spirit divine attributes, works, and powers. How then could the Father, the Son, and the Holy Spirit be defined as distinct from each other and yet be one true God?

In searching the scriptures for answers, orthodox theologians became aware that they stood before a profound mystery that could not be explained and understood in earthly terms. God is one God only and yet three in person. Here the word *person* is determinative. Only when the church came to understand the word could it define properly the biblical teaching concerning God.

Even though the word *person* had no clear meaning in the ancient church, a person is the *subject of all the activities of the nature.* As a person, I am born; I eat; I grow up; I go to school; I work; I die. In God there are three that say "I"; each in his own way, but together with one mind, one will, one course of action. That is the doctrine of the Trinity.

Theologians over the years have attempted to make this clear by means of analogies with human life and relationships,[10] but these analogies fail. God is completely Other. He is so different from anything in this world, from any person, from any human relationship, that no comparison is possible. Aware of this, the church has bowed in worship before an infinitely great God and has said, "Thou great three in one, we worship and adore thee!"

Because God is three in person and one in essence, God is a covenantal God who has blessed fellowship within himself. The covenantal fellowship that God eternally enjoys within himself makes it possible for God to have covenantal fellowship with his people through Christ, who is in our flesh "very God of very God."

From the controversies surrounding the Council of Nicaea emerged the doctrine of the Trinity and its incomparable blessedness for the church.

---

9 Belgic Confession 9, in *Confessions and Church Order*, 31.
10 For two such analogies, see Shelley, *Church History in Plain Language*, 104–6.

THE ATHANASIAN CREED

Although the great church father Athanasius did not write this ancient creed, it is fitting that this confession bears his name. Throughout his long and tumultuous life, Athanasius fought tenaciously and suffered immensely in defense of the very doctrines established in the creed. The Athanasian Creed systematically and musically proclaims the doctrines of the Trinity (vv. 3–28) and of the incarnation (vv. 29–43). It was originally written in the fifth century by an unknown Latin author. Due to the opening words in the Latin original, the creed has sometimes been referred to as the *Symbolum Quicunque* ("Whosoever Creed") and the *Quicunque Vult* ("Whosoever Will"). Reaching its final form in the eighth century, the Athanasian Creed is the latest, longest, fullest, and most rhythmic of all the ecumenical creeds. Along with the Apostles' Creed and the Nicene Creed, this creed is mentioned in the Belgic Confession, article 9. The first 28 verses are included below.

Whosoever will be saved, before all things it is necessary that he hold the catholic faith;

Which faith except every one do keep whole and undefiled, without doubt he shall perish everlastingly.

And the catholic faith is this: That we worship one God in Trinity, and Trinity in Unity;

Neither confounding the persons nor dividing the essence.

For there is one person of the Father, another of the Son, and another of the Holy Ghost.

But the Godhead of the Father, of the Son, and of the Holy Ghost is all one, the glory equal, the majesty coeternal.

Such as the Father is, such is the Son, and such is the Holy Ghost.

The Father uncreated, the Son uncreated, and the Holy Ghost uncreated.

The Father infinite, the Son infinite, and the Holy Ghost infinite.

The Father eternal, the Son eternal, and the Holy Ghost eternal.

And yet they are not three eternals, but one eternal.

As also there are not three uncreated nor three infinites, but one uncreated and one infinite.

So likewise the Father is almighty, the Son almighty, and the Holy Ghost almighty.

And yet they are not three almighties, but one almighty.

So the Father is God, the Son is God, and the Holy Ghost is God.

And yet they are not three Gods, but one God.

So likewise the Father is Lord, the Son is Lord, and the Holy Ghost Lord.

And yet not three Lords, but one Lord.

For like as we are compelled by the Christian truth to acknowledge every person by Himself to be God and Lord:

So are we forbidden by the catholic religion to say, There are three Gods or three Lords.

The Father is made of none, neither created nor begotten.

The Son is of the Father alone, not made nor created, but begotten.

The Holy Ghost is of the Father and of the Son, neither made, nor created, nor begotten, but proceeding.

So there is one Father, not three Fathers; one Son, not three Sons; one Holy Ghost, not three Holy Ghosts.

And in this Trinity none is before or after; none is greater or less.

But the whole three persons are coeternal and coequal.

So that in all things, as aforesaid, the Unity in Trinity and the Trinity in Unity is to be worshiped.

He therefore that will be saved, let him thus think of the Trinity.[11]

11 Athanasian Creed 1–28, in *Confessions and Church Order*, 13–14.

CHAPTER 13:
THE CHRISTOLOGICAL CONTROVERSIES

For verily he took not on him the nature of angels; but he took on him the seed of
Abraham. Wherefore in all things it behoved him to be made like unto his brethren,
that he might be a merciful and faithful high priest in things pertaining to God, to
make reconciliation for the sins of the people.

—Hebrews 2:16–17

CHRISTOLOGICAL QUESTIONS

The difficult problem of the divinity of our Lord Jesus Christ was settled by the decisions of the councils of Nicaea and Constantinople. Yet problems arose regarding the possibility and manner of Christ being both wholly and truly God and, at the same time, truly man. To this the church had as yet no answer. That it is true, she realized. Nicaea and Constantinople had said that Christ is wholly God. But he is also a man, born of a virgin, who lived with the Jews, ate with them, talked with them, healed their sick, and wept with them. He suffered as any man suffered, and he died at the relatively young age of thirty-three years old. Besides being God, Christ is also truly man. How best to explain this truth?

Various solutions were proposed, but most of them were wrong. After the Council of Nicaea, the church was embroiled in especially three Christological controversies: Apollinarianism, Nestorianism, and Eutychianism. Throughout these grueling theological battles, God led his church to understand more fully the doctrine regarding the person and natures of the Lord Jesus Christ and to declare these doctrines definitively with another ecumenical creed.

159

THE APOLLINARIAN CONTROVERSY

Apollinaris of Laodicea (c. 310–90) proposed one solution to the problem of Christ's divinity and humanity. A bishop of Laodicea, Apollinaris was well known for his piety and orthodoxy, as well as his love of classical culture, which may have been his undoing. An enemy of Arianism, he was highly respected in the church. Even the hard-hitting Athanasius did not mention Apollinaris by name when attacking his views.

Apollinaris looked at the relation between Christ's humanity and divinity from a philosophical and rationalistic viewpoint. He said it was logically impossible that two wholes (the humanity and the divinity of Christ) could be found in one whole (Christ's person). He proposed an ingenious, but wrong, solution. He said that the divine Logos (the Word, Christ) assumed the nature of a man, but did so by taking the place of man's spirit. He claimed that Christ possesses a human body and a human soul, but not a human spirit.

Athanasius, again the chief defender of biblical truth, refused to be drawn into the debate by making use of philosophical terms and categories. He insisted, as scripture does, that all truth must be understood in the light of God's work of salvation in Christ. It was obvious to Athanasius that Apollinaris denied that Christ possesses a *complete* human nature. Since our sins have corrupted us in body, soul, and spirit, we need to be saved in body, soul, and spirit. Therefore, in order to save us, Christ had to be like us in all things except our sin. He had to be a man with a human body, a human soul, and a human spirit. If that is not true, he argued, our salvation is impossible.

The Council of Constantinople, AD 381

Up to this point, Apollinaris was incorrect, but he was not a heretic. He was wrong but not sinful. His views were condemned by a provincial synod in Alexandria in 362, by bishop Damasus of Rome in 377, by a synod in Antioch in 378, and finally at the great Council of Constantinople in 381, the same council that had modified the Nicene Creed. This second ecumenical council represented the whole church. When it condemned Apollinaris's views, it made the condemnation of

Apollinarianism the official teaching of the church; and when Apollinaris still insisted on his error after it was shown to conflict with scripture, he became a heretic. Apollinaris died in 390, less than ten years after the Council of Constantinople.

Athanasius was right: scripture repeatedly insists that Christ is like us in all things, except for our sin (Rom. 8:3; Heb. 4:15). Christ possessed a human body, a human soul, and a human spirit. At the moment of his death, Christ commended his spirit to his Father in heaven.

The church had advanced in its development of the doctrine of Christ.

THE NESTORIAN CONTROVERSY

The second Christological controversy after Nicaea was the Nestorian controversy. Perhaps no single event in the history of the church demonstrates so clearly the truth of an old proverb: "God can draw a straight line with a crooked stick." God does use sinful men to accomplish his purpose, and the Nestorian controversy is proof of this. Both of the outstanding men in the controversy were notorious for their ugly characters and were wrong in their theological positions. Only God could make something good emerge from the mess that these two men made.

Sometimes people in the church support a heretic because of his charisma and pleasant character and oppose a defender of the truth because of his unpleasant personality. In the case of the Nestorian controversy, neither of the chief antagonists was very pleasant. Those who had to determine right and wrong had to do so in spite of the personalities of the antagonists.

Nestorius (c. 386–451) was a monk brought to prominence by his excellent voice and fluent speech. But he was unbearably vain, a superficial thinker, impetuous, and intemperately hostile to anyone who opposed his violence. He was too rigorous in his pursuit of orthodoxy. Only a few days after his consecration as patriarch of

Apollinaris of Laodicea (c. 310–90)

Apollinaris was a respected theologian and bishop of Laodicea in Asia Minor. An enemy of Arianism and a champion of the Nicene Creed, he was highly esteemed by the church fathers Athanasius, Basil, and Jerome. But when Apollinaris later denied Christ's full humanity by insisting that Christ has a human body and a human soul but not a human spirit, his teachings were condemned by the ecumenical Council of Constantinople (381). Although Apollinaris died a heretic, stubbornly refusing to accept the council's decision, his teachings served to sharpen the church's understanding of the doctrine of Christ. To learn more, read "Apollinaris and the Doctrine of Christ," chapter 6 of Herman Hanko's *Contending for the Faith*.

Constantinople, he burned down the chapel of an Arian congregation; yet he sheltered Pelagians who had fled to the East when the heresy of Pelagianism had been condemned in the West.

His theological opponent was Cyril (c. 376–444) from the hot sands of Egypt. For over thirty years, he was the patriarch of the prestigious city of Alexandria. Cyril was learned, astute, energetic, and the intellectual superior of Nestorius. But Cyril was also shrewd, haughty, selfish, and ready to use means both fair and foul in his efforts to overthrow Nestorius. Cyril and Nestorius were like two boxers in a ring, both so utterly distasteful that one can hardly decide for whom to cheer.

Nestorius taught that Christ possessed two persons, a divine person and a human person. The divine person was the eternal Son of God. The human person was active in Christ's human nature and was the subject of some of Christ's actions. Nestorius insisted that the union between Christ's two natures was analogous to the way a man and a woman are united in marriage. This was a fatal flaw. In a marriage, husband and wife become one flesh, something that did not happen between the two natures of Christ; and in a marriage, husband and wife both retain their own persons.

Cyril, however, saw a real union between the divine and human natures, so that the divine person used the human nature as one through which to accomplish his work. He correctly saw that a union of the two natures was necessary and that Christ had only one person, the divine person of the Son of God. But in his determination to view the two natures of Christ as related to each other, Cyril viewed the union of the two natures as a mixture of the divine and the human. That was his weakness.

Cyril of Alexandria

The question at issue was, "Does Christ have two persons, one divine, the other human? Or is Christ one divine person with a divine nature and a human nature?"

The dispute turned ugly. Both damned the other, and both excommunicated each other and their followers. Both spent a great deal of time stating their own views with a lot of smoke but not much fire. The result was a religious dispute characterized by fierce argumentation, hurling of anathemas, political intrigue, and perpetual jockeying for a favorable position with the current emperor. It was unseemly in the extreme.

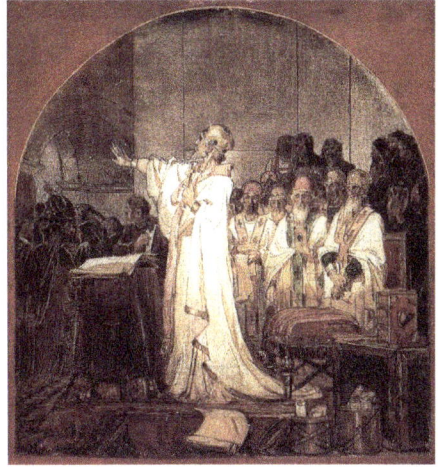

The Council of Ephesus, AD 431

A strange element entered the controversy that did little to settle the debate. Among the monks and ascetics in Egypt, the exaltation and worship of Mary (Mariolatry) had become common. In their growing doctrine of Mary (Mariology), the monks used an ambiguous term that became the watchword of orthodoxy. The term was *theotokos* ("God-bearer"); it meant that Mary was the mother of God.[1] *Theotokos* became the password of orthodoxy in the Nestorian controversy, as *homo-ousios* had been the password of orthodoxy in the Arian controversy. Cyril and his followers used the term to mean that Mary gave birth to God. Nestorius repudiated the term because he believed it confused Christ's humanity and divinity.

Nestorius was wrong, and Cyril was closer to the truth. Emperor Theodosius II called the third ecumenical council, the Council of Ephesus (431), to settle the controversy. At the council, Cyril's views were adopted, Nestorianism was condemned, and Nestorius was deposed from office. Nestorius left Constantinople, sought retreat in a monastery near Antioch, and died in exile in the year of the ecumenical Council of Chalcedon (451), which council finally brought the controversy to a close.

THE EUTYCHIAN CONTROVERSY

The Nestorian controversy produced other Christological disagreements. Nestorius had indeed separated the two natures of Christ and taught two persons, but Cyril had

---

1 *Theotokos* is composed of *theos*, which means "God," and *tokos*, which means "one who gives birth to."

so emphasized the union of the two natures of Christ that he came close to teaching the confusion or the mixture of the two natures of our Lord.

Eutyches (c. 375–454) was a monk and the abbot of a large monastery in Constantinople. Although he was under the jurisdiction and rule of the patriarch of Constantinople, he was influenced by Cyril and the Alexandrian school of theology. In stressing the union of the two natures, Eutyches concluded that Christ, after his birth, had one nature, because the impersonal human nature was assimilated into and absorbed by the divine. Christ was some sort of God-man.

Under the leadership of the orthodox patriarch Flavian of Constantinople (d. 449), a successor of Nestorius, a council met in Constantinople in 448 and deposed Eutyches for heresy. The result was two parties in the church: an orthodox party and a Eutychian party.

Both parties promptly appealed to the bishop Leo I of Rome (c. 400–461), who knew how to use these appeals to enhance the prestige of his own bishopric and decided in favor of the orthodox party. Leo wrote an influential letter ("The Tome of Leo") to Flavian, in which he defended orthodox Christology over against the heresy of Eutychianism. In spite of his extravagant claims of superior authority in the church, Leo was the calmest voice in the whole controversy. A man of great ability, he has rightly been called the first real pope. The orthodox looked to him for leadership, and the prestige of his position as bishop of Rome gave the orthodox an edge over the Eutychians.

However, the scheming patriarch Dioscorus of Alexandria (d. 454), a supporter of Eutyches and an enemy of Flavian, convinced Emperor Theodosius II to summon another council, which met in Ephesus in 449 and upheld Eutyches and denounced Flavian. At the council, a mob of Eutychian monks mercilessly beat Flavian, who died three days later from his injuries. The council has gone down in history as the "Robber Council," a term coined by Leo. The "Robber Council" resulted in a split between the churches of Rome and Alexandria. At this point in the controversy, one council had approved of Eutyches and one council had condemned him, manifesting serious disunity over a crucially important doctrine.

CHRISTOLOGICAL HERESIES IN THE ANCIENT CHURCH

Heresy	Proponent	Summary	Problem
ARIANISM	Arius (c. 250–336)	Christ was an eternally created being, less than God but more than man.	Denied the full divinity of Christ.
APOLLINARIANISM	Apollinaris (c. 310–90)	Christ had a human body and a human soul, but his human spirit (mind) was replaced by the divine nature.	Denied the full humanity of Christ.
NESTORIANISM	Nestorius (c. 386–451)	Christ had two separate persons, one human and the other divine.	Denied the union of Christ's two natures in one person.
EUTYCHIANISM	Eutyches (c. 375–454)	The human nature of Christ was absorbed by the divine nature.	Denied the distinction of Christ's two natures.

THE COUNCIL OF CHALCEDON

In 450, Emperor Theodosius II died after falling from his horse. Because he had no successor, his sister Pulcheria and her husband Marcian ruled. They favored the orthodox position, as Theodosius had, and they called for the fourth ecumenical council to meet in Chalcedon, a city in Asia Minor located almost directly across the Bosporus from Constantinople.

The Council of Chalcedon met in 451. It annulled the decisions of the "Robber Council" of Ephesus (449); it condemned Eutyches and his followers; and it condemned Nestorianism once again. The council also drew up a creed that correctly defined the doctrine of Christ in this way: Our Mediator is the eternal Son of God. With his entire divine nature, he entered into our flesh. He took on a complete human nature that was united with the divine nature in the one divine person of the Son of God. Christ united the two natures in such a way that they are both "without confusion, without change, without division, without separation."[2] These decisions settled the controversy officially.

The Council of Chalcedon, AD 451

---

2   Creed of Chalcedon, in *Confessions and Church Order*, 17.

It is interesting that the church after the Protestant Reformation considered the Creed of Chalcedon to be part of its creedal heritage, along with the Nicene Creed and the Athanasian Creed. However, after the Reformation, although the term *theotokos* remained in the Creed of Chalcedon, the Reformed churches did not often refer to it. While the Nicene Creed and the Athanasian Creed are mentioned by name in the Belgic Confession, the Creed of Chalcedon is not.

The Council of Chalcedon was a major milestone in the history of the church. The final decision embodied in the Creed of Chalcedon stated correctly that our Lord Jesus Christ is fully God and fully man; Immanuel, God with us; God dwelling with his people in covenantal fellowship; hence, he is the head of the covenant.[3]

THE CREED OF CHALCEDON

After over a hundred years of fierce controversy, the ecumenical Council of Chalcedon (451) settled the doctrine of the person and the natures of our Lord Jesus Christ. The creed establishes that Jesus Christ is fully God (over against Arianism) and fully man (over against Apollinarianism), having two distinct natures (over against Eutychianism) in one divine person (over against Nestorianism). Although the Creed of Chalcedon is not mentioned in the Belgic Confession, the trinitarian and Christological truths proclaimed within are clearly echoed in the Reformed confessions and have been confessed by the universal church ever since.

We, then, following the holy fathers, all with one consent teach men to confess one and the same Son, our Lord Jesus Christ, the same perfect in Godhead and also perfect in manhood; truly God and truly man, of a rational soul and body; coessential with the Father according to the Godhead, and consubstantial with us according to the manhood; in all things like unto us, without sin; begotten before all ages of the Father according to the Godhead, and in these latter days, for us and for our salvation, born of the Virgin Mary, the mother of God [theotokos], according to the manhood; one and the same Christ, Son, Lord, Only-begotten, to be acknowledged in two natures, without confusion, without change, without division, without separation; the distinction of natures being by no means taken away by the union, but rather the property of each nature being preserved, and concurring in

---

3   The Heidelberg Catechism in Lord's Days 5 and 6 teaches why Christ must be both God and man. See *Confessions and Church Order*, 87–89.

one person and one subsistence, not parted or divided into two persons, but one and the same Son, and only begotten, God the Word, the Lord Jesus Christ; as the prophets from the beginning have declared concerning Him, and the Lord Jesus Christ Himself has taught us, and the creed of the holy fathers has handed down to us.[4]

THE MONOPHYSITE CONTROVERSY

While Chalcedon adopted the definitive statement concerning the truth, controversy continued for many years. These controversies produced only bitterness, barren theological speculation, and deeper division. In the years after Chalcedon, the followers of Eutyches became known as monophysites because they believed in "one nature." The church made many attempts to heal the breach. In 553, Emperor Justinian I called the fifth ecumenical council, the Second Council of Constantinople, for this very purpose. This council condemned the monophysites, who subsequently broke away from the rest of the church. Their teachings live on today in the Coptic Church of Egypt and the Jacobite Church of Syria.

It is neither profitable nor edifying to enter into the controversies that characterized the schismatic churches of the East that did not accept the decisions made at the Council of Chalcedon. The East lost sight of the fact that the doctrine of Christ is the salvation of the church. Many disagreements were rooted in abstract philosophizing and meaningless distinctions, for the mere purpose of displaying the learning of the theologians. In its speculative debates, the Eastern church forgot Athanasius's insistence that the doctrine of Christ is inseparable from the doctrine of salvation.

Other pressures on the church demanded a great deal of attention as well. The pressure of the barbarians finally resulted in the fall of the Western Roman Empire, and secular rule passed over to the barbarian chieftains. The emperors in the East managed to withstand these barbarian pressures on the eastern frontier, but they finally succumbed to Islamic conquests, which were the judgment of God on a church that had lost its theological and spiritual bearings.

---

4   Creed of Chalcedon, in *Confessions and Church Order*, 17.

IMPORTANCE OF THE CONTROVERSIES

While the Arian controversy brought the church to confess the truth of Christ's divinity, the decisions relating to the Christological controversies expressed the truths concerning the person and natures of Christ. The Creed of Chalcedon is the fullest expression of the truth concerning these questions. It has stood the test of time and remains the confession of the church today. Nor has the truth been developed beyond this expression of Chalcedon. Usually doctrines are developed over a period of years and continue to be developed throughout every age. But this doctrine is an exception to that. The church has never added to what Chalcedon stated as the truth.

There is good reason for this. The confession concerning Jesus Christ is the fundamental confession of the truth. It is the final dividing line between the true and false church. For "every spirit that confesseth not that Jesus Christ is come in the flesh is not of God, and this is that spirit of Antichrist" (1 John 4:3). On this confession is built the entire structure of the Christian faith. When Peter confessed that Jesus was the Christ, the Son of the living God, Christ answered that upon this rock (Peter's confession) he would build his church. Through Christ, God reveals himself as the God who saves his church. That this doctrine be established definitely and completely was essential for subsequent development of the truth.

Although the errors condemned by Chalcedon have appeared again in the church, they have never constituted a dire threat to the church's existence. They arise on the periphery of the church. They are the marks of a church that has become apostate.

Throughout these Christological controversies, it became apparent that the gates of hell cannot prevail against the church of Jesus Christ. Against all the opposition of Satan and wicked men, God gave the church an astonishing victory. Sometimes victory seemed impossible, and the wicked seemed to triumph. Sometimes victory was brought about by weakest means. But always the church emerged triumphant. God used the evils of heresy to establish the truth, and the church prevailed through the darkest hours. Christ gave this victory by the gift of the Spirit of truth who never forsakes the saints. "The foundation of God standeth sure" (2 Tim. 2:19).

THE ECUMENICAL COUNCILS OF THE EARLY CHURCH[5]

LOCATION	DATE	EMPEROR	KEY PARTICIPANTS	MAJOR OUTCOMES
NICAEA	325	Constantine	Arius Alexander Eusebius of Nicomedia Eusebius of Caesarea Hosius Athanasius	Declared Son *homoousios* (coequal, consubstantial, and coeternal) with Father. Condemned Arius. Drafted original form of Nicene Creed.
CONSTANTINOPLE	381	Theodosius I	Meletius Gregory of Nazianzus Gregory of Nyssa	Confirmed results of Council of Nicaea. Produced revised Nicene Creed. Ended Trinitarian controversy. Affirmed deity of Holy Spirit. Condemned Apollinarianism.
EPHESUS	431	Theodosius II	Cyril Nestorius	Declared Nestorianism heretical. Accepted by implication Alexandrian Christology. Condemned Pelagius.
CHALCEDON	451	Marcian	Leo I Dioscorus Eutyches	Declared Christ's two natures "unmixed, unchanged, undivided, inseparable." Condemned Eutychianism.
CONSTANTINOPLE	553	Justinian	Eutychius	Condemned "Three Chapters" to gain support of Monophysites. Affirmed Cyrillian interpretation of Chalcedon.

---

5 Chart taken from Walton, *Chronological and Background Charts*, chart 28.

CHAPTER 14:
THE WORSHIP OF THE IMPERIAL CHURCH

*And I John saw these things, and heard them. And when I had heard and seen, I fell
down to worship before the feet of the angel which shewed me these things. Then saith
he unto me, See thou do it not: for I am thy fellowservant, and of thy brethren the
prophets, and of them which keep the sayings of this book: worship God.*

—REVELATION 22:8–9

INTRODUCTION

As could be expected, the worship of the church changed substantially, though not
for the better, after Emperor Constantine legalized and favored Christianity in 313.

During the years of persecution, worship services had been simple. The church had possessed no elaborate and costly structures, and the buildings they had possessed before the Great Persecution were taken from them.

But as the temper of the times changed and persecution disappeared in the Roman Empire, the church enjoyed rapid growth under the benign rule of the emperors. The imperial church increased in wealth and popularity, and the worship services gradually lost their former simplicity and became increasingly liturgical, visually imposing, outwardly ceremonial, and even theatrical. Church buildings became large, costly, and elaborately furnished.

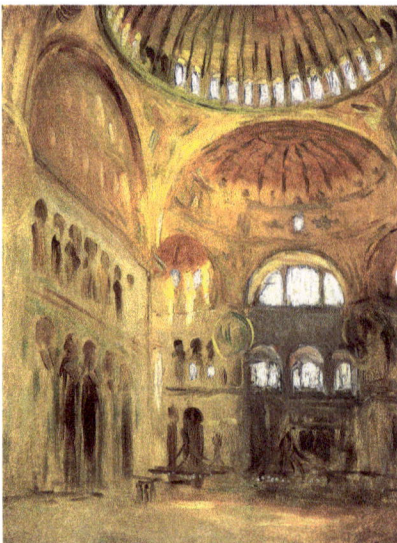
The interior of the Hagia Sophia

Liturgical vesture became rich and imposing. Worship services made greater appeal to the senses than to the inward worship of the heart. Although these changes took place over a long period of time and were more or less limited to different areas in the church, they became increasingly widespread as time wore on.

SUNDAY WORSHIP

Ever since the days of the apostles, the church had faithfully maintained the weekly worship of God on the Sabbath. Sunday was a holy day on which the church met for public worship, read the word of God, listened to the preaching, participated in the sacraments, prayed and sang together, collected alms for the poor, and enjoyed the fellowship of the saints. While the church continued these practices after Constantine, it introduced many new practices into the worship services on the sabbath day.

Although congregational singing was retained, special choirs and antiphonal singing (alternate singing by two choirs) became common. Although scripture reading was continued, fixed passages (called lectionaries) were read in the worship services and on Christian holidays. Although the basic elements of worship remained, heathen customs were introduced as concessions to the large numbers of "converts" from paganism.

With the rapid growth of the church, faithful Sabbath observance became a problem. Many considered the day to be a time of escape from the drudgery of work and an occasion for merriment. Constantine had declared Sunday to be a legal holiday and had passed laws concerning proper Sabbath observance. In 321, he prohibited manual labor, juridical transactions, and military exercises on the Sabbath. This general policy was strengthened by succeeding emperors. However, by 401, the Council of Carthage requested the emperors to prohibit public shows and special feast days on the Sabbath because the churches were empty and the people were busy with the worldly pursuit of pleasure.

PREACHING AND SACRAMENTS

During this period, preaching continued to be an integral part of the worship services. Although there was a gradual decline in some areas of the church as a reliance on liturgy became more common, preaching flourished in other areas of the church under the influence of such great pulpiteers as Gregory of Nazianzus (c. 330–90), Ambrose of Milan (c. 339–97), John Chrysostom (c. 349–407), and Augustine of Hippo (354–430).

THE "GOLDEN-MOUTHED" PREACHER

Preaching has always been the lifeblood of the church. From the preaching of the apostles in the early church to the pulpits of God's church today, preaching has always occupied a central and important place…

It is not amiss, therefore, to consider the greatest preacher of the ancient church, John Chrysostom. Not only has his name become synonymous with preaching, but the last part of his name, "Chrysostom," was given him because it means "golden-mouthed," and was indicative of the high respect granted him as a minister of the gospel…

For twelve years Chrysostom occupied the pulpit in the church of Antioch. It was his custom, as it has been in our own Reformed tradition, to preach series on a given book of the Bible or on one theme. Many of his sermons are still extant. He preached sixty-seven sermons on Genesis, ninety on Matthew, eighty-eight on John, thirty-two on Romans, seventy-four on I and II Corinthians, as well as series on other books. He preached not only on the Lord's day but also during the week, sometimes five days in succession. His auditorium was always packed with people, and sometimes the congregation, appreciative of his preaching, would break out in spontaneous applause—of which he severely reprimanded them.

One noteworthy incident demonstrates the power of Chrysostom's preaching. During the Lenten season of 387, the people of Antioch rioted over new taxes imposed upon them by the emperor Theodosius and burned a number of statues of the emperor and his family. Theodosius threatened to destroy the city in his anger and sent troops into the city to quell the rioting and judges to try the instigators. Chrysostom took the occasion to preach twenty sermons on the subject "On the Statutes" in which he reminded the people of their responsibilities to those whom God had put over them and reminded the emperor of the evils of undue cruelty. These sermons served to bring about a quietness in the city and an amnesty from the emperor. One writer of the time said of these sermons, "Though such a crowd had come together, the silence was as deep as though not a single person had been present." One is reminded of Luther's sermons which quelled the disorders in Wittenberg, brought on by the unruly Zwickau prophets.

Because of his great preaching powers, Chrysostom was appointed by the agent of the emperor to be minister in Constantinople. He had to be escorted out of Antioch by troops because of the great devotion of the people in whose midst he had labored for twelve years.

—Herman Hanko, *Portraits of Faithful Saints*, 34–37.

John Chrysostom

Little development took place during this period in the doctrine of the sacraments, but various practices were joined to both baptism and the Lord's supper. Baptism was generally conducted by immersion in the baptismal font and sometimes by pouring or sprinkling water over the head. The sacrament often included exorcism (the casting out of devils), breathing on the one baptized as a sign of the gift of the Holy Spirit, touching the ears as a sign of the power given through baptism to hear the gospel, using the sign of the cross on the forehead and breast, giving salt as an emblem of the word, anointing with oil, and changing of garments. The sacrament became a complicated and time-consuming ceremony.

Although the church practiced infant baptism, people frequently neglected baptism for themselves and their children. This was partly due to the mistaken notion that baptism washes away all sin committed before baptism, but also due to spiritual carelessness and indifference to spiritual things. However, in times of calamities and catastrophes, the churches were packed with people demanding baptism.

The celebration of the Lord's supper was, from the time of the apostles, an important part of the worship of the church. It was typically celebrated every Sunday. Already in the early church it was known as the *Eucharist*, by which the church meant a sacrifice of "thanksgiving."[1] But the superstitious and half-pagan mind of many in the church of this period could not distinguish between a sacrifice of thanksgiving and a sacrifice to God, such as our Lord made on the cross. This wrong idea was encouraged by the fact that the clergy who were of a lesser sort and under the rule of bishops were called priests, as they are today. Priests, after all, make sacrifices.

Thus the idea developed that the Lord's supper was an unbloody sacrifice that repeated the sacrifice Christ offered on the cross. The doctrine of transubstantiation was not developed and adopted until the Middle Ages, and so no one in the early church claimed that the bread and wine of the Lord's supper were actually changed into the body and blood of Christ. Yet some maintained that Christ's real body and real blood did come along with the bread and wine. This strongest view of the Lord's supper, sometimes called the "mystical view," taught that the sacrament created the relation between Christ and his church and made it real. This view was widely taught by most of the outstanding church fathers of the period, including Cyril of Jerusalem, Gregory of Nyssa, John Chrysostom, Hilary of Poitiers, Ambrose of Milan, Eusebius of Caesarea, Athanasius of Alexandria, Gregory Nazianzus, Basil of Caesarea, and Theodoret of Cyrus.

---

1   *Eucharist* comes from the Greek word *euchairstein* (to give thanks).

At the outset of the Middle Ages, Pope Gregory the Great (c. 540–604) declared that the Eucharist was an unbloody sacrifice offered by the priest. This sacrifice, he said, could be made for the living and for the dead. This erroneous doctrine led to masses for the dead, prayers for the dead, and eventually the doctrine of purgatory.

We must not suppose that all the liturgical corruption that was piled on the sacraments actually made the true worship of God impossible. Church history is something like our present-day media, which generally reports only the bad news, for the good news is normal and unnewsworthy. So it is in church history: the bad is underscored, and it is sometimes forgotten that God preserves his church. In many places, the gospel was preached and the sacraments were administered according to the command of Christ.

THE CHRISTIAN CALENDAR

The church set aside various dates as Christian holidays to commemorate important events in the life of Christ and leading events in the history of the church. But soon the annual Christian calendar became clogged with a multitude of festivals and feasts commemorating many different events. By the end of the fourth century, there were feasts for Mary, the apostles, various martyrs, saints, the see (bishopric) of St. Peter in Rome, Stephen, John the Baptist, Michael, Gabriel, and many others. Some of the feasts began as local events, but even such local feasts soon became customary throughout the empire. Under the influence of new converts, these feast days became occasions for parades, banqueting, and drunkenness.[2]

By the end of this period, the Christian calendar contained three cycles: the Christmas cycle, the Easter cycle, and the Pentecost cycle. The Christmas cycle, which included the celebration of Christ's birth on Christmas (December 25), was a Christian transformation of several pagan festivals. In addition to Christmas, the cycle included Advent (the four special Sundays prior to Christmas); Christmas vigils on Christmas Eve (December 24); St. Stephen's Day, which commemorated the earliest Christian martyr (December 26); the Feast of the Holy Innocents, which commemorated the slaughter of the children of Bethlehem by Herod the Great

---

2 Neander, *History of the Christian Religion*, has an interesting section on the relation between Christian and pagan festivals (2:311–12).

(December 28);[3] the observance of the circumcision and the naming of Christ eight days after Christmas; New Year's Day, which was formerly a pagan festival (January 1); and Epiphany, which celebrated the baptism of Christ and later the visit of the wise men from the East (January 6).[4]

The Easter cycle began on Ash Wednesday and included a six-week period of fasting, called Lent. The fasting came to a climax during Easter week, which included Palm Sunday (celebrating Christ's triumphal entry into Jerusalem), Maundy Thursday (celebrating the Last Supper), and Good Friday (celebrating Christ's death on the cross), during which services were often held in a graveyard. Easter Sunday (celebrating Christ's resurrection from the dead) was celebrated with an end of fasting, an all-night festival, and a week of celebration filled with festivities, various ceremonies, and the wearing of white robes by the newly baptized.

The Pentecost cycle extended from Easter to Pentecost. It was a period of rejoicing and banqueting in distinction from the period of fasting preceding Easter, and it soon degenerated into a time of wanton merrymaking. The cycle included Ascension Day (celebrating Christ's bodily ascension to heaven) and Pentecost, or Whitsunday (celebrating the outpouring of the Holy Spirit), and ended on the Sunday after Pentecost with the Feast of All Saints (celebrating the saints and martyrs) in the East and the Feast of the Holy Trinity (celebrating the doctrine of the Trinity) in the West.

Many of these feast days remain a part of Roman Catholicism to the present. They were a burden to the faithful, a destruction of the true worship of God, and a bold step in the direction of formal lip service, which God abhors. The situation in the church was almost worse than in Judah prior to the captivity. We must be thankful for the Reformation's deliverance from the bondage of Roman Catholic lip service in feasts and holy days.

---

3   It was called "the slaughter of the innocents" because of a misinterpretation of Herod's murder of the babies in Bethlehem. While the murder of these babies was a dreadful crime, it was also God's judgment on Bethlehem for rejecting Christ.

4   I well remember while going to college that our Roman Catholic neighbors would have a crèche on the mantel of their fireplace and three wise men some distance from the crèche. Each day between Christmas and what was called Epiphany, the wise men would be moved a little closer to the crèche until on January 6, they were at the side of the manger.

WORSHIP IN THE EARLY CHURCH[5]			
Observance	Time	Practice	Historical Notes
SABBATH	Weekly	Singing, scripture reading, exhortation, prayer, Communion.	Adapted from Jewish synagogue service. Moved to Sunday to commemorate Christ's resurrection. Sunday declared a legal holiday under Constantine.
EASTER	Annually	Observance of the death and resurrection of Christ. Easter preceded in early days by 40-hour fast to commemorate Christ's time in the tomb and identify with catechumens who were preparing for baptism.	First appears in the 2nd century. Quartodeciman Controversy (189) over date of observance—should it be on the day of the Jewish Passover, the 14th of Nisan—or the following Sunday? Finally observed on first Sunday after first full moon after vernal equinox. Symbols such as eggs and rabbits derived from pagan fertility rites after conversion of barbarian tribes.
LENT	Annually	Abstinence before Easter later expanded to 40-day partial fast and time of penitence.	First mentioned in writings of Council of Nicaea in 325. Also associated with the temptation of Christ in the wilderness.
ASCENSION	Annually	Observance of the ascension of Christ into heaven following his resurrection. Celebrated 40 days after Easter.	Observed on the sixth Thursday after Easter from the late 4th century. Often accompanied by processional to commemorate Christ's journey to the Mount of Olives.
PENTECOST	Annually	Observance of the coming of the Holy Spirit. Celebrated 50 days (seven weeks) after Easter. Along with Easter, popular time for baptisms.	First mentioned in the writings of the 4th century. Also known as Whitsunday.
CHRISTMAS	Annually	Observance of the birth of Christ. Accompanied by the giving of gifts.	Date or even time of year of Christ's birth unknown. Observance began in 4th century. Date of December 25th chosen to counter pagan Saturnalia observance of winter solstice. Armenian Church celebrates Christmas on January 6th.

---

5   Chart taken from Walton, *Chronological and Background Charts*, chart 12.

EPIPHANY	Annually	Observance of the baptism of Christ. Later associated with the visit of the magi.	Evidence for observance as early as the 3rd century. Celebrated on January 6th. Initially given more importance than Christmas in the East.
SAINTS' DAYS	Annually	Remembrance of the life, or more commonly death, of a significant member of the church.	Initially served as a way to remember the sacrifices of martyrs in the congregation. Later expanded to ascetics as well, with the end of the persecutions in the fourth century. (Martin of Tours, in the 5th century, was the first non-martyr to be recognized as a "saint.") Relics and pilgrimages associated with holy people and places became common after the Edict of Milan, spurred to a significant extent by Constantine's mother, Helena.

IDOLATROUS PRACTICES

During the age of the Christian Roman Empire, the pagan world of the empire and the barbarian tribes increasingly impacted the life of the church. As a result, idolatrous practices of every sort gradually crept into the church, including the worship of the virgin Mary, saints and martyrs, holy relics, and sacred images.

It is likely that the monks were primarily responsible for the introduction of the worship of Mary, the mother of Jesus. It appears that this abominable practice was introduced to placate converted pagans who worshiped female gods.[6]

In the earlier years of this period, Mary was honored because of the angel Gabriel's words to her, "Hail, thou that art highly favoured, the Lord is with thee: blessed art thou among women" (Luke 1:28). Before long, Mary was exalted beyond what scripture permits. In time, the honoring of Mary became Mariolatry (the worship of Mary). She was said to be the counterpart of Eve (as sin came through Eve, so salvation came through Mary); to have brought forth Christ in different ways than by normal conception and birth; and to have remained a sinless virgin all her life.

The worship of Mary began with the theologian and hymnwriter Ephraem Syrus (c. 306–373), but it blossomed during the Nestorian controversy, during which the orthodox applied the word *theotokos* ("mother of God") to Mary as a test of orthodoxy.

---

6 Schaff, *History of the Christian Church*, 3:411.

"Procession of the Holy Martyrs"

Churches were dedicated to her, images were made of her, and miracles were ascribed to her. Feast days were held for her too, including the Feast of the Annunciation on March 25, celebrating the angel Gabriel's announcement that she would be the mother of Jesus, and the Feast of the Assumption on August 15, celebrating Mary's supposed ascension into heaven without dying.

The curse of idolatry spread rapidly in the church. Evangelists, the deacon and martyr Stephen, the martyrs of the first three centuries, famous patriarchs, prophets, popular monks, theologians, and angels were also worshiped.

Added to the worship of people was the worship of relics. The bones of Ignatius in Antioch and the half-burnt bones of Polycarp in Smyrna were supposedly preserved and soon became objects of superstition and idolatrous worship. The same worship was given to bodies, bones, blood, ashes, and furniture of departed martyrs, to instruments of martyrdom, and to Jesus' coat and crown of thorns. The cross of Jesus, supposedly discovered in 326 by Helena, Constantine's mother, was a special relic that claimed the veneration of many. Miracles of healing were ascribed to relics, a practice justified by similar miracles wrought by the bones of Elisha, the coat of Jesus, and the shadow of Peter, as recorded in scripture. So much wood was claimed to be from the cross of Christ that the church was compelled to believe that the wood had miraculously multiplied like the bread and fish with which Jesus fed five thousand men in Galilee.

Gradually the worship of images came into practice as well. Many in the church condemned image worship as idolatrous and pagan; but it was widely condoned on the grounds that the poor and uneducated could better worship if visible objects were used. At first only symbols, such as a lamb, were constructed; but soon pictures and images of Jesus and the angels were brought into use for purposes of worship.

Attempting to justify the practice of image worship, the church made a distinction between *veneration* and *adoration* with the Greek words *douleia* and *latreia*. *Douleia* means "to venerate" and was to be given to Mary, saints, and images; while *latreia* means "adoration" and could be given to God alone. The people on the whole, however, could not understand these hair-splitting distinctions, with the result that the people worshiped objects, images, saints, angels, and relics even as they worshiped God.

These idolatrous practices lasted in the church until the time of the Reformation, and they remain common in both the Eastern and Western branches of the church.[7] Especially the Calvinistic Reformation sharply condemned these practices; the Heidelberg Catechism explicitly condemns the Roman Catholic justification for image worship.[8]

Rome called images "books for the laity," meaning that images help in worship by teaching illiterate people. God is invisible, and people find it easier to worship an invisible God when they have something visible in their hands to represent him. But "God is a spirit: and they that worship him must worship him in spirit and in truth" (John 4:24).

CONCLUSION

During the Nicene and Post-Nicene Period (313–590), the ceremonies of the church were gradually corrupted because many of them were derived directly from paganism and because the church was filled with hypocrites who do not love the worship of God. The imperial church, even in her liturgical usages, became worldly and pleasure-minded, and she adapted to the corruptions of paganism about her. Unfortunately, many of the doctrines that the church developed fully in the Middle Ages began in this period.

It is important to remember that in many parts of the church, the true worship of God was preserved. Through it all, God always preserves his church. Many bishops, church fathers, and conscientious laymen protested vehemently and, to some extent, successfully against the abuses. Beneath the layers of externalism, the true church possessed spiritual strength, as is evident from the sturdy battles fought and won at this time in defense of the faith.

---

7 I recall being in places of worship of the Western church and the Eastern church: St. Patrick's Cathedral in New York City and an Eastern Orthodox church on the island of Patmos. Both were crowded with images, pictures, icons, and relics. It was enough to make one sick.
8 Heidelberg Catechism Q&A 96–98, in *Confessions and Church Order*, 125–26.

CHAPTER 15:
THE BEGINNINGS OF MONASTICISM

*Now the Spirit speaketh expressly, that in the latter times some shall depart
from the faith, giving heed to seducing spirits, and doctrines of devils; speaking lies
in hypocrisy; having their conscience seared with a hot iron; forbidding to marry,
and commanding to abstain from meats, which God hath created to be received
with thanksgiving of them which believe and know the truth. For every creature
of God is good, and nothing to be refused, if it be received with thanksgiving:
for it is sanctified by the word of God and prayer.*

—1 Timothy 4:1–5

ANTHONY OF EGYPT

Around the beginning of the third century, some Christians began to live a solitary life. Leaving the cities and the fertile land that bordered the Nile River in Egypt for the vast wasteland on either side, these individuals lived in caves or other sheltered places and refused to move into the company of other people. They were the first Christian monks, the founders of the monastic movement. In time, monasteries in Egypt, Palestine, Asia Minor, Greece, Italy, Spain, and the rest of Europe would be filled with men and women who followed their example.

This lonely life in the desert became popular when one man from a wealthy family living in the Nile Delta decided to take literally Jesus' words to the rich young ruler: "If thou wilt be perfect, go and sell that thou hast, and give to the poor, and thou shalt have treasure in heaven: and come and follow me" (Matt. 19:21). This one man's name was Anthony.

Born around 251, Anthony was shy and retiring. He was never very learned, yet he memorized entire books of the Bible. As a young man, he lost his parents and was left to care for his sister. Taking the words of the Lord to the rich young ruler seriously, he provided for his sister's needs, gave away all his remaining possessions, and entered a life of seclusion in the desert. He ate only once a day; he slept on bare ground; he never combed or cut his hair, nor washed his hands and feet; and he spent his time struggling with temptation through prayer and meditation on the scriptures. Considered the holiest of men, Anthony was constantly visited by admirers who wanted to see him in his retreat. He came briefly out of his seclusion at the age of 100 to support the orthodox faith against Arianism. He died at the age of 105.

The Torment of Saint Anthony

Anthony made popular a solitary life apart from society. Living alone, he practiced extreme self-denial, a lifestyle sometimes called *asceticism* (from the Greek word *askesis,* which means "practice," "training," or "exercise"). One who severely denies himself is called an *ascetic.* Although asceticism began already in the age prior to Constantine, this lonely, rigid way of life attained popularity during the days of Anthony, when persecution ceased and the church was free from the threat of the emperor's sword.

THE ANCHORITES

Asceticism in the early church took two forms: *anchoritism* (solitary life) and *cenobitism* (communal life). Anthony was an anchorite. The solitary ascetic life he lived was called *anchoritism* (from the Greek word *anachoreo,* which means "to retire") and sometimes *eremitism* (from the Greek word *eremia,* which means "desert," from which we derive our English word *hermit*). The anchorites, or eremites (hermits), retired from society to practice a rigid and external separation from the whole of society's life. Anchorites found Egypt conducive to this way of life both because the climate was warm throughout the year and because large stretches of desert on each side of the Nile River made solitude possible.

This solitude was a protest against the formalism, worldliness, lack of genuine spirituality, and hypocrisy that increasingly characterized the church. For the ascetics, the way to escape the spiritual trap of carnality was to separate from all who

Anthony of Egypt
(c. 251–356)

As a young man, Anthony was moved when he heard from scripture the words of Jesus to the rich young ruler. Selling his possessions, he fled society for a harsh life as a hermit in the deserts of Egypt. Living alone in a tomb, fasting, and battling devils, wild beasts, and the temptations of the flesh, Anthony became a legendary hero for believers disillusioned by an increasingly carnal church. Scores of Christians followed his ascetic example. Before he died at the advanced age of 105, Anthony organized his followers into monastic communities. His popularity soared when his friend Athanasius wrote a glowing biography about him, called the *Life of Anthony*. Today, Anthony is remembered as the father of monasticism. To learn more, read "Anthony: Ascetic among Ascetics," chapter 4 of Herman Hanko's *Portraits of Faithful Saints*.

lived evil lives and from the things of the world that turned people away from spiritual realities.

Most church members considered such a life of self-sacrifice a spiritual ideal. The majority of people honored the ascetics as having attained a level of holiness that others could not attain. The anchorites also considered themselves to be closer to God, to be living in a way that was more pleasing to God than the normal way of living.

From the time of Anthony, anchoritism spread like wildfire in the lands south and east of the Mediterranean.

A few examples of these hermits, though admittedly extreme, indicate to what ends asceticism drove people. Paul the Simple prayed three hundred times a day, counting each prayer with pebbles, and probably concentrating more on moving the pebbles from one pile to another than on the contents of his prayers. Macarius ate once a week and slept standing and leaning on a staff; when he did lie down, it was for six months, at which time he lay naked in the desert, allowing gnats to attack him incessantly. Ptolemy lived in the desert alone for three years, drinking only dew collected in December and January. Many anchorites never washed, shaved, or combed. Others braved the elements almost naked, living on precipices and in caves.

One of the most memorable of the anchorites was Simeon Stylites (c. 390–459), who founded an ascetic movement in

Simeon Stylites

Syria known as the Stylites (pillar saints). Each of his followers decided to live atop a pillar on a small platform, on which they prayed, fasted, and ate the bits of food passed up to them with a rope and a pail. Simeon lived for thirty-six years on his pillar and kept increasing the pillar's height until it was over sixty feet above the ground. From the top of the platform he preached and exhorted the crowds that came to see him and to witness his alleged miracles. Simeon died at the age of sixty-nine and was hailed as a saint of extraordinary piety.[1]

MONASTICISM IN THE ANCIENT CHURCH[2]				
NAME	DATES	LOCATION	TYPE OF MONK	CONTRIBUTIONS
Anthony of Thebes	c. 251–356	Egypt	Anchorite	Initiated anchoritic practice as first hermit monk. Influenced many to practice monasticism. Encouraged martyrs during persecution of church in 311. Biography written by Athanasius.
Pachomius	c. 290–346	Egypt	Cenobite	Initiated cenobite practice by founding first monasteries. By his death, led nine cloisters for men, two for women.
Hilarion	c. 291–371	Palestine	Anchorite	Influenced by Anthony. First to bring anchorite practice to Palestine.
Basil the Great	c. 329–379	Cappadocia	Cenobite	Founded monastery in Pontus. Founded first Christian hospital for care of lepers. His monastic rule still used in Eastern church.
Macarius	d. c. 390	Egypt	Anchorite	Influenced by Anthony. Supervised group of hermits in Libyan desert.
Martin of Tours	c. 335–400	Gaul	Cenobite	Missionary to Franks. First to bring monasticism to the West. Served as bishop of Tours while living monastic life. First monk to be canonized.

---

1 Picture taken from https://www.flickr.com/photos/internetarchivebookimages/14763254291/, (accessed November 3, 2020).

2 Chart taken from Walton, *Chronological and Background Charts*, chart 29.

MONASTICISM IN THE ANCIENT CHURCH[2]

NAME	DATES	LOCATION	TYPE OF MONK	CONTRIBUTIONS
Jerome	c. 345–420	Syria Rome Bethlehem	Cenobite	Lived as an anchorite in Syria early in life. Encouraged asceticism in Rome. Founded monastery in a cave in Bethlehem, where he lived for 35 years while translating Vulgate.
Augustine of Hippo	354–430	North Africa	Cenobite	Converted under Ambrose in Milan after dissolute youth. Founded monasteries in North Africa as bishop of Hippo. Rule of St. Augustine influenced later ascetics.
John Cassian	c. 360–435	Gaul	Cenobite	Educated in monastery in Bethlehem. Founded monastery of St. Victor near Marseilles. Wrote in support of Semi-Pelagians.
Patrick	c. 389–461	Ireland	Cenobite	Born in Britain, taken as slave to Ireland, where he later returned as missionary, converted over 100,000 Irish. Founded monastery at Armagh. Irish monasteries provided many missionaries for conversion of barbarian tribes.
Simeon Stylites	c. 390–459	Syria	Anchorite	First of the pillar monks. Lived on a 50-foot pillar for the last 36 years of his life. Influenced many other stylites.
Cassiodorus	c. 477–570	Rome	Cenobite	Wealthy nobleman who founded monastery on his own estate. Introduced practice of copying manuscripts to monastic life.
Benedict of Nursia	c. 480–547	Monte Cassino	Cenobite	Began as a hermit in Subiaco. Founded monastery at Monte Cassino, which became first monastery of Benedictine Order. Wrote Benedictine Rule.

THE CENOBITES

A second form of asceticism is called *cenobitism*, which comes from the Greek words *koinos* (common) and *bios* (life). Cenobitism refers to a life of self-denial in the company of other people. It was a further development of asceticism in which a group of people lived together, bound by monastic rules.

In its earliest stages, the solitary ascetic life of the anchorites was called *monasticism* (from the Greek word *monachos*, which means "living alone"); and the one who lived a solitary life was called a *monk*. But as cenobitism became popular, the term *monasticism* came to include this communal life of monks as well. Cenobitism was the form of monasticism that became common throughout Europe and is still practiced today.

Pachomius (c. 290–346), the founder of cenobitism, was born from heathen parents and was converted at the age of twenty while serving as a Roman soldier in Thebes. In 313, he became a disciple of Anthony and an anchorite ascetic. Shortly after becoming a monk, Pachomius claimed that an angel visited him and commanded him to found a community of monks. This suited him, and he obeyed the command. At Tabennisi on the Nile River, Pachomius founded the very first Christian monastery. He drew up a set of written regulations, called a *rule*, for his cenobites. The monks were given fixed times for work and for prayer. By the end of his life, Pachomius had established an order of nine monasteries for men and two convents for women.

Many anchorites wanted to practice extreme self-denial but could not endure the solitary life and the rigors of the more fanatical ascetics. After all, God created man as a social creature. It was not good for Adam to be alone, and it is never good for any person to live alone. So these people desired a communal way in which to practice self-denial. In addition, while a hermit life in the open was possible in the warm climate of Egypt, the harsher climate of Europe made the anchorite life almost impossible. Cenobitism was more moderate than a life of loneliness out in the desert under the blazing sun and in waterless sands.

Although cenobitic asceticism had all the theological weaknesses of anchoritic asceticism, it also had a good side. Monasteries became centers of learning, of study, of the copying of scripture,[3] and of the care of the poor. Many monasteries were expected to be self-sufficient. They raised vegetables and tended cows and sheep. They made their own clothing from wool that they sheared and combed and from

---

3 The ancient texts of the holy scriptures were accurately preserved by the painstaking labor of many monks in many monasteries.

which they wove cloth. Some even engaged in weaving baskets and preparing other products to be sold outside the monastery.

Saint Catherine's Monastery at Mount Sinai

Some outstanding Christian men of the period lived in monasteries. In the East, the most outstanding cenobite was Basil of Caesarea (c. 329–79), one of the three Cappadocian Fathers who defended the Nicene Creed. He introduced monasticism into Cappadocia in Asia Minor after having studied the practice in Egypt. He encouraged and supported the growth of the communal ascetic life in many other areas. Basil was also influential in developing for the monasteries a corporate discipline, which involved much prayer, Bible reading, and studying of sacred writings, but which also emphasized manual labor in agricultural pursuits and the nursing of the sick. Basil is sometimes called the father of Eastern monasticism.

Jerome reading in the countryside

Athanasius (c. 296–373), the great defender of orthodoxy at the Council of Nicaea, was a friend of Anthony and introduced anchoritic monasticism into Western Europe during one of his many exiles. He was especially influential in this field because he wrote his *Life of Anthony*, a biography of the first notable ascetic. Martin of Tours (c. 335–400), the first to bring cenobitic monasticism to the West, was a leading figure in monasticism as well. He started a monastery in France and became a missionary to the barbarian Franks. Augustine of

Hippo (354–430), after his conversion, also lived as a cenobite and founded monastic communities in Thagaste and Hippo, where he taught prospective members of the clergy. Augustine wrote the first monastic rule of the West, which proved to be extremely influential.

Perhaps the most productive monk of the period was Jerome (c. 345–420). He was born in Stridon of Dalmatia and was raised a pagan. Wealthy and well-educated, he was converted and became an anchorite ascetic in Syria after sinning against the seventh commandment. He vowed from henceforth to read only the Bible. After becoming a presbyter in Rome, he traveled widely and became acquainted with the church throughout the empire. Jerome later became a cenobite and founded a monastery in Bethlehem in 386. His greatest achievement was a Latin translation of the Bible, which became known as the Vulgate. Jerome was a learned scholar but arrogant, harsh, intolerant, and passionate.

JEROME'S LATIN VULGATE

In 382, the bishop Damasus of Rome (c. 304–384) commissioned his secretary, the brilliant scholar and strict monk Jerome, to produce a reliable, standard Latin translation of the Bible. Over the next twenty-three years, Jerome exerted his scholarly mind and used his monastic retreat to produce a monumental translation called the Vulgate.

Jerome began his work in Rome and continued to work on the project over the next two decades, while living as a cenobite in Bethlehem. Translating from the Hebrew Old Testament and the Greek New Testament, Jerome worked with a team of translators to complete the task around 405. When it was finished, his Latin Bible became known as the Vulgate, which means *common*, because he put the scriptures into the common language of the people: Latin.

The translation contained all sixty-six books of sacred scripture along with a handful of books called the Apocrypha. These uninspired apocryphal books had been written in the four hundred years before Christ and were included in the Greek Septuagint. Although Jerome made it clear that he did not consider these books to be part of the canon of scripture, they were in time considered scripture by the church in the Middle Ages.

The Latin Vulgate became the most influential Bible translation in history. Its wide acceptance in the church helps to explain why Latin remained the language of the Western church, even after Latin fell out of common use. For a millennium, until the Renaissance and the Protestant Reformation, the Vulgate was the definitive Bible translation of the entire Western church. In the late four-teenth century, when the pre-reformer John Wycliffe translated the Bible into English for the first time, he worked from Jerome's Latin Vulgate. In 1455, the Vulgate was the first book to be printed by Johannes Gutenberg on his new printing press. In 1546, at the Council of Trent, the Roman Catholic Church declared the Vulgate to be the only authentic Latin translation of the Bible, a status it still maintains in that church today.

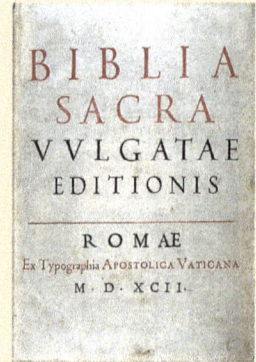

BIBLIA
SACRA
VVLGATAE
EDITIONIS

ROMAE
Ex Typographia Apostolica Vaticana
M · D · XCII.

The 1592 Vulgate

MONASTIC ORDERS

The rise of monastic orders (a group of monks living under a religious rule) belongs more to the medieval age than the ancient age. However, one order began in this period that was to determine the character of communal monasticism for many centuries: the Benedictine Order.

The order was founded by Benedict of Nursia (c. 480–547), who first lived as a hermit in a cave east of Rome, but in 529 founded a monastery on Monte Cassino in Italy.[4] Here Benedict wrote his famous *Rule* and led his monks effectively for the rest of his life. This was the beginning of the Benedictine Order. The monastery of Monte Cassino soon became the headquarters of a vast network of monasteries throughout Europe.

The Benedictine Order had rigid rules. The abbot (leader of the monks) was elected by the other monks. Although the monks made all internal decisions together, the decrees and orders of the abbot had to be strictly obeyed. Entrance into the monastery as a member could only be gained after one year of probation and, if the probation were successfully completed, by irrevocable vows of poverty, chastity, and obedience. All

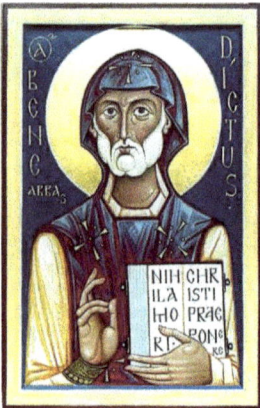

Benedict of Nursia

---

4 Those who are acquainted with the Italian campaign in World War II will recall that the Allies bombed this monastery because they were convinced that the Germans were using it to store ammunition and to shell Allied positions. The Allies were bitterly criticized for bombing this very famous and very old monastery, which was still in use.

the monks had to engage in spiritual exercises and manual labor. Four hours a day were devoted to prayer, seven hours to manual labor or the instruction of children from surrounding areas, and extra time had to be spent in reading. The monks might own no personal property, nor have any contact with the world outside the monastery, although they were required to do works of love.

Benedict's monastery at Monte Cassino and his *Rule* became an attractive model for monasteries throughout the West. The Benedictine Order was organized and practical, providing spiritual guidance for generations of monks until the present time. For this reason, Benedict is often called the father of Western monasticism.

As monastic orders developed throughout the ancient and medieval periods, monasteries held worldliness in check, showed hospitality to strangers and travelers, cared for the poor, educated future clergy, became schools for the education of children, and built libraries for the preservation of learning.

Benedict delivers his rule

The influence of these monasteries expanded rapidly. As a result, the monks in these orders came to occupy an ambiguous place in the growing hierarchy of the church. Although not considered members of the clergy, they occupied a sort of middle ground between the clergy and the laity. By the Middle Ages, they became a quasi-clergy who, although not ordained, could preach, administer the sacraments, and perform other ecclesiastical functions. More importantly, they became a kind of standing army for the popes to enforce their decisions.

BIBLICAL EVALUATION

Asceticism was spiritually dangerous. It encouraged superstition and idolatry, undermined the church institute, taught a meritorious two-level morality, disdained the body and rejected the good gifts of God, and promoted the error of world flight. The movement as a whole cannot stand the sharp scrutiny of scripture.

In its attempts to be holy, monasticism often became superstitious and idolatrous. It promoted demonology, angelology, Mariolatry, image worship, saint worship, relic worship, and the cluttering of the church calendar with endless feast days. It encouraged belief in miracles, visions, and dreams and in the appearances of angels, devils, and saints. In its most radical forms, it led to madness, despair, and suicide; and in some instances to licentiousness. In spite of all the good that monasteries accomplished, in the Middle Ages they often became cesspools of wickedness, and reform orders were repeatedly created because of monasteries' moral degeneracy.

To the extent that monks separated from the institutional life of the church, monasticism became a church within the church. It was an undermining of the communion of the saints and a derogation of the importance of the institute of the church of Christ. Already in this period, the monks attempted to be independent and used their independence to dictate to bishops. In 451, the Council of Chalcedon put them under the firm jurisdiction of bishops and would not allow them to challenge clerical prerogatives. Monasticism neglected the preaching of the word and the sacraments, means that God ordained for the exercise and strengthening of our faith. It had no room for the quiet and unnoticed works of charity and the care of the poor that are crucial to the welfare of the church. It was a self-centered exercise of religion when it professed to be the ultimate in piety.

The idea that the monk was especially holy led to another evil in the church, a two-level morality. The common people who went to work every day, married, had children, took care of their families, and lived a life of godliness in a wicked world were living on one level of morality, which no doubt was pleasing to God. But it was thought that the ascetic lived on a higher level of morality, more pleasing to God and therefore also meritorious with God. Thus crept into the church the whole idea of merit, which has had such an insidious influence on Roman Catholicism to this day. The notion of man's ability to merit with God prevented the medieval church from adopting pure Augustinianism, with its doctrine of sovereign grace. This idea of merit drove Martin Luther frantic in the monastery prior to his understanding of justification by faith alone, without any works. The allurement of being able to merit with God has coaxed multitudes to follow Rome.

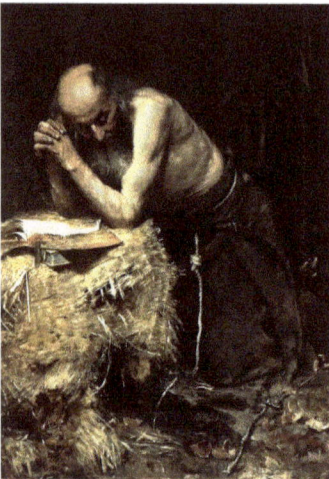

An anchorite

With this idea of a two-level morality also came the influence of gnostic thinking, which continued to plague the church. Gnosticism considered matter (the stuff of which this creation consists) to be inherently evil, or at least a powerful barrier toward the attainment of holiness. Ascetics believed that because matter was inherently evil, and because the body consisted of matter, one could attain a genuinely spiritual contemplative life by escaping not only from society, but from one's own body. The way to escape the body was to deny as much as possible the needs of the body and the comforts that the body enjoyed. Mystical contemplation and spiritual meditation were considered morally superior to active virtue. So the monks refused to treat the human body with respect, even though Christ died to save it.

In addition, world flight is not an option for the child of God. Holiness cannot be obtained by keeping the world outside the walls of the monastery, living in holy isolation, and claiming that one's activities in isolation are actually spiritual practices of value to God. Worldliness is repeatedly and sharply condemned by scripture, but so is world flight. Jesus prays for his saints to the Father, "I pray not that thou shouldest take them out of the world, but that thou shouldest keep them from the evil" (John 17:15). To seek holiness by world flight is to consider God's creatures to be in themselves sinful and to be shunned as dangerous to one's spiritual wellbeing. This is despising the good gifts God gives. Paul makes clear to Timothy, "Every creature of God is good, and nothing to be refused, if it be received with thanksgiving: for it is sanctified by the word of God and prayer" (1 Tim. 4:4–5).

Further, to crawl behind the walls of a monastery and seek holiness in a cold and dank cell is impossible. The enemies of the Christian soldier are the devil and the wicked world; but a third enemy, and the most dangerous, is our own depraved and corrupt nature. We cannot leave him behind when we enter the door of a monastery. He goes along wherever we go, and the battle against him continues no matter in what monastery we seek escape.

It is not holiness to pray four hours a day in a monastery. It is holiness to go to work every morning at six or seven o'clock, to marry, to love one's spouse and raise and teach a family, to wash the dirty dishes and mop the floors of the kitchen, and to be busy in the affairs of the church—when doing all these things to God's glory. There is no holiness in wearing a cowl and refusing to see other people. To teach covenantal children to lisp, "Bless this food, for Jesus' sake" is holier than to pray for many hours behind damp walls. To punch a time clock in a factory is more pleasing to God than to grow potatoes for one's fellow monks. God calls us to be in the world, but not be of the world. He calls us to seek the kingdom of heaven, not in isolation, but in working for the extension of Christ's kingdom and the holy gospel. To recognize the halo of holiness that sanctifies a covenantal mother's daily chores in the home and a father's daily work to support his family and Christian schools is to recognize a genuine holiness that is performed only by the power of grace earned in the cross of Jesus Christ.

CHAPTER 16: **THE DONATIST SCHISM**

*Another parable put he forth unto them, saying, The kingdom of heaven is likened
unto a man which sowed good seed in his field: but while men slept, his enemy came
and sowed tares among the wheat, and went his way. But when the blade was
sprung up, and brought forth fruit, then appeared the tares also. So the servants of the
householder came and said unto him, Sir, didst not thou sow good seed in thy field?
From whence then hath it tares? He said unto them, An enemy hath done this.
The servants said unto him, Wilt thou then that we go and gather them up?
But he said, Nay; lest while ye gather up the tares, ye root up also the wheat
with them. Let both grow together until the harvest: and in the time of harvest
I will say to the reapers, Gather ye together first the tares, and bind them
in bundles to burn them: but gather the wheat into my barn.*

—MATTHEW 13:24–30

THE ISSUE OF APOSTASY

The Donatist Schism in the fourth century was not the first schism that troubled
the ancient church, but it was the most important. Prior to it had been the Novatian
Schism in Rome (see chapter 9) and alongside it was the Meletian Schism in Egypt,
but the issues were basically the same as in the Donatist Schism. For over a century,
the Donatist Schism divided the church of North Africa into two warring parties
with radically different convictions about the purity of the church, the nature of the
sacraments, the exercise of church discipline, and the relationship of the church and
the state.

The Post-Apostolic Period that preceded the Edict of Milan (313) had been a
time of severe persecution by the pagan Roman Empire against the church of Jesus
Christ. At various times throughout this period, the empire had tested the loyalty of

the church. Christian citizens had been forced to choose between the worship of the emperor or torture and death. During the empire-wide Decian Persecution (250–51), the authorities required citizens throughout the empire to recite the words "Caesar is lord" and burn a pinch of incense before the emperor's image. Fifty years later, during the initial stages of the Diocletian Persecution (303–311), the authorities commanded the churches to turn over the sacred scriptures for burning. Would Christian bishops give their Bibles to the Roman soldiers, or would they face the dreadful consequences? Would Christians maintain that Jesus Christ is lord and die for their convictions?

Throughout these persecutions, many faithful saints had suffered terrible tortures before they died as *martyrs*. Under almost unbearable pain they had not denied their Lord. Others, known as *confessors*, survived their tortures and spent the rest of their lives with broken bodies for their refusal to deny their Savior. However, still others denied their faith and agreed to worship Caesar or the heathen gods. They were called the *lapsed* or the *apostates* because they had fallen from the faith. When the persecutions were over, they knocked on the door of the church, asking for readmittance. However, their request raised many questions, one of which was whether a mere confession of sin was sufficient for readmittance.

The martyrs in the catacombs

Many in those days believed apostasy to be a far more serious sin than others. Was it perhaps true that apostasy during persecution was a sin against the Holy Spirit and therefore the unforgivable sin (Matt. 12:31–32; Mark 3:28–29; Luke 12:10)? Or that, while the apostates who wanted to return could be forgiven in heaven, they had lost their right to be members of the church here on earth? Because they had left the church under the duress of persecution and wanted to return only when persecution eased, should they be allowed to return?

Further, because some of the lapsed were bishops who had proved themselves unfaithful, were the baptisms they had performed before leaving the church still valid? Did those who had been baptized by unfaithful bishops have to be rebaptized? In some instances, lapsed bishops who had left their churches and wanted to return were refused and started new churches. Were their baptisms in these new churches legitimate? Did those who had belonged to these new churches but now wanted to return have to be rebaptized? Some bishops had been faithful in persecution and then left the church to form new churches because they believed the church had erred in taking unfaithful members back upon confession. Were the baptisms of their bishops legitimate?

These questions demonstrated vividly that the church did not really agree on how to treat those who had apostatized during times of persecution. The question of how to treat apostates was basically a question of Christian discipline. The ancient church generally agreed that such sinners had to be disciplined and put out of the church, and that if they did repent, they could be restored in the way of confession. But there were other opinions, and these differences of opinion led to a number of schisms in the ancient church.

THE HISTORY OF THE SCHISM

The Donatist Schism began during the Diocletian Persecution (303–311). During this final and terrible empire-wide wave of Roman persecution, Christians were ordered to turn over to the government all sacred writings in their possession. The authorities

Emperor Constantine

then promptly burned these books. While some bishops refused to hand over the scriptures, others complied with the demand in order to avoid persecution.

Mensurius, the bishop of Carthage in North Africa, used a rather clever deceit to avoid both persecution and the loss of sacred books. Rather than give up his sacred writings, he hid them and instead turned over the heretical writings in his library to be burned. Mensurius was convinced that the pagans would not understand the difference between Christian and pagan writings, even if they happened to read them. He made this decision on the grounds that it is not the calling of believers actively to seek persecution. In fact, he condemned those who actively sought martyrdom.

But Mensurius's actions were instrumental in creating two parties in the North African church: one that thought his ruse acceptable and even clever, another that considered his actions as bad as denying outright his Lord and Savior. The party that would be known as the Donatists considered obedience to these orders from a wicked government to be a sin as great as apostasy. They called those who turned over religious books to the police *traditors*, or traitors; and they claimed that these *traditors* had apostatized and forever forfeited their rights to be church members.

The matter came to a head when Mensurius died in 311. The party that favored Mensurius's views elected his archdeacon Caecilian as the new bishop of Carthage. But the party that opposed Mensurius claimed that Caecilian's ordination was invalid because he had been ordained by a *traditor*. They elected their own bishop instead, a man by the name of Majorinus, who deposed Caecilian from office and was supported by no less than seventy Numidian bishops.[1] In 313, Majorinus was succeeded by Donatus, who ruled as the rival bishop in Carthage for about forty years and gave the Donatist Schism its name. Carthage now had two bishops and two churches: the Catholic church led by Caecilian and the Donatist church led by Donatus. The schism spread quickly throughout the rest of North Africa and beyond.

Many efforts were made to heal the breach. The Christian emperor Constantine ordered Miltiades, the bishop of Rome, to settle the dispute. Miltiades was more than happy to do so because his involvement in the schism could only enhance his claims to be the bishop of all bishops. But Miltiades failed in his efforts; although he decided against the schismatic Donatists at the Synod of Rome in 313, the Donatists paid no attention.

In spite of their abhorrence of governmental interference in ecclesiastical matters, the Donatists appealed to Constantine himself. In 314, Constantine summoned the Western bishops to the Synod of Arles in Gaul. Attended by delegates from Gaul, Sicily, Italy, North Africa, and Britain, the synod supported Caecilian and repudiated the claims of Donatus.

Still dissatisfied, the Donatists appealed to Constantine again. Deeply concerned about unity in the church, and perhaps convinced the Donatist fanatics were wrong, Constantine finally ruled against them in 316. Constantine authorized the use of force to suppress the Donatists, who were subsequently persecuted by local government authorities with the assistance of church leaders.

The Donatists stubbornly insisted that they were the only true church. They rejected the Catholic churches of the West and the East and considered all their ordinations and sacraments to be invalid and ineffectual. A fanatical group of Donatist peasants, called Circumcellions, even armed themselves with clubs and terrorized the Catholics of North Africa in the following years.

---

1   Numidia was an ancient country in North Africa, roughly comparable to today's Algeria.

Because the Donatists became even more fanatical, an exasperated Constantine issued an edict of toleration in 321. However, this edict was later overruled by Emperor Constans I, one of Constantine's sons, and Donatus was banished. The persecution of the Donatists continued off and on throughout the fourth century.

EVALUATION OF THE SCHISM

What particularly attracts the Reformed believer to this chapter of ancient church history is the involvement of Augustine of Hippo (354–430). In 395, Augustine became the bishop of Hippo in North Africa at a time when many Donatists lived in and around the city. Augustine was at first convinced that the Donatists could be wooed back into the church by careful argumentation, and he tried to prove to them from scripture and tradition that they were wrong. In many books and in public debate, Augustine made strenuous efforts to bring them back to the fellowship of the church.

His efforts did not work. The Donatists were hard to persuade. Augustine eventually recommended the use of force to bring them back into the church. To justify the use of force, Augustine appealed to Luke 14:23, where the Lord commands his servants to go into the byways to bring guests to his wedding supper. The servants are commanded to "compel them to come in." It was a remarkable bit of poor exegesis on the part of this great church father. The medieval church would later use this exegesis to justify the atrocities of the Inquisition against those it deemed a threat.

In 411, the Synod of Carthage met at the request of Emperor Honorius (r. 395–423) to bring the century-long Donatist Schism to an end. Augustine played a crucial role at this synod, which condemned Donatism yet again. Donatists were fined and banished, and they lost their churches and their right to worship. In the following years, the Donatist sect was gradually weakened through state suppression, internal dissension, and the barbarian invasions.

Augustine debates the Donatists

In connection with the controversy with the Donatists, Augustine developed his views of the church. Along with some earlier church fathers, such as Cyprian of Carthage (c. 200–258), Augustine believed that there is one universal church institute. Augustine believed that the Catholic church of his day was that church; and outside it there was no salvation. He taught correctly that the validity of the sacraments does not depend upon the holiness and worthiness of the ministers who administer them; but he erred in teaching that only the sacraments of the Catholic church have efficacy. The Romish church of later years would lean heavily on Augustine's doctrine of the church.

But Augustine also made an important distinction between the visible church (the institution) and the invisible church (the body of Christ). As an institution, the church has a visible form; possesses a constitution that defines its purpose, work, and goals; has officers; and has a membership roll. As the body of Christ, the church is made up of an invisible number of elect known only to God. Indeed, scripture and the Reformed confessions speak highly of the institute of the church, calling it the mother of believers and insisting on the utter urgency and necessity of having membership in it.[2] But the scriptures also teach that the church institute manifests the church as the body of Christ. The church as the body of Christ is the full number of the elect, chosen eternally by God and united to Christ by faith. Sadly, this truth was lost by the church of the Middle Ages and not recovered until the time of John Wycliffe (c. 1330–84), after which it became a part of Reformational theology.

Furthermore, Augustine disagreed with the Donatists on the matter of the holiness

Augustine of Hippo
(354–430)

Raised in Thagaste, North Africa, by his godly mother, Monica, Augustine spurned the Christian faith for earthly pleasures. At school in Carthage, he lived with a mistress, fathered a son out of wedlock, and joined a gnostic sect called the Manichaeans. His brilliance and ambition eventually brought him to Milan, Italy, as a famous teacher of rhetoric; but it was here, under the preaching of Ambrose of Milan, that God converted him. A changed man, Augustine moved back to Thagaste to live as a monk. Reluctantly, he became a priest and then the bishop of Hippo Regius, North Africa, where he served for the last thirty-five years of his life. Augustine wrote voluminously, producing *Confessions* and *The City of God*, two of the most important books in Christian history. He skillfully defended the faith against the gnostic Manichaeans, the schismatic Donatists, and the heretical Pelagians. Above all, he championed the beautiful doctrine of sovereign grace. Augustine died in Hippo reciting the psalms as the barbarian Vandals besieged the city. To learn more, read "Augustine: Theologian of Sovereign Grace," chapter 7 of Herman Hanko's *Portraits of Faithful Saints*.

---

2 Belgic Confession 28–29, in *Confessions and Church Order*, 60–64.

and purity of the church. The Donatists had an idealistic conception of the church. They blamed Constantine, who had brought about a union between church and state, for the presence of wicked and righteous, unbelievers and believers, unholy and holy in the same church. They considered the church on earth to be holy in an absolute sense. In fact, the Donatists wanted a pure church, a church composed only of true believers. In keeping with this, they did not receive apostates back into their fold, they maintained the strictest discipline, and they insisted that salvation was only found within their communion.

Others throughout history have maintained the idea of a pure church. The Novatianists at the time of the Decian Persecution wanted a pure church; the Anabaptists who would not join the Reformation churches were of this mind; and this idea persists in Baptist thinking.[3] In fact, some claim that the history of the Baptist church can be traced through the Donatists back to the Apostolic Period.[4]

However, Augustine disagreed with the idea of a pure church. He maintained that until the end of the world, the church on earth will always be made up of believers and unbelievers. He appealed to the parable of the wheat and the tares. Here the Lord reminds the church that it is not God's will to have a pure church, one composed of only believers, in this world. Both the wheat and the tares must grow together until the harvest. Christ's instituted church is composed not only of believers, but also of unbelievers who outwardly profess faith but do not possess a true faith in Christ (Matt. 13:24–30, 36–43, 47–52).

Tares are always present in the wheat field. Tares are sometimes born in covenantal lines as the children of believers, and tares sometimes enter the church from outside under false colors and for reasons other than firm belief of the truth.

Their presence does not mean that the church of which they are a part is lacking in discipline. For, as Jesus points out, tares and wheat look alike until they ripen. Those who are not true believers are hypocrites who mask their unbelieving hearts. When and if they manifest themselves to be unbelievers, they rightly become the objects of discipline.

The warning for the church is that it must not judge who are tares and who are wheat. God will take care of that. It is the calling of the church to forgive sins, no matter how great, and to bring repentant sinners back into the church; but never to judge the heart, unless it be with the judgment of love.

---

3   See David Kingdon, *Children of Abraham: A Reformed Baptist View of Baptism, the Covenant, and Children* (Foxton, England: Carey Publications Ltd., 1975), 59–60.

4   Cushing Biggs Hassell and Sylvester Hassell, *History of the Church of God: From the Creation to A. D. 1885* (New York: Gilbert Beebe's Sons Publishers, 1886), 389.

CHAPTER 17: **THE PELAGIAN CONTROVERSY**

For by grace are ye saved through faith; and that not of yourselves:
it is the gift of God.

—Ephesians 2:8

THE HOTTEST BATTLE IN HISTORY

It was necessary in the wisdom of Almighty God that the trinitarian and Christological controversies took place before the Pelagian controversy. The biblical doctrines of the Trinity and of our Lord are the foundation of the church. The Pelagian controversy dealt with a different problem: the extent of sinful man's depravity and what was necessary for him to be saved.[1]

The correct understanding of the doctrines of God and of Christ are necessary for a biblical understanding of the doctrines of man and of salvation. To develop the biblical doctrines of man and salvation without first establishing the truths of God and his Christ would be the same as trying to build a house on sandy soil and without a foundation.

The opposite also holds true. If the church goes astray in the doctrines of man and his salvation, it will soon go astray in the doctrines of God and of Christ. To put it bluntly: if a man denies total depravity and sovereign grace, as the heretic Pelagius did, he will soon deny Christ's divinity and the Trinity.

From the time of Augustine to the present, the church's hottest battles have been fought over the doctrines of man's depravity and of salvation by sovereign and

---

1   In Reformed dogmatics these doctrines are given specific names. The doctrines of God and Christ are, respectively, theology and Christology. The doctrines of man and salvation are called anthropology and soteriology.

irresistible grace. The issue of sovereign grace was the great issue in the battle of Pelagius versus Augustine (fifth century), Rome versus Gottschalk (ninth century), the pope versus Luther and Calvin (sixteenth century), the Arminians versus the Synod of Dordrecht (seventeenth century), and the Christian Reformed Church with its doctrine of common grace versus the Protestant Reformed Churches (twentieth century). The battle for sovereign grace that began against the Pelagians is still going on today.

EARLY DEVELOPMENTS

Prior to the fifth century, the church had not paid much attention to the questions that Pelagius would raise. In general, the church taught that salvation was by grace alone and only on the basis of the suffering and death of Christ on the cross. The difficulty was that, especially in the East, the church also held to the doctrine of the freedom of man's will. That is, the church taught that although man is depraved, he is not so bad that he cannot still make a choice for good or evil, on which choice his salvation depends.

Bear in mind that because the church had not thought the matter through, it considered the doctrine of the free will of man important as a defense against the heresies of gnosticism and Manicheanism, which both taught the terrible error of fatalism. Fatalism teaches that man is nothing but a chip of wood, riding the tossing waves of the sea, over which he has no control, and going where he does not know. The early church thought it necessary to insist that man has some control over where he is going and what happens to him along the way to his destination.

The early church also had been concentrating on defending the truth concerning our Lord Jesus Christ. In the preoccupation with questions concerning the person and natures of Christ, the early church gave little thought to the question of how salvation in the cross of Christ alone stands connected to the doctrine of man's free will.[2]

Nevertheless, a few early theologians in the West saw the problem. Tertullian of Carthage (c. 160–225), the great theologian and apologist who had much influence on the development of biblical truth in the trinitarian and Christological controversies,

---

2 Augustine brought up this very question and answered it. All those who defend the doctrine of the free will of men must face the question of the relation between Christ's work and man's depravity. Today those who want to hold both the truth of salvation by grace alone and the doctrine of free will shrug off the question by saying that it is an apparent contradiction that we cannot solve.

taught the doctrine of original sin—in the sense of inherited sin from one's parents all the way back to Adam. Hilary of Poitier (c. 291–371), "the Hammer of the Arians" and "the Athanasius of the West" who attacked Arianism fiercely in his defense of the truth, taught that all men sinned in Adam when Adam ate of the forbidden tree. Ambrose of Milan (c. 339–97), the powerful preacher who humbled Emperor Theodosius and was used for the conversion of Augustine, taught the sovereignty of grace as the fountain of all goodness in man. Yet each of these theologians, to one extent

Hilary of Poitier

or another, left room for man to exercise his free will in the choice of good or evil.

It would be left to another theologian of the West to develop the truth of sovereign grace more fully. That theologian was Augustine.

AUGUSTINE OF HIPPO

Augustine of Hippo (354–430) was, without doubt, the greatest theologian of the ancient period. He was born on November 13, 354, in the province of Numidia, North Africa, in the town of Thagaste, from an unbelieving father named Patricius and a devout and pious mother named Monica. The Lord led Augustine through a time of youth and early manhood that prepared him for his life's calling.

Though Augustine was a brilliant student, he lived a wicked and immoral life until the time of his conversion in 386. At school in Carthage, he took a mistress and fathered an illegitimate son named Adeodatus. He also dipped into and tasted the waters of pagan philosophy. He was first a classicist, that is, one who reveled in pagan classical writings; then he dabbled in Manicheanism, an early gnostic sect; and then in skepticism, which claimed that knowledge is not possible. He flitted from one school of thought to another as a bumblebee flits from one flower to another in search of nectar.

Manicheanism especially appealed to him. The founder of the movement was a teacher named Mani (c. 216–74), whose Persian parents raised him near Babylon in an area where Eastern Orientalism and Western Christianity met. Mani was influenced by Zoroastrianism (a pagan mystical religion from the Orient), gnosticism, and Christianity. He claimed Zoroaster, Buddha, and Jesus as his spiritual ancestors. He taught that the history of the world is characterized by a massive and vicious struggle between Good (the spiritual world) and Evil (the material world), with the outcome uncertain. Mani gained a wide following and his views spread all the way to the Western church. Although he died a natural death, his followers claimed that he was crucified, in conscious imitation of Jesus' death.

Augustine was a Manichean for nine years and only gradually freed himself from its chains. He experienced a dreadful spiritual struggle in his life. Evil tugged irresistibly at him and pulled him in the direction of lust. That which was morally good seemed to him to be only an inward awareness and vague knowledge that in some sense good was preferable. Even when the Holy Spirit began his work in Augustine's heart, the great obstacle to a godly life was his burning desire to satisfy the lusts of his flesh in spite of his new knowledge that holiness was pleasing to God.

After teaching in his hometown for a bit, Augustine moved to Rome and then to Milan, where he acquired a position teaching rhetoric. There he met Ambrose, the bishop in Milan, a man noted for his rhetorical ability. Led by God's providence to learn more about rhetoric, Augustine went to hear Ambrose preach. God used his attention to Ambrose's sermons to stir in Augustine the beginnings of a new spiritual life.

Still he struggled, until his conversion in a garden, when he heard a child's voice singing *"tolle lege, tolle lege"* (take up and read, take up and read). Interpreting the voice as a command, Augustine took up a Bible lying on the table and read. The verses upon which the Bible opened were: "Let us walk honestly, as in the day; not in rioting and drunkenness, not in chambering and wantonness, not in strife and envying. But put ye on the Lord Jesus Christ, and make not provision for the flesh, to fulfill the lusts thereof" (Rom. 13:13–14). From that point on, Augustine was a different man. The Holy Spirit conquered his lustful flesh by an irresistible work of grace.

Ambrose of Milan

Over the years of his spiritual wandering, his acquaintance with pagan philosophy taught him the futility of human thought. His dabbling in Manicheanism showed him that the fatalism taught by this sect did not necessarily imply that man had to have a free will, a view held by most in the church. His deliverance from an immoral life, which he had so much difficulty resisting, was to Augustine a testimony to the power of grace and the inability of man to do anything to save himself. As God used the apostle Paul's early life of rebellion against Christ to prepare him to be a missionary to the Gentiles, so God used Augustine's sinful life to lead him to the doctrines of sovereign grace. Other men whom God appointed as stirring leaders in the battle to defend sovereign grace, he similarly prepared. It was in the monastery, as Martin Luther struggled to come to peace with God by his own works, that he learned the truth that smashed the citadel of Roman Catholicism: justification is by faith alone, without the works of the law.

After his conversion, Augustine was baptized with his son, Adeodatus, by Ambrose of Milan. He soon left Milan to return to North Africa. His overjoyed mother, Monica, who had followed him to Italy, set out to travel with him.

The baptism of Augustine

Church historian Philip Schaff calls Monica "one of the noblest women in the history of Christianity."[3] She was married to an unbeliever and considered it her obligation before God to pray without him for her wandering son. So anguished were her prayers for his conversion that Augustine became known as the "son of my tears." She lived long enough to see her prayers answered. Monica died in Ostia, at the mouth of the Tiber River, in the arms of her son. Their last conversation is described by Schaff as "a glorious conversation that soared above the confines of space and time, and was a foretaste of the eternal Sabbath-rest of the saints."[4]

Shortly after his return to North Africa, Augustine was, against his own desire, ordained a presbyter and later a bishop in the church of Hippo, North Africa. Here he spent the rest of

Augustine and Monica

his life. He established a monastery in Hippo to train prospective ministers of the gospel, and he pastored his large congregation as a prolific writer, ardent defender of the faith, and faithful man of God in the service of the church. Augustine died in Hippo when the barbarian Vandals were knocking on the gates of the city.

The major works for which Augustine is best known are his *Confessions*, a powerful and moving doxology of praise to God for rescuing him from his sin; *The Enchiridion*, a dogmatics; *The Trinity*, the clearest exposition of this doctrine prior to the writings of John Calvin; and *The City of God*, a masterful philosophy of history based on scripture and demonstrating the eternal divide of the city of the world and the city of God. The book was prompted by the fall of Rome in 410 and the stream of refugees that poured into Hippo and the surrounding areas. In addition to these books, Augustine's many anti-Pelagian writings developed his convictions regarding the absolute sovereignty of God in the work of salvation.

3 Schaff, *History of the Christian Church*, 3:990.
4 Schaff, *History of the Christian Church*, 3:991.

During his lifetime, Augustine engaged in several theological battles. He battled first with the Manicheans, whose wicked philosophy had been such a danger to his soul that, after his conversion, he wrote a book against the heresy to warn people of its attractiveness.

Augustine also battled the Donatists, the sect that believed that the pure church was composed only of true believers (see chapter 16). He wrote several books against the Donatists and developed his doctrine of the church.

But Augustine's greatest battle was with the Pelagians and the semi-Pelagians.

THE PELAGIAN CONTROVERSY

Pelagius (c. 354–420) was born in Britain or Ireland, where he became a monk at an early age. He moved to Rome about 400 and was known as a pious and learned man. During the next ten years, he began to teach his views and gained an important disciple, a former lawyer by the name of Celestius, who also became the chief propagator and the intellectual defender of what later became known as Pelagianism.

Pelagius and Celestius denied original sin and taught that Adam's fall did not affect the rest of humanity. Man, they believed, is born good and capable of meriting salvation apart from the sovereign grace of God. They insisted that Christ did not come to die on the cross for the sins of his elect people, but to give humanity an excellent example of righteous living.

Around 410, Pelagius and Celestius left Rome for North Africa, where they continued to spread their views. But Celestius made a mistake when he tried to become a presbyter in Carthage under bishop Aurelius. Upon examination, he was charged with teaching heretical views, which he would not retract. The Synod of Carthage condemned and excommunicated him in 412. Both he and Pelagius fled to the East, where they found the church much more sympathetic to their views. Pelagius traveled to Palestine and Celestius to Asia Minor, where he became a presbyter in the church of Ephesus.

However, the decisions of the Synod of Carthage soon became known in the Eastern church. Pelagius was the first one to get into trouble. He was opposed by Jerome (c. 345–420), who was also in Palestine at this time, and by Paulus Orosius (c. 375–418), a Spanish theologian and historian, who brought charges against Pelagius to the Synod of Jerusalem in 415. Pelagius was exonerated and escaped condemnation

PELAGIVS

Accurst Pelagius with what false pretence
Durst thou excuse Mans foule Concupiscence:
Or sow slowen [?] Origieall, or that
The Loue of God did Man predestinate.

Pelagius

chiefly because he repudiated Celestius, equivocated in his views, and insisted that he believed that the help of divine grace was necessary to do good. It seems that as long as Pelagius was willing to say the word "grace," he found supporters among the theologians of the Eastern church, which had long held the doctrine of the free will of man.

As the controversy developed in the Western church, a settlement seemed beyond reach. African synods in Carthage and Mileve, both held in 416, condemned Pelagius *in absentia* and asked the bishop of Rome, Innocent I (r. 401–417), to confirm their decisions. The strong-willed Innocent was more than willing to do this. He excommunicated Pelagius and Celestius and took the opportunity to commend the African bishops for recognizing the superiority of the Roman bishop, something they never intended to do.

When Innocent died in 417, the tyrannical Zosimus took his place as bishop of Rome. Pelagius and Celestius persuaded Zosimus to declare them orthodox. Zosimus even reprimanded the African bishops for condemning Pelagius and Celestius—a veiled threat that they had better change their decisions. But, faced with the anger of the African bishops, Zosimus changed his mind and decided after all to condemn Pelagius—a change of mind that makes mockery of claims to papal infallibility in matters of doctrine.

The Synod of Carthage in 418 again condemned the position of Pelagius and informed Zosimus that they repudiated his approval of Pelagius and would not support it. The decision of Carthage, which condemned Pelagius, was confirmed by the Emperor Honorius and by most of the Italian bishops. The few who disagreed fled to the East.

The final condemnation of Pelagianism took place at the ecumenical Council of Ephesus in 431, a year after the death of Augustine, who had battled the heresy valiantly and for nearly two decades. The Council of Ephesus lumped together the errors of Nestorius and Pelagius and condemned them both. The Council of Ephesus also read and approved the actions of the Western churches in their condemnation of Pelagius. However, these repeated condemnations of Pelagianism were not the end of the matter. In fact, Pelagianism eventually won.

The unexpected triumph of Pelagianism was due to several factors. First, the bishops who condemned Pelagius failed to make positive statements of the truth against the heresy of Pelagianism. Second, the church was saddled with the error of monasticism and its teaching that man is able to merit with God by doing good. But the idea of merit and the doctrine of sovereign grace cannot be harmonized. Third, a

Pelagius (c. 354–420) and Celestius (d. c. 431)

Pelagius was a British monk who rejected the doctrines of original sin and sovereign grace and taught instead that man has a free will, a natural capacity for good, and an ability to live in sinless perfection. He traveled first to Rome, where he gained a following; then to North Africa, where he was opposed by Augustine; and finally to Palestine, where he was opposed by Jerome. The chief disciple of Pelagius was a Roman lawyer named Celestius. Having traveled with Pelagius from Rome to North Africa, Celestius tirelessly promoted Pelagianism and tried unsuccessfully to be ordained in Carthage before moving to Asia Minor. The teachings of Pelagius and Celestius were condemned at a number of synods throughout the church and finally at the ecumenical Council of Ephesus in 431. To learn more, read "Pelagius and Celestius: Enemies of the Doctrines of Grace," chapter 8 of Herman Hanko's *Contending for the Faith*.

modification of Pelagianism arose, called semi-Pelagianism, which was a persuasive attempt to merge Pelagianism with Augustine's teachings. The Western church of the Middle Ages would eventually adopt this compromise. In the Pelagian controversy, the battle was won, but the war was lost.

THE ISSUE OF SOVEREIGN GRACE

The battle lines were drawn in the Pelagian controversy. The war in defense of the truth of sovereign and particular grace has been fought along these lines to the present day.[5]

Pelagius and his friend Celestius had an exaggerated view of man's goodness. Even though both believed the scriptural narrative of the fall of Adam and Eve in paradise, they insisted that the fall did not have a damaging effect on human nature. Nor did the fall of Adam and Eve have any moral effect on the world's population, all of which came from Adam and Eve. Every baby is born with a nature that is neither good nor bad, though capable of doing good or bad. What a child does in life depends primarily on the examples of the conduct of others. One can easily follow the examples of good people and remain good, or one can follow the examples of bad people and sin. Sin can become habitual, if committed often enough, and the habit of a given sin may become so strong that it requires considerable effort to break the habit.

Pelagius and Celestius believed that perfection was possible in this life and that scripture contains examples of people who never sinned. Because sin is no more than an imitation of a bad deed, sinful man has no need of a Savior either. They taught that Christ was a good man who never sinned, nor did he die for the sins of others. He did

---

5   For a detailed study of the doctrinal issues involved, see Hanko, *Contending for the Faith*, 63–81.

not represent anyone in his death; he did not make atonement for sin; he did not earn salvation by his death and resurrection; and he was only one of many who did good and whose example we ought to follow.

Hence, they taught that our salvation is not necessarily in Christ, but in our own free will and in our own innate ability to break bad habits and follow good examples. Grace is not necessary for salvation, but one can be and often is saved merely by keeping the law. God gives grace to people sometimes, but only when they ask for it and then only as a help.

These ideas showed how superficial and shallow Pelagius and Celestius were in their conception of sin. Augustine, who had struggled with the dreadful power of sin in his own life, knew that Pelagius lived in an ethical dream world far removed from reality.

Augustine, taking his starting point from scripture, understood that deliverance from sin came only by the grace of God. God's grace was not a shot of penicillin to help one on the road to recovery, but grace was God's unmerited favor and his divine power to deliver from the dreadful power of sin. Augustine had experienced this grace of God, which is irresistible in its power and able to accomplish for a man what he cannot do himself in delivering him from the bondage of licentiousness.

Augustine of Hippo

Grace was necessary because when Adam sinned, he died, as God said he would. He died spiritually and physically. The death of his body was the door to hell. His spiritual death included his total depravity, from which he could not deliver himself, nor even desire to escape death. His will was also dead. He could will only to sin.

Adam's sin affected the whole human race. The guilt of Adam's sin came upon everyone born from Adam and Eve, and the corruption of a totally depraved nature was passed on from parents to children. Humans are so completely incapable of doing any good that only divine grace could save us.

But God gives that grace because Jesus Christ, who himself was without sin and is the eternal Son of God, died for sin, paid the price of hell, and earned the grace that saves.

Is everyone saved? Augustine said that the reason why not everyone is saved is that Christ did not die for everyone. In fact, Christ died for only certain people, the elect, according to God's own plan. Here Augustine saw the biblical teaching of election and reprobation, and he saw clearly that scripture teaches that God himself determined and executes salvation.[6] Augustine was the first to develop clearly the doctrines of sovereign and particular grace.

AUGUSTINE AND CALVINISM

Augustine emphatically taught everything concerning the doctrines of grace that Calvinists hold dear today. He believed in sovereign predestination—election and reprobation. He believed that Adam's fall brought both the guilt of sin and the corruption of sin on the whole human race. The result of the fall was the total depravity of man, so that Adam's descendants are unable to do any good.

Christ died on the cross only for the elect. By his death Christ earned grace for the elect and for them only. Grace is sovereignly given and bestowed only on God's elect. Grace provides the power for all the good that the people of God do. The elect are preserved throughout all their lives and brought faithfully to glory. In short, Augustine held to what are now called the five points of Calvinism.

—Herman Hanko, *Contending for the Faith*, 69.

THE SEMI-PELAGIAN CONTROVERSY

Pelagius's views were so naïve regarding sin and so distant from what scripture teaches that even the Eastern church, with its view of the free will of man, did not swallow them. A certain modification arose as a result, which, though closer to Augustine's teachings than to those of Pelagius, was still not biblical. Some have called this view *semi-Augustinianism*, but the better (and more accurate) name is *semi-Pelagianism*. It is, after all, still based on the fundamental error of Pelagius, who taught the free will of man, and not on the theology of Augustine, who taught salvation by grace alone.

---

6   In an unpublished paper entitled "Double Predestination: Augustine, the Synod of Orange, and Gotteschalk, A Historical Analysis," written for a master's degree, I demonstrated, contrary to the opinion of many church historians, that Augustine taught what has become known as double predestination.

POSITION	MAJOR PROPONENTS	SUMMARY
PELAGIANISM	Pelagius Julian of Eclanum Celestius	Man is born essentially good and capable of doing what is necessary for salvation. He sins because he follows bad examples, but Christ came to set a good example.
AUGUSTINIANISM	Augustine of Hippo	Man is dead in sin; salvation is totally by the grace of God, which is given only to the elect.
SEMI-PELAGIANISM	John Cassian Vincent of Lerins	The grace of God and the will of man work together in salvation, in which man must take the initiative.

THE PELAGIAN CONTROVERSY[7]

The doctrine of semi-Pelagianism first arose in Gaul. John Cassian (c. 360–435), a mystical monk who had lived as a cenobite in Bethlehem and an anchorite in Egypt, started it. He was a cultivated Greek, a deacon and presbyter, and the founder of a famous cloister in Marseilles. His semi-Pelagian views were adopted by others in Gaul, so that opposition to the teachings of Augustine grew.

Cassian taught that salvation was a work of God and man, the two working together for a common goal, like a team of horses pulling a wagon. He said that grace is the creative power that saves man, but the initiative must come from man, not God. Man is not *dead* in sin, although he is so sick that without a cure he will die. He has a terminal illness; but in his sickness man must call the divine Physician. God makes his services available and even assures man that he can cure him, but God will not help unless man wants him. Grace can help man along, but it can be resisted.

Following from this, Cassian taught that God wants all men to be saved and that Christ earned salvation for all men. Predestination was God's work of electing those whom he foresaw would believe. So predestination was still based on man's will.

The error of semi-Pelagianism was brought to Augustine's attention by Prosper of Aquitaine (c. 390–463), a historian from Gaul who recorded the events and effects of the barbarian invasions. It is hard to tell whether Prosper himself defended semi-Pelagianism, or whether he was merely asking Augustine questions in an effort to understand better. But his questions make clear that the opposition in Gaul to Augustine's teachings centered on the doctrine of predestination.

This opposition of the semi-Pelagians to the truth of sovereign predestination set a pattern for succeeding history. Enemies of the truth always attack the doctrine of

---

7   Chart taken from Walton, *Chronological and Background Charts*, chart 27.

John Cassian (c. 360–435) and Faustus of Riez (c. 405–490)

In his early years, John Cassian joined a monastery in Bethlehem and lived among the hermits of Egypt. In later years, he befriended John Chrysostom in Constantinople, became a priest in Rome, and introduced monasticism to the West by writing books and founding the famous Abbey of St. Victor near Marseilles. Sadly, Cassian used his influence to promote the heresy of semi-Pelagianism, which teaches that God and man cooperate in salvation. His views were reinforced by the bishop Faustus of Riez, who strongly disagreed with Augustine's doctrine of sovereign grace. At the Synod of Orange in 529, the semi-Pelagianism of Cassian and Faustus was condemned as heresy. To learn more, read "Cassianus, Faustus, and Semi-Pelagianism," chapter 9 of Herman Hanko's *Contending for the Faith*.

sovereign grace by attacking predestination, because this doctrine, above all others, is an uncompromising statement of God's absolute sovereignty. God eternally determines who will be saved and who will not be saved.

Augustine also refuted this error, which he dreaded as much as Pelagianism, in his last writings. These attacks against his views served to sharpen his thinking so that he emphasized more strongly and clearly the doctrines of grace alone.

But Augustine's views did not prevail in the Roman Catholic Church. In a way, this is not surprising. Augustine's views were astonishingly biblical, and one can only give thanks to God for enlightening the church father to see so clearly truths that were not again taught in the church (with a few notable exceptions) until the reformers Martin Luther (1483–1546) and John Calvin (1509–1564).[8]

The controversy over Augustine's teachings regarding sovereign grace continued after his death in 430. In fact, the semi-Pelagian views of John Cassian were approved by two synods in Gaul: the Synod of Arles in 472 and the Synod of Lyons in 475. After many years of heated debate, the Synod of Orange in 529 officially settled the problem. This synod, presided over by Caesarius of Arles (c. 470–542), condemned the semi-Pelagianism of John Cassian and Faustus of Riez and approved Augustinianism, although in a very weak way. The synod's refusal

---

8 Although in his *Institutes of the Christian Religion* John Calvin quotes many of the ancient church fathers, his quotations from Augustine are the most copious. He consciously reached back to Augustine to show that his teachings were those of one whom, although over a thousand years earlier, the Roman Catholic Church itself called "Doctor of Grace."

to mention the doctrine of reprobation was its great defect. In fact, the Synod of Orange was a victory for semi-Pelagianism and paved the way for this error to prevail in the entire medieval church. It was really a compromise; and compromises of the truth are always victories for heresy.

THE SYNOD OF ORANGE (529)

The synod, in itself, was of very minor importance. It was a local gathering attended by only thirteen or fourteen bishops. It could not speak for all of Gaul, much less the whole western church. What makes it important is Pope Boniface II's endorsement of its decisions, making them binding on the western church. Pope Boniface II thereby officially committed the Roman Catholic Church, at least in the West, to semi-Pelagianism, and Pelagianism has remained official Roman Catholic doctrine.

Even before the synod met, a certain consensus emerged among Gaul's theologians. The consensus acknowledged, generally speaking, that election was indeed true and that grace was necessary to salvation because of man's sinful condition with which he was born. But having tipped the hat, so to speak, toward Augustine, the consensus also thought reprobation to be wrong. It made a caricature of Augustine's views by condemning the idea that men are predestined to evil and that damnation belongs to the will of God apart from sin. Such views, which Augustine never taught, attempted to make the doctrine of sovereign reprobation, which he did teach, to be reprehensible in the minds of men. The theologians mostly agreed that even though predestination in a limited sense is true, nevertheless God wills the salvation of all men, and baptism enables a person to do what is necessary for the salvation of his soul.

The Synod of Orange went in the direction of this consensus. As if to prove its orthodox character, the synod insisted on original sin, total depravity, and the inability of the natural man to do any good. It felt perfectly free to anathematize anyone who denied these truths. But in the same decision, with a complete about-face, the synod also spoke of the ability of any baptized person to work out his own salvation. And so the synod said that God gives the beginning of faith and charity, with an emphasis on the word *beginning*, which made it clear that the synod meant to teach that from thereon in, salvation was up to man.

More crucially, the synod refused to adopt the doctrine of reprobation and would only

Pope Boniface II

pour its anathemas upon the heads of all who taught the doctrine. With this thundering anathema, the synod anathematized its own Augustine, whom the Roman Catholic Church had declared a saint.

Herman Hoeksema makes this comment on the Synod of Orange: "It appears very clearly that they were afraid to maintain the strict doctrine of Augustine. The synod assumed an apologetic attitude. And although it opposed the doctrine of the Semi-Pelagians, it nevertheless was far from maintaining the positive doctrine of predestination and sovereign grace."

—Herman Hanko, *Contending for the Faith*, 80–81.

The trouble was that the ancient church had already approved of monasticism and its two-level morality. The idea that monastics were holier than ordinary people of God had led to the fatal doctrine of merit: man, by his holiness, can and does merit with God. He earns some special place in heaven to which he is brought at death. But the idea of merit is repugnant to those who hold to sovereign grace. No one, not even Adam in paradise, merits with God. Everything man receives is given without merit.

Man merits with God when he does something on his own, which God has not enabled him to do. Jesus reminds us: "So likewise ye, when ye shall have done all those things which are commanded you, say, We are unprofitable servants: we have done that which was our duty to do" (Luke 17:10).

God used Augustine to lay the groundwork for the doctrines of sovereign and particular grace. Few have taught these truths, but those who did were an illustrious group of saints: Gottschalk, Luther, Calvin, Knox, the fathers at Dordt, the Westminster divines, some outstanding Dutch and English theologians, Abraham Kuyper (before he spoiled it all with his common grace), and Herman Hoeksema. That is a noble company indeed!

CHAPTER 18: **THE RISE OF THE PAPACY**

And there was also a strife among them, which of them should be accounted the greatest.
And he said unto them, The kings of the Gentiles exercise lordship over them; and they
that exercise authority upon them are called benefactors. But ye shall not be so: but he
that is greatest among you, let him be as the younger; and he that is chief, as he that
doth serve. For whether is greater, he that sitteth at meat, or he that serveth?
is not he that sitteth at meat? but I am among you as he that serveth.

—LUKE 22:24–27

No church shall in any way lord it over other churches, no minister
over other ministers, no elder or deacon over other elders or deacons.

—ARTICLE 84 OF THE CHURCH ORDER OF THE PROTESTANT REFORMED CHURCHES[1]

THE INCREASING POWER OF BISHOPS

During the Nicene and Post-Nicene Period, the concept of the papacy began to take shape. Throughout the period, the bishop of Rome gained power over the other bishops of the church. By the end of the period, the bishop of Rome, who came to be identified as "the pope" (from the Latin *papa*, meaning "father"), became the unchallenged hierarchical leader of the Western church. The papacy would dominate the history of the church in the Middle Ages until the time of the Protestant Reformation.

During this period, several important factors contributed to the growing power of the bishops. Although many of these trends began in the Post-Apostolic Period and were noted in chapter 8, the power and prestige of bishops increased dramatically in the Nicene and Post-Nicene Period.

---

1   Church Order 84, in *Confessions and Church Order*, 403.

First, the bishops began to train and appoint the officebearers of the church. The church increasingly emphasized the need for an educated clergy. More and more converts who had acquired extensive education in pagan schools prior to their conversions entered the church, and some wanted to be ministers. In the Eastern church, the Alexandrian School and the Antiochian School had been established to train them. But no theological schools of note were found in the Western church. Clerics in the West were trained in cloisters and private schools or by gifted bishops.

The laity usually participated in the appointment to the office of the ministry, as in most Reformed and Presbyterian churches today. The churches held elections, and the chosen man was asked to be the shepherd of the flock that had elected him. These elections were not always under the control of elders and bishops; sometimes men were appointed by popular acclaim, and charisma and popularity were viewed as more important than the qualifications for the office listed in 1 Timothy 3. This practice led to some distressing situations in which unworthy men were installed into office. This resulted in increased reluctance to entrust this work to the laity and an increased desire to give this task to the bishops.

Second, the celibacy (abstaining from marriage) of the bishops set them apart from the laity of the church. The idea of a celibate clergy gained ground as the hierarchical structure of the church became more complex. Already in 305, the Synod of Elvira made clerical celibacy a law but limited the practice to the three lowest levels of clergy. In 325, the Council of Nicaea rejected clerical celibacy as a general rule. However, it was assumed in most parts of the church that those who entered the clergy without being married had to remain unmarried, and that if a cleric's wife died during his tenure of office, he was not permitted to remarry. Celibacy arose in connection with the *sacerdotal* idea of the priesthood, that is, the idea that priests stand between God and the members of the church, speaking for and acting on behalf of God to the people, and speaking for the people to God. In the minds of the laity, celibacy set the clergy apart from the members of the church and placed them on a higher level of holiness.

Third, the bishops ruled over an increasing number of subordinate offices of the church. The office of elder (or presbyter) gradually disappeared. The elder's office of oversight and rule was abandoned as the bishops gained more power; and soon these elders or presbyters became known as *priests*.

The office of deacon remained, but it became a channel for the bishop himself to distribute money from collected funds and from the imperial treasury. Deaconesses remained as helpers of the deacons in the care of female sick and poor and as assistants in the baptism of women converts.

Other church offices were introduced as well, including stewards, who administered church affairs; secretaries, who took care of the protocol in public ecclesiastical assemblies; parabolani, who cared for the sick in church-operated hospitals and even served as bodyguards for the bishop; and buriers of the dead. All these offices were under the supervision of the bishop.

The bishops stood as sovereign authorities within their dioceses. They filled church vacancies within their spheres of jurisdiction, appointed all the lesser clergy, made all the necessary decisions for the operation of affairs within the diocese, and in some instances even ruled in the secular sphere. Unfortunately, all of this led to ambition, avarice, luxury, and intrigue among the clergy.

Throughout the period some thoughtful clergymen, such as Jerome (c. 345–420), John Chrysostom (c. 349–407), and Theodoret of Cyrus (c. 393–457), opposed the bishops' grab for power, but their objections were drowned in the increasingly popular notion of apostolic succession; that is, that the bishops of the churches followed in an unbroken line from the apostles.

THE DEVELOPING HIERARCHY OF THE CHURCH

In time, several tiers of officebearers became common in the ancient church. Already in the Post-Apostolic Period (100–313), the church came to be governed by multiple levels of bishops. On level one were the *priests*, formerly known as presbyters or elders, who each served a small territory of the church called a parish. Level two consisted of *country bishops* who ruled rural dioceses that included small villages and towns. The third level was composed of *city bishops* who ruled in their cities and over surrounding country bishops.

By the Nicene and Post-Nicene Period (313–590), a fourth level of clergy came to rule in the capital cities of the Roman provinces. These officebearers, called *archbishops* or *metropolitans*, ruled over all ecclesiastical affairs in a given province, including all the lesser bishops within their sphere. They had authority to call a provincial synod, to preside over its meetings, and to exercise enormous influence on decisions. Yet their authority was also somewhat curbed. Their own appointment to office required the presence of all the lesser bishops. They could not act independently in provincial affairs. If they were guilty of sin or negligence, they could be tried by a provincial synod. All the appointments they made to lower offices had to be approved.

The fifth level of the church hierarchy consisted of powerful bishops called *patriarchs*, who ruled the entire church from five patriarchal cities: Rome, Constantinople,

Alexandria, Jerusalem, and Antioch. Gradually, the patriarch of Rome in the West and the patriarch of Constantinople in the East emerged as the most powerful, but constant strife, bitterness, and political intrigue characterized their relationship as both struggled for supreme mastery in the church.

The Major Bishoprics in the Roman Empire

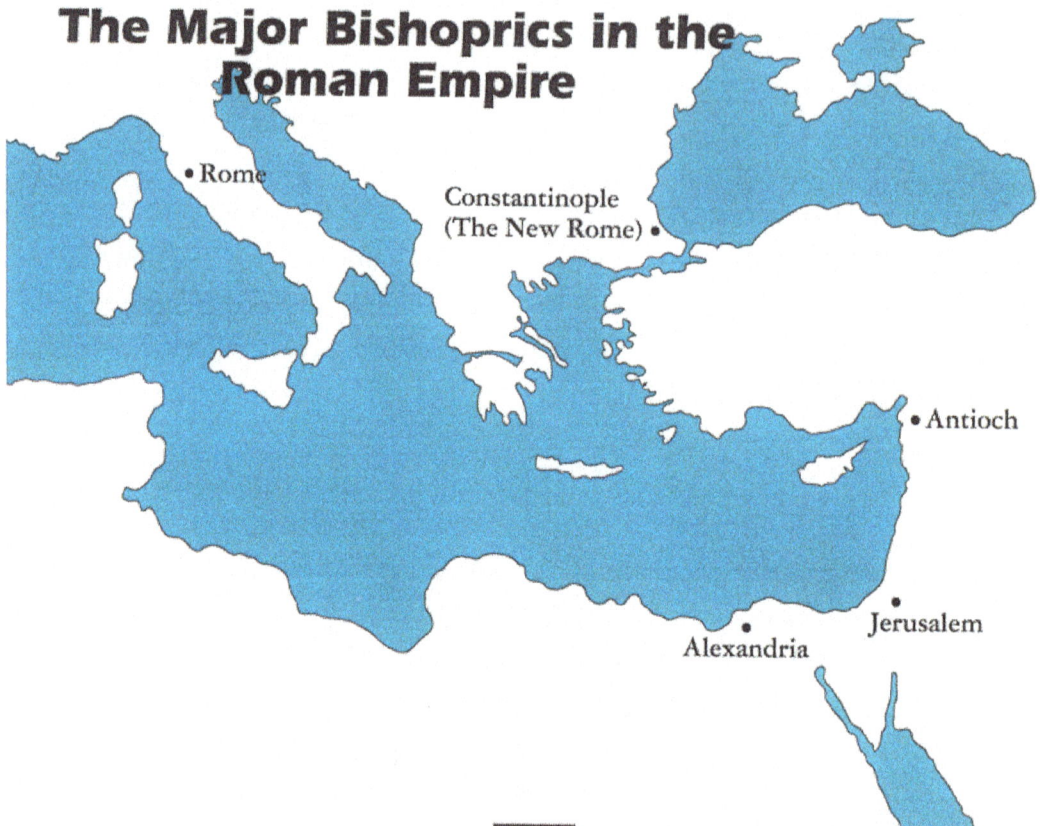

Chart 53

The Major Bishoprics in the Roman Church. Taken from *Charts of Ancient and Medieval Church History* by John D. Hannah. Copyright @ 2001 by John David Hannah. Used by permission of Zondervan, www.zondervan.com.

Various elements contributed to the prestige of Constantinople. In 330, Constantine the Great made this city his imperial capital and named it "New Rome." In addition, the trinitarian and Christological controversies were primarily in the East, and the great ecumenical councils were under the rule of clerics in the East, especially in Constantinople. Two ecumenical councils were held there, while none were held in Rome. Furthermore, as the power of the other Eastern patriarchal cities—Jerusalem, Alexandria, and Antioch—decreased, that of Constantinople increased.

But Rome had its own claim to fame. When Constantine moved the capital of the empire from Rome to Constantinople, Constantinople became the political center of the empire. This left the bishop of Rome with all the political power in the West. Further, Rome claimed the right to primacy because its bishop was, supposedly, through his ordination, directly in the line of the apostle Peter. Finally, Rome had a long history of orthodoxy in doctrinal disputes, a history that Constantinople did not have.

Some of the church fathers were appalled by the struggle for primacy. Gregory of Nazianzus (c. 330–90) wrote:

> Would to Heaven there were no primacy, no eminence of place, and no tyrannical precedence of rank; that we might be known by eminence of virtue alone! But, as the case now stands, the distinction of a seat at the right hand or the left, or in the middle; at a higher or a lower place; of going before or aside of each other, has given rise to many disorders among us to no salutary purpose whatever, and plunged multitudes in ruin.[2]

ROME'S EMERGENCE AS SUPREME

Although the controversy between Rome and Constantinople did not end until the schism between the Western and Eastern branches of Christendom in 1054, Rome did gain ascendancy in the West.

Bishop Victor I

Already during the Post-Apostolic Period, in the controversy over the date of Easter, the bishop of Rome had asserted his power. Bishop Victor of Rome (d. 199) argued that the bishop of Rome had jurisdiction over all other bishops and arrogantly decreed that the date observed in Rome was correct and that all who disagreed were heretics. Irenaeus of Lyons (c. 130–202), one of the early apologists, wrote against his domineering ways:

> The apostles have ordered that we should "judge no one in meat or in drink, or in respect to a feast-day or a new moon or a sabbath day" (Col. 2:16). Whence then these wars? Whence these schisms? We keep the feasts, but in

2 Neander, *History of the Christian Religion*, 2:165.

the leaven of malice by tearing the church of God and observing what is outward, in order to reject what is better, faith and charity.[3]

By the fourth century, the Roman bishop had won the battle over Easter.

Especially during the Nicene and Post-Nicene Period, the bishop of Rome succeeded in gaining the position of primacy in the church. Several factors contributed to this.

Powerful men who served as bishops of Rome were not afraid to do what they could to extend their authority over the entire West and even, in some instances, over the East. Further, several of the church councils (Nicaea, Constantinople, Ephesus, and Chalcedon) had given the bishop of Rome a precedence of honor. This was meant as a gesture of goodwill without ecclesiastical or political significance, but shrewd bishops from Rome appealed to these decisions in support of their claims. Finally, the destruction of the secular government in the West by the barbarians left the church with the bishop of Rome as the only head of the city and in a position to exercise political rule.

Many years passed before Rome could consolidate its claim. In the meantime, several church fathers resisted and rejected these papal claims: notably Basil of Caesarea (c. 329–79), Augustine of Hippo (354–430), and Hilary of Arles (401–449).

THE FIRST POPE: LEO THE GREAT

Three bishops of Rome during this period are especially noteworthy for their extravagant papal claims: Damasus I (c. 304–384), Innocent I (d. 417), and Leo I (c. 400–461).

S · DAMASVS · PP · LVSITANVS

Bishop Damasus I

Damasus I ruled as bishop of Rome from 366 to 384. He was the first to argue that the bishops of Rome have primacy over all other bishops because the church of Rome was established by the apostle Peter. Although the struggle between Rome and Constantinople had begun earlier, it took on greater importance when Emperor Theodosius called a council meeting in Constantinople in 381. This was the same meeting that confirmed and modified the Nicene Creed. The council also decided, "The bishop of Constantinople shall take precedence immediately after the bishop of Rome, because his city (Constantinople) is the New Rome."[4]

---

3 Schaff, *History of the Christian Church*, 3:217–18.
4 Shelley, *Church History in Plain Language*, 136.

Viewing the increasing power of the bishop of Constantinople as a threat, Bishop Damasus immediately protested the council's decision. His position was made official by the Synod of Rome in 382, which declared: "The Holy Roman Church takes precedence over the other churches, not on the ground of any synodical decisions, but because it was given the primacy by the words of our Lord and Redeemer in the gospel, when he said, 'Thou art Peter, and upon this rock I will build my church.'"[5]

Innocent I, who ruled as bishop of Rome from 401 to 417, built on this theme. He claimed to be the sole caretaker of apostolic tradition and authority, and he used every available opportunity to press and expand his papal claims. He approved of synodical decisions that pleased him and emphasized his rights and claims to be the head of the whole church when asked for advice. Always with one eye in the direction of Constantinople, Innocent did everything possible to outdo his rival. He even approved the condemnation of the views of Pelagius by a synod in North Africa, which later popes ignored.

Bishop Innocent I

However, Leo I, who ruled as bishop from 440 to 461, was the first real pope. No one in the ancient period did more to consolidate power in the hands of the papacy than Leo. Circumstances were in his favor: the East was torn by doctrinal controversy, Africa was devastated by the barbarians, and the West had weak emperors and few influential bishops. The way was open for Leo to pursue his papal goals with cunning, diplomacy, and zeal.

In his inaugural sermon as bishop of Rome, Leo put the case for the primacy of Rome frankly, extolling "the glory of the blessed Apostle Peter...in whose chair his power lives on and his authority shines forth."[6] Appealing to the words of Jesus to the apostle Peter in Matthew 16:17–19, Leo claimed that Peter is the rock of the church and that the bishops of Rome are his apostolic successors who exercise hierarchical authority over the entire church and exclusive control over the keys of the kingdom.

Pope Leo I

Leo's influence at the Council of Chalcedon, which formulated the creedal statement concerning the union of Christ's two natures in the person of the Son, was

---

5 Shelley, *Church History in Plain Language*, 136.
6 Shelley, *Church History in Plain Language*, 137.

Gaiseric the Vandal sacks Rome

great and decisive. His doctrinal credentials were impeccable, and he prepared a paper on the subject of Christ's person and natures that became the basis for the decisions of the council. However, the council also decided that the bishop of Constantinople had authority equal to the authority of the bishop of Rome. Leo's representative protested vehemently, but to no avail. The decision stood.

Leo was also revered for his success in turning away the barbarians. In 452, he convinced the fearsome Attila the Hun (c. 406–453) to spare the city of Rome. His prestige rose even higher when Gaiseric (c. 389–477), the Arian leader of the barbarian Vandals, approached Rome in 455, when the city was helpless to defend itself. Leo went out to meet Gaiseric, and the result of their meeting was that the Vandals demanded fourteen days in which to plunder Rome. They made good use of their time but did not burn the city, did not massacre the people, and plundered only two churches. Leo had survived, now not only as the head of the church, but also as the effective savior of the city.

LEO THE GREAT AND THE SCOURGE OF GOD

Attila the Hun (c. 406–453) was the most feared of all the barbarian invaders of the fifth century. Christian writers called him the "Scourge of God." Sweeping through Europe from across the Danube, Attila invaded and terrorized the Balkans, Greece, Gaul, and Italy. In 452, he was marching to the ancient capital of Rome when a peace delegation from Rome met him in northern Italy.

Representing the Roman emperor, bishop Leo of Rome (c. 400–461) pleaded with the barbarian conqueror to spare Rome and leave Italy. Surprisingly, Attila agreed and marched his armies north. He died less than a year later, and the fearsome Huns soon lost their influence.

Attila may have actually been looking for reasons to abandon his Italian campaign. Far from home, plague-ridden, and suffering

The meeting of Pope Leo and Attila

from widespread famine, his weary army of Huns was ready to mutiny. But in the popular mind, Leo had saved the city of Rome and the Western Roman Empire. The same bishop of Rome who had argued at his inauguration that he was the successor of Peter (440), whose papal claims had been enforced by an edict of Emperor Valentinian III (445), and whose orthodox theology had prevailed at the Council of Chalcedon (451) now turned back the "Scourge of God" and the dreaded barbarian hordes. God seemed to be on Leo's side. This amazing turn of events made Leo a legendary hero, strengthened his extraordinary papal claims, and earned him the title "Leo the Great."

At the end of this period of church history, another pope would exert even greater influence than Leo: Gregory I ("the Great"), who ruled as bishop of Rome from 590 to 604. Gregory was a transition pope between the ancient and medieval periods of church history. His period of power belongs to the medieval times, and his grab for papal power will be discussed later.

FACTORS CONTRIBUTING TO THE SUPREMACY OF THE BISHOP OF ROME [7]	
FACTOR	RESULT
MATTHEW 16:17–19	Papal claims rest on the assertion that Peter was given authority by Jesus over the entire church. This claim was first officially recognized during the papacy of Leo I.
APOSTOLIC SUCCESSION	The teaching that the apostles passed their authority to their successors led to the conclusion that Peter's supreme authority had been perpetuated in the bishops of Rome.
MARTYRDOM OF PETER AND PAUL	With the rise of the veneration of martyred saints, Rome gained prestige as the site of the deaths of the two principal apostles. The persecution under Nero also gave to the Roman church a special prominence by virtue of its suffering.
POPULATION OF ROME	Both the size of the city and the size of the church contributed to the authority of the bishop.
IMPERIAL CAPITAL	After the Edict of Milan, the emperors often sought advice on religious matters from the bishops of Rome.
LANGUAGE	The Latin-speaking West, led by the bishop of Rome, was often able to cut through the knotty theological dilemmas that incapacitated the Greek-speaking East, because of the lesser ability of the Latin language to express subtle shades of meaning.
LOCATION	Of the five patriarchal cities, only Rome was in the West; thus the bishop of Rome exercised authority over much more territory than did the other patriarchs.

---

7   Chart taken from Walton, *Chronological and Background Charts*, chart 23.

FACTORS CONTRIBUTING TO THE SUPREMACY OF THE BISHOP OF ROME	
FACTOR	**RESULT**
MISSIONARY OUTREACH	The bishops of Rome, such as Gregory the Great, encouraged successful missionary work among the barbarian tribes, who then looked to Rome with great respect. The Eastern patriarchs were much less successful in evangelizing the Persians and later the Muslims.
BARBARIAN INVASIONS	The collapse of the Western Empire under the barbarian invasions left the church as the major integrating force in society—in the empire as well as among the "Christian" barbarians.
MUSLIM CONQUESTS	The loss of the territories of the patriarchs of Antioch, Alexandria, and Jerusalem to Islam and the continual pressure exerted against Constantinople also increased the authority of the bishop of Rome.
LEADERSHIP	Leo I played a major role in resolving the Christological controversy. Gregory I acted to protect Rome against the Lombards, encouraged missions to England, and contributed pastoral and theological writings.

EVALUATION OF PAPAL CLAIMS

The popes based their arguments for supremacy on scripture as well as history. The argument, still used today, was that Peter was the first bishop of Rome. While in Rome, he represented all the apostles as chief among them. His position of preeminence among the other apostles was based on Matthew 16:17–19, where the Lord says, according to Rome, that on Peter he would build his church. As the first bishop of Rome, Peter transferred his position to subsequent bishops of Rome, who received their preeminence through apostolic succession.

However, this claim of Rome is spurious, unbiblical, and responsible for the deception of millions who perish.[8] It is factually untrue and exegetically wrong. Although scripture does not mention Peter's presence in Rome, early tradition says that he was, and this is probably reliable. But there is no proof that Peter represented the apostles in his visit, that he was the first bishop of the church in Rome, or that he transferred any position of authority to anyone else.

The exegetical grounds for Rome's claims are also fallacious. Matthew 16:13–19 states:

---

8 An interesting book and a careful examination of papal claims is William Shaw Kerr, *A Handbook on the Papacy* (New York: Philosophical Library, 1951).

13. When Jesus came into the coasts of Caesarea Philippi, he asked his disciples, saying, Whom do men say that I the Son of man am?

14. And they said, Some say that thou are John the Baptist: some, Elias; and others, Jeremias, or one of the prophets.

15. He saith unto them, But whom say ye that I am?

16. And Simon Peter answered and said, Thou art the Christ, the Son of the living God.

17. And Jesus answered and said unto him, Blessed art thou, Simon Barjona: for flesh and blood hath not revealed it unto thee, but my Father which is in heaven.

18. And I say also unto thee, that thou art Peter, and upon this rock I will build my church; and the gates of hell shall not prevail against it.

19. And I will give unto thee the keys of the kingdom of heaven: and whatsoever thou shalt bind on earth shall be bound in heaven: and whatsoever thou shalt loose on earth shall be loosed in heaven.

When the Lord said, "Upon this rock I will build my church," the Lord was referring to Peter's confession that Jesus was "the Christ, the Son of the living God." The Lord was not referring to Peter at all, as is evident from the fact that Peter's name in Greek is *petros*, a masculine noun, which means "rock," while the word used by the Lord when speaking of Peter's confession was *petra*, a feminine form of the noun and in agreement in gender with "confession," which is also feminine. That Christ would build his church on a man does not even make sense. That Jesus would build his church on the rock of a confession makes sense and agrees with Paul's doctrine of the church in Ephesians 2:19–22:

19. Now therefore ye are no more strangers and foreigners, but fellowcitizens with the saints, and of the household of God.

20. And are built upon the foundation of the apostles and prophets, Jesus Christ himself being the chief corner stone;

21. In whom all the building fitly framed together groweth unto an holy temple in the Lord:

22. In whom ye also are builded together for an habitation of God through the spirit.

Nevertheless, the text does contain a play on the name Peter, which means "rock." This too is significant. The Lord means to say that this fundamental confession of

Christ as the Son of God upon which will be built the entire church is a truth revealed through the apostles as the infallibly guided instruments of revelation. The apostolic succession is not the personal succession of the bishops of Rome but is a succession of doctrine. The doctrine that Christ is the Son of God, which truth has come to the church through the apostles, is the foundation for all doctrine that the church has received in the holy scriptures. This doctrine of the apostles is the confession of the church throughout every age of the new dispensation.

CHAPTER 19: **THE BARBARIAN INVASIONS**

And I say unto you, that many shall come from the east and west,
and shall sit down with Abraham, and Isaac, and Jacob, in the kingdom of heaven.
—MATTHEW 8:11

THE FALL OF THE ROMAN EMPIRE

The barbarian invasions of the fourth and fifth centuries changed the face of Europe, destroyed the Roman Empire, and made the church a missionary church. The resulting Christianizing of Europe altered the character of the ancient church and paved the way for Europe to become the cradle of Christianity.

The barbarians had been exerting pressure on the Roman frontier since the middle of the second century. But their invasions did not involve any major incursion until the Goths, fleeing the fierce and warlike Huns, took refuge on the Roman side of the frontier. These Goths were badly treated by the Romans and finally, almost in desperation, turned against the Romans and attacked their mighty legions. The Goths were spectacularly successful, annihilating the Roman army and killing the emperor Valens at the Battle of Adrianople in 378.

The succeeding emperor Theodosius I held the barbarians in check during his lifetime, but after he died in 395, the frontier could no longer be held. A door to the heart of the Roman Empire had been opened through which the barbarians streamed.

Sometimes more honorable men can be found among the heathen than in a morally corrupt but civilized empire and in a church deeply involved in politics. Alaric I (c. 370–410), king of the Visigoths (Western Goths), was such a man. Under the influence of Arian Christianity, Alaric at first helped the Nicene emperor

Theodosius hold back the barbarians on the Roman frontier. But Alaric received no recognition for his valor and his help, and in bitterness he became the enemy of the Romans.

Alaric conquered and plundered the eastern part of the empire almost to the gates of Constantinople. He drove into Greece and finally marched into Italy. After being defeated twice, Alaric and the Visigoths settled in the valleys of northern Italy. Emperor Honorius ordered the slaughter of the Goths, and thousands were butchered. In anger Alaric and the Visigoth army turned once again toward Rome to seek revenge. To the shock of the empire, they sacked Rome in 410. The ancient capital of the empire was now in the hands of barbarians. The houses and palaces of the rich were plundered, but Alaric spared the churches because he was acquainted with Christianity.

Alaric the Visigoth sacks Rome

Terrorizing Romans and barbarians alike, the fierce Huns invaded the Roman Empire as well. Led by Attila (c. 406–453), the Huns swept from Asia through the Balkans, Greece, and Gaul. After a defeat at the Battle of Chalons in 451, the Huns crossed the Alps and threatened to sack Rome again in 452. But after meeting with Pope Leo the Great and suffering from pestilence and famine, the Huns abandoned Italy and never returned.

Another tribe, called the Vandals, had invaded Gaul already in 406. From Gaul they entered Spain and crossed the Mediterranean Sea into North Africa, arriving at the gates of Hippo as Augustine lay dying in 430, and conquering Carthage by 439. Under the leadership of king Gaiseric (c. 389–477), the Vandals sailed from North Africa to Italy and sacked Rome a second time in 455. After Pope Leo begged Gaiseric to spare the lives of the people, the Vandals looted the city for two weeks before leaving on their ships.

Other tribes also took part in these invasions and conquered the rest of Europe. The Alans and Suebi invaded southern Gaul; the Franks occupied northern Gaul; and the Burgundians took over eastern Gaul. The Angles, Saxons, and Jutes settled in Britain. While the Western Roman Empire was at the mercy of the barbarians, it kept its own emperor until 476, when the Gothic king Odoacer (c. 433–93) dethroned the emperor Romulus Augustulus at Ravenna and brought the Western Empire officially to its end.

The Eastern Roman Empire, now called the Byzantine Empire, survived for another millennium. Justinian I (r. 527–65), the greatest of the Byzantine emperors, reconquered much of the Western Roman Empire for a short time. After his reign, the Lombards pressed into Italy; the Visigoths conquered Spain; the Persians conquered Syria, Palestine, and Egypt; the Croats and Serbs conquered the Balkans; and the Muslims swept through North Africa and beyond. For many years, Constantinople could not be conquered because of its strategic position on the Bosporus; but in 1453 the city finally fell to the Muslim Turks.

The Barbarian Invasions, 4th and 5th Centuries. Tim Dowley, *Baker Atlas of Christian History* (Grand Rapids, MI: Baker Books, 1997), 76–77. Used with permission from 1517 Media.

SIGNIFICANCE OF THE INVASIONS

Momentous changes took place in Europe through these barbarian invasions, which were significant for several reasons.

Attila the Hun, "The Scourge of God"

First, the fall of the Roman Empire was the judgment of God on an empire that had become morally rotten. The empire was filled with horrible vice, indescribable corruption, and moral stupor. Christianity had not been able to restrain the moral decline of what was once a mighty kingdom. We must note that the destruction of the Roman Empire speaks to us of the inevitable judgment of God upon all the kingdoms of this world founded on the principle of opposition to the Lord of lords and the King of kings.

Second, the fall of the Roman Empire paved the way for tremendous increases in papal power. When the Western Empire disintegrated, the church survived intact. This gave the church enormous influence and paved the way for the ecclesiastical domination of the whole of Western Europe. Because the power of the empire had vanished before the barbarian hordes and because no civil rule was left in Rome, the pope emerged as the most powerful figure in the West. The result was the rapid development of the Romish hierarchical system.

Finally, God used the fall of the Roman Empire to preserve and gather his church. Through the barbarian invasions, the church spread into Europe proper and embraced at last all the barbarian tribes. As a result, the church lost her Graeco-Roman character and became Romano-Germanic instead. In the providence of God, Europe became the center of the church and the stronghold of the faith for many succeeding centuries.

ULFILAS AND THE GOTHS

The church found in the barbarian invaders a fertile field for missions. From the early fourth century to late in the medieval period, the church spent her energies on bringing these uncivilized and fierce barbarians into the Christian faith. This great work of the church can best be described by meeting the most important missionaries.

Prior to the invasion of the empire by barbarian tribes from the north of Europe, the steppes of Russia, and lands to the east, missionaries from the churches in the Roman Empire had brought Christianity to many areas of Europe.

One of the earliest and most influential of these missionaries was Ulfilas (c. 311–83). Ulfilas's parents were part of the Roman Empire in Cappadocia, a large province south of the Black Sea in what is now Turkey. It is likely that young Ulfilas and his family were captured by a band of Gothic invaders and carried away north of the Danube River. The barbarian Goths, originally from Scandinavia, had settled here in Eastern Europe, north of the Black Sea.

Ulfilas returned to the Roman Empire from his captivity when the Arian controversy after Nicaea was at its peak. He studied theology in Constantinople. Eusebius of Nicomedia, the influential Arian bishop who had defended the heretic Arius at the Council of Nicaea, appointed him a bishop in 341.

Soon after his ordination, Ulfilas returned to the land of the Goths, where he engaged in rigorous mission work. He invented an alphabet for the Goths and translated the Bible into the Gothic language. The result of his work was that many were brought to the faith, although it was an Arian version of Christianity.

Ulfilas preaches to the Goths

In the fifth and sixth centuries the Arian Goths split into the Ostrogoths (Eastern Goths) and the Visigoths (Western Goths). The Visigoths pushed west, and under their ruler, Alaric I, they sacked Rome in 410. In the years that followed, the Arian Christianity of Ulfilas spread from the Goths to many other barbarian tribes, including the Vandals, Burgundians, and Lombards. Only the Franks and Saxons remained completely pagan.

CLOVIS AND THE FRANKS

The Franks were the first barbarians to be Christianized in the interior of Europe, and their conversion to orthodox Christianity prepared the way for the downfall of Arianism among the barbarians. The Franks had settled in Gaul (modern France) after other tribes had passed through. In the fourth and fifth centuries, Gaul was the most advanced of all the Roman provinces on the northern frontier.

Clovis (c. 466–511), the founder of the Merovingian dynasty, ruled the Franks

The Battle of Tolbiac

The baptism of Clovis

from 481 until his death and became the first barbarian king to be converted. He married a devout Christian princess, Clotilda (c. 475–545), the daughter of a Burgundian king. Legend has it that when he was losing against the Alemanni at the Battle of Tolbiac, Clovis promised Christ that he would become a Christian if Christ granted him the victory.

Clovis won the battle and was baptized, along with three thousand of his warriors, on Christmas day in 496.

Although he was instructed in the orthodox Christian faith by bishop Remigius of Reims (c. 437–533), Clovis remained brutal and became guilty of the most atrocious crimes. He used his orthodox Christianity as an excuse to conquer Arian barbarians and helped defeat Arianism among the Germans.

In the following years, Benedictine monks from the south brought order, civilization, and Christianity to the Franks through the establishment of numerous monasteries. Later, Irish monks from the north also worked among the Franks, the most famous of whom was Columbanus (c. 543–615), who in 590 established the first of many Celtic monasteries in the land of the Franks. The Franks would play an extremely important role in the history of the medieval church. They would rescue Europe from Muslim invasion, defend the Roman papacy, and establish the powerful Holy Roman Empire.

PATRICK AND THE IRISH

Mission work in Ireland began with Patrick (c. 389–461), who was born and raised in a Christian home on the west coast of Britain. Tragedy struck when fierce Celtic raiders sailed across the Irish Sea, sacked villages along the coast, and took Patrick captive. He lived as a slave in Ireland for six years but took the opportunity to learn the language of his captors. By ways known only to God, Patrick was converted to Christianity.

Patrick escaped from his Irish master and fled back to Britain after a particularly hazardous trip across the Irish Sea. His stay in Ireland had created in him, in spite of his slavery, a love for the land and the people, a love that would not go away. Patrick resolved to return as an ambassador of the gospel of Christ. He entered the ministry and was ordained a missionary to Ireland.

To Ireland he sailed to take up the work. It was filled with danger and hardship. Most of Patrick's mission work took place in the northern part of the island, in what is now known as Ulster, and the center of his work was Armagh. God preserved Patrick from danger and used his ministry to bring thousands to faith in Christ.

The result was a Celtic church established in Ireland that was largely independent and quite different from Rome in practice and ritual, as well as in the doctrine of scripture. Patrick had only scripture as his teacher, and he was not weighted down with the baggage that had already become part of the religion brought to continental Europe by missionaries from Rome.

Further missionary work was carried on in Ireland by Christian Britons who were driven from England. A woman named Bridget (c. 452–523) contributed to the work in Ireland as well. An illegitimate child of a chieftain and a slave, Bridget established the first nunnery in Ireland, at Kildare, which was of some assistance in the progress of missionary work in that country. By the sixth and seventh centuries, Ireland sent missionaries of her own to the interior of the continent.

Patrick (c. 389–461)

In the early 400s, the Roman army abandoned Britain to defend the empire from barbarian invasion. Taking advantage of Britain's vulnerability, Irish pirates raided the coast, kidnapped Patrick from his British home when he was sixteen, and enslaved him on a farm in northern Ireland. After six long years and a life-changing conversion, Patrick escaped Ireland and found his way home. Unable to ignore dreams that the Irish were calling him to bring them the gospel, Patrick trained for the ministry and returned to Ireland as a missionary for the last thirty years of his life. Armed with his Bible, Patrick brought the good news to Irish kings and commoners alike, establishing strong and flourishing Celtic churches and monasteries. Before he died, Patrick wrote *Confessions*, an autobiography that exemplifies Christian humility and steadfastness and celebrates God's grace to undeserving sinners. To learn more, read "Patrick: Missionary to Ireland," chapter 8 of Herman Hanko's *Portraits of Faithful Saints*.

Columba (521–97)

Columba, the great missionary to Scotland, grew up in the Celtic church established by Patrick a hundred years earlier. An Irishman of royal blood, Columba became a respected Christian scholar, a notable preacher, and a founder of churches and monasteries in Ireland. In 563, he sailed with a band of twelve monks for Scotland and established a missionary headquarters on the desolate island of Iona. For the next thirty-five years, Columba brought the gospel to the barbarian Scots and Picts by preaching throughout the country, training missionary monks, and copying the scriptures by hand. Inspired by Columba's example, scores of Celtic missionaries from Iona established churches, monasteries, and schools throughout the British Isles and even on the continent. Spending himself in the cause of the proclamation of God's word, Columba died copying the scriptures. To learn more, read "Columba: Missionary to Scotland," chapter 9 of Herman Hanko's *Portraits of Faithful Saints*.

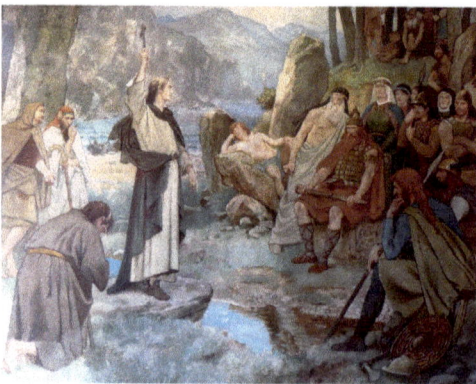
Columba converts the Picts

COLUMBA AND THE SCOTS

A British missionary named Ninian (c. 360–432) was the first to bring Christianity to Scotland. Ninian worked among the barbarian Picts of southern Scotland, in areas Roman legions had penetrated. In Whithorn, Ninian built a stone church called Candida Casa ("the White House"), which became his missionary base. The monastery he founded there attracted students from Ireland and Wales.

But the greatest missionary to Scotland was Columba (521–97). A native of Ireland, Columba traveled at the age of forty-two to the island of Iona, off the western Scottish coast, and established a famous monastery there in 563.

Columba's missionary work in Scotland was forced upon him. Although he had been instrumental in the establishment of several monasteries and churches in northern Ireland, he became involved in a dispute over a biblical manuscript that led to war. Many were killed. Smitten with remorse, Columba promised to go into exile. He kept this promise and spent the rest of his life in missionary work among the Scots and the Picts, some of the most fierce and warlike people in all the British Isles.

Columba's missionary labors in Scotland were blessed by God so that the true gospel was proclaimed there and the church of Jesus Christ was gathered. The monastery of Iona became a center of Christianity, a base for mission work, a holy spot long revered by Christians from Scotland, and a haven for many in a land that was in almost constant turmoil. Iona was known as "The Light of the Western World."

As in Ireland, the Celtic church in Scotland was independent of Rome. The men of Iona refused to submit to the episcopal authority of Rome. They celebrated Easter at a different time; permitted priests to marry; and kept a simpler liturgy and worship. Although the conflict between Iona and Rome was finally settled at the Synod of Whitby in 664, the differences remained, and the church in Scotland never submitted entirely to Rome's practices.

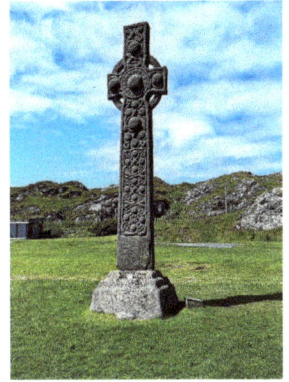

The Celtic cross at Iona

IONA: THE LIGHT OF THE WESTERN WORLD

Noah, after awakening from his drunken stupor, blessed his two sons, Shem and Japheth. Japheth's blessing was that the day would come when he would dwell in the tents of Shem. With the work of the apostle Paul, and in subsequent centuries, God brought Japheth into the tents of Shem as the church was established first in Antioch, Syria, Greece, and Italy, and then in the whole of Europe. Gradually Europe, where cruel and fierce barbarians lived, was brought the gospel, was Christianized, and in time became the center of the church.

...When Columba was over forty years old, he took with him twelve companions and sailed for the coast of Scotland. After a rough and perilous journey and a lengthy search for a good place to settle, he found the small island of Hy, now known as Iona, where he determined to live. The island was

a treeless, barren piece of land measuring about three miles in length by one mile in width with a breath-taking view of the sea and of the coast of Scotland.

Iona Abbey in Scotland

Here, on this small island, Columba built a monastery. It was not an imposing structure but a small group of huts which included a refectory, a library, a guesthouse, a kiln, a mill, two barns, and a small church. Here was organized around Columba a monastic life

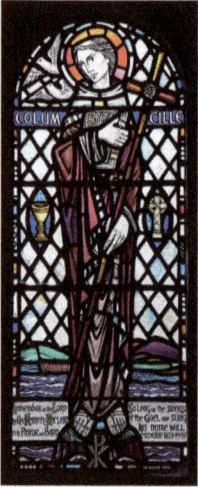

Columba (Columcille)

consisting of three groups of residents: the seniors, who were responsible for leading in worship, preserving manuscripts, and teaching the other residents; the workers, who performed the manual labor necessary to keep the monastery functioning; and the juniors, who were responsible for miscellaneous tasks. It was a hive of activity but was devoted especially to the training of missionaries who would be sent out to the inhabitants of what is now Scotland. Columba, in his own words, had now dedicated his life to bringing as many heathen to Christ as were killed in the battle with his cousin, the king.

Missionary work in those days was difficult. It required that the monks who were trained at Iona, and Columba himself, go to the mainland, where they were in constant peril of fierce people, wild animals, rugged terrain, an unforgiving climate, and the enmity of the Druids (the priests of pagan religion who hated with all their souls the arrival of Christianity). Here too lived the Picts and Scots, who—though Christianity had made some inroads into their land—were still basically the race of barbarians they had been long before our Lord was born in Bethlehem.

The stories that are told of the work of Columba are, in many instances, legendary. His biographers relate how he counteracted the magic of the Druids with miracles of healing; how he drowned out the chanting voices of the Druid priests with songs of praise to God and sung in his own booming voice; how he gained the respect of Brude the king of the Picts who lived in a castle on the shores of Loch Ness; and how he labored with unrestrained zeal for the cause of the gospel. Stripped of all the legendary stories, the work of Columba shines as a light in the midst of the darkness of heathendom. His missionary labors were blessed by God in Scotland so that he true gospel was proclaimed there and the church of Jesus Christ was gathered. His missionary zeal is an example to all those whom God throughout the years calls to this difficult work.

...Through the labors of Columba and others who braved the dangers of heathen lands to bring the gospel to barbarians—for Columba is only one example among many—God was pleased to begin to bring Japheth into the tents of Shem.

—Herman Hanko, *Portraits of Faithful Saints*, 51, 53–55.

INDEX

E

Easter, 57, 67, 95, 106, 116, 174, 175, 176, 217, 218, 233
Eastern Orientalism, 201
Eastern Roman Empire, 142, 227
Ebionism, 81–82
Ebionites, 82
Ecclesiastical History (Eusebius of Caesarea), 131
Edessa, 47
Edict of Milan, 57, 110, 129, 131, 138, 177, 192, 221
Edict of Thessalonica, 131
Egypt, 22, 39, 49, 95, 98, 99, 120, 137n2, 147, 162, 163, 167, 180, 181, 182, 183, 185, 186, 192, 209, 210, 227
Egyptians, 39, 40
Elisha, 178
The Enchiridion (Augustine of Hippo), 203
England, 222
Ephesus, 17, 36, 37, 44, 46, 47, 61, 79, 106, 106n11, 164, 165, 169, 204, 218
Ephraem Syrus, 177
Epiphany, 175, 177
Epistle of Barnabas (Barnabas of Alexandria), 103
Epistle to the Philippians (Polycarp), 104
Ethiopia, 47
Ethiopian eunuch, 49, 112
Eudoxia (Empress), 141
Europe, 44, 47, 85, 137n2, 138, 180, 185, 225, 233
Eusebius of Caesarea, 64, 68, 96, 131, 149–51, 169, 173
Eusebius of Nicomedia, 148, 151, 169, 229
Eutyches, 164, 165, 167, 169
Eutychianism, 132, 159, 163–64, 165, 166, 169
Eutychius, 169
Eve, 5, 20, 21, 177, 206
Exposition of the Oracles of Our Lord (Papias of Hierapolis), 103

F

Fabianus, 65
fatalism, 200, 202
Fausta, 139
Faustus of Riez, 210
Feast of All Saints, 175

Feast of Firstfruits, 15
Feast of the Annunciation, 178
Feast of the Assumption, 178
Feast of the Holy Innocents, 174
Feast of the Holy Trinity, 175
Feast of Weeks, 15
Felicitas, 67
First Apology (Justin Martyr), 57, 78
Flavian of Constantinople, 164
For Thy Truth's Sake (Hanko), 35
France, 186, 229. *See also* Gaul
Franks, 132, 183, 186, 226, 229–30

G

Gabriel (angel), 174, 177, 178
Gaiseric the Vandal, 132, 220, 226
Galatia, 35
the Galatians, 42, 70, 71, 73, 93
Galerius (Emperor), 65, 68–69, 110, 129, 136, 138
Galilee, 178
Gaul, 47, 79, 120, 132, 136, 183, 184, 195, 209, 210, 211, 220, 226, 229
Geneva, 116
Genevan Reformation, 101
Gentiles, 15, 22, 33, 40, 41–43, 51
Germans, 188n4
Gibeonites, 40
gnosticism, 56, 190, 200, 201
God, 1, 4–5, 6, 7, 8, 16, 19, 20–25, 27, 34, 36, 39, 42, 46–47, 49, 61, 63, 83–84, 91, 94, 100, 110, 117, 118, 119, 122, 123, 124–25, 137, 145, 148, 150, 152, 157, 159, 160, 161–63, 168, 171, 174, 175, 179, 185, 191, 197, 198, 199, 202, 207, 208, 209, 210, 211, 212, 228, 232, 233, 234
Good Friday, 175
Gospel of Mary, 85
Gospel of Philip, 85
Gospel of Thomas, 85
Gospel of Truth (Valentinus), 57, 85, 96
Goths, 140, 225, 228–29
Gottschalk of Orbais, 200, 212
Great Persecution, 57, 68, 110, 129, 135, 136
Greece, 17, 44, 47, 51, 75, 120, 138, 180, 220, 226, 233
Greeks, 117
Gregory I ("the Great"), 130, 132, 174, 221, 222

www.ingramcontent.com/pod-product-compliance
Lightning Source LLC
Chambersburg PA
CBHW041609260326
41914CB00012B/1442